Mordaunt Roger Barnard, Carl Wilhelm Paijkull

A Summer in Iceland

Mordaunt Roger Barnard, Carl Wilhelm Paijkull

A Summer in Iceland

ISBN/EAN: 9783337316273

Printed in Europe, USA, Canada, Australia, Japan

Cover: Foto ©Andreas Hilbeck / pixelio.de

More available books at **www.hansebooks.com**

A SUMMER IN ICELAND.

C. W. PAIJKULL,
PROFESSOR OF GEOLOGY AT THE UNIVERSITY OF UPSALA.

TRANSLATED BY

REV. M. R. BARNARD, B.A.,
VICAR OF MARGARETTING, ESSEX,
AND AUTHOR OF "SPORT IN NORWAY, AND WHERE TO FIND IT," "LIFE OF THORVALDSEN," ETC.

ILLUSTRATED.

LONDON:
CHAPMAN AND HALL, 193, PICCADILLY.
1868.

PREFACE.

ICELAND and the Icelanders are comparatively but little known to us. Those of our countrymen who have visited the island have, from their inability to speak the language, to a great extent, been precluded from acquiring that intimate acquaintance with the manners, and the public and private life of the inhabitants, which a knowledge of the vernacular alone can ensure.

It occurred to me, therefore, that by translating "A Summer in Iceland," the author of which seems to have made it his business to pass nothing by unobserved, I might be doing good service; and if I have only succeeded in rendering it in a style as readable and agreeable as is the case in the original, the many pleasant hours I have passed in imagination with the Author on the snow-clad " Jökuls " and the sandy " heiði " of Iceland will not have been thrown away.

M. R. B.

1st June, 1868.

P.S.—In order to render the volume more complete, I have appended a list of the Fauna and Botany of the country, from Gaimard's voluminous work. The woodcuts, I should state, are the same which are used in the original, and were executed in Sweden.

CONTENTS.

CHAPTER I.

Voyage from Copenhagen to Iceland—Great Auk—Ice-mountains—Reykjavik—Description of Town—Icelandic Officials—Schools—Clergy—Newspapers—Mode of Travelling—An Icelandic House—A Dilemma—Style of Building—A Parsonage—Internal Arrangement of Houses—Strange Fuel—Stables—Agriculture—Mode of Salutation—Mount Esja—National Costume—Everyday Dress—Physical Appearance and the Darwinian Theory—Icelanders warm-blooded—Icelandic Shoemakers . . 1

CHAPTER II.

Leave Reykjavik—Lava Streams—An unpleasant Ride—Thunder and its Effects—Guides—Letters of Recommendation—Fording a River—View of Hekla—A Paradise—Position of Clergy—Their Income—Similarity between Icelandic and Swedish Accent—Hrútshellir—Skógafoss—Sólheima-Jökul—Jökul Floods—Þrasi and Loðmundr—Dyrhólarey or Portland—A Patent Saddle—Víksdalr—Curious Rock Formations—The Volcano Katla—Its Eruptions—The Sea becomes Land—Valleys filled up—View from Mýrdals-Jökul—Mýrdalssandr—Passage over the Kuda—Icelandic Churches—An Epitaph—Strange Incident—A Proselyte—Magnus Eiriksson, the Colenso of Iceland—Icelandic Intolerance—A Man eaten up by Horses 46

CHAPTER III.

Skaptar Volcano—Eruption in 1783—A River dried up—Enormous Lava Stream—Fearful Devastations—Consequences of the Eruption—Pestilence among Animals and Men—New Rivers formed—Bread and Butter—A Fairy Tale—Icelandic Fare—The Meaning of the word "Beg"—Snuff Horns and Powder Flasks—Remarks on Brandy Imports—Strange Advertisement—Articles of Import—Reppstyrer or Constable—A Farmhouse in the Eastern Districts—Fording Places—Skeidarar-Jökul—Progressive Motion of Glaciers—Iceland formerly a Wooded Country—Skeidararsandr—Svinafells-Jökul—Crevices—Danger of falling into them—Glaciers melting on the Surface—Öræfa-Jökul and Volcano—Eruption in 1727 described—Terrific Results—Great Mortality—Journey Continued—Bird Rocks—Bird-catching in the Færoe Islands—Great Dimon—Insect Powder—Its Blessings—Mercantile Caravans—Icelandic Whip . . . 92

CONTENTS.

CHAPTER IV.

Volcanic Systems—Basaltic Formations—Tufa—Geological Age of Iceland—A Dog on Horseback—Remarks on Dogs—Tape-worms—Mountain Passes—Dangerous Mountain Excursions—Roadside Flowers—Sira Bjarni and his Eider Ducks—Fishery and the Frenchmen—Icelanders not a race of Sailors—French Companies—Eider Down—A Wooden House—Lonsheiði—Absence of Woodland not depressing—A Natural Crinoline—Wages of Guides—Price of Horses—Hippophagy—Recipe for a good Complexion—A Bishop with Nine Hundred Children—Remarks on Birds—Plants . 142

CHAPTER V.

The Mineralogy of Iceland—Zeolites—The Darwinian Theory again—Búlandstindr—Mountain Guides—Fissures and Mountain Slips—Mountain Formations—Valleys—Glacial Age—Phenomenon of Friction—Lava from the Glacial Age—The Glacial Age and the Fjords—Expedition to Greenland—Drift Ice—Discovery of Greenland—Discovery of America due to Iceland—Traits of Character—Glorious Sunsets—Reyðarfjörðr—Icelandic Spar—"Lausna" Stone—Mountain Passes—Legend of Hrútafjarðarháls—Whale Fisheries—Novel Harpoon—A whole Nation fed by a Whale—Fishery of the Færoe Islands—Húskerðingr—A New Prophet in the Whale's Belly—Delicacies of the Sea—Mode of Preserving Fish—Fresh-water Fish 178

CHAPTER VI.

Surturbrandr—Its Origin—Snow Fonds—Journey over the Heiði—Alftaviksfjall—Hvítserkr—Sheep-farming and Agriculture—From Hjaltastaðr to Vopnafjörðr—An Adventure—Passage across Jökulsá—Curious way of Crossing a River—Basaltic Columns—Grímsstaðir—Peasant Girls on Horseback—Jökulsá, in Axafirði—Reykjahlíd—Krafla—Sulphur Springs—Mud Springs—Geysirs—Journey to Húsavík—Return to Reykjahlíd—Volcanic Crater "Cauldron"—Herðubreið—Solfataras—Excursion on a Lava Stream—Volcanic Craters of Leirhnúkr—Eruptions of 1724-1730—Mývatn or "Mosquito Lake"—Reindeer 216

CHAPTER VII.

From Reykjahlíd to Akureyri—Akureyri—Medical Staff—Homœopathy—Epidemics—Icelanders and Scandinavianism—Emigration to Brazil—Iceland "The Best Land under the Sun"—Wood-carving—Painting—Icelandic Foxes—Tales about Foxes—Catching Ptarmigan—Hot-springs of Reykir—A Night-Ride over the Heiði—A Night under the Open Sky—Storisandur—Surtshellir—Its Origin—Legend of Surtshellir—Geitlandsjökul—Legend of Throndalr—Attempts to re-discover it—Cracks in a Lava Stream—Almannagjá—Pre-historic Lava Stream—Return to Reykjavik . 256

CONTENTS.

CHAPTER VIII.

Discovery of Iceland—Colonisation of the Country—Political Divisions—Ancient Laws—Lost Independence—Iceland and Denmark—Iceland under the Norwegian Kings—Calmar Union—What country is Iceland?—Financial Matters—Iceland's Decadence—Monopoly: Its Effects—Free Trade: Its Happy Results—Brandy Imports—A Banquet—The Dessert . 285

CHAPTER IX.

Days of the Week—Þingvalla Church—Laugardalr—Subaqueous Bridge—The Geysir System—Great Geysir—Strokkr—Eruptions of Strokkr—Subterranean Noises—Origin of Geysirs—The Geysir not of great Date—A Night by the Geysir—Journey to Hekla—Hekla—Eruption in 1766—Eruption in 1845—Premonitory Symptoms—First Effects—Showers of Ashes—Continuation of Eruption—Lava Stream—Cessation of Eruption—Return to Reykjavik—From Eyrarbakki to Krisuvík—Dangerous Coast—Shipwrecks—Oil on the Waters—Sulphur Springs at Krisuvík—Farewell to Iceland 316

LIST OF PLATES.

Skógafoss	*Frontispiece.*
	PAGE
Dyrhólarey, or Portland	71
Drying Fish	214
Crossing a River	229
Almannagjá	283
Hekla	332

ICELANDIC PRONUNCIATION.

á	is pronounced like		ow
æ	"	"	ai in *said*.
è	"	"	yed
ei	"	"	ei ⎫
ó	"	"	ou ⎬ Dipthong.
ú	"	"	u in fool.
au	"	"	eui
ð	"	"	d pronounced soft.
fl, fn	"	"	bl, bn
h	"	"	aspirated.
ll	"	"	dl
nn	"	"	dn
þ	"	"	th in *the*.

WEIGHTS (Danish).

The Danish pound is equal to $1\frac{1}{10}$ lbs. English avoirdupois.

MONEY (Danish).

			s.	d.	
1 skilling	is equal to about		0	$\frac{1}{4}$	English
1 mark	"	"	0	$4\frac{1}{2}$	"
1 rix-dollar	"	"	2	3	"
1 Sp. dollar	"	"	4	6	"

MEASURES.

The Danish foot is $12\frac{3}{4}$ English inches. The Danish mile equals 8,244 English yards, or $4\frac{1}{2}$ English miles and 330 yards.

Fifteen geographical miles (Danish) equal one degree.

N.B.—English measurement is used throughout, unless when the reverse is expressly stated.

LIST OF WORDS USED.

Amtmand, *deputy governor;* dalr, *valley;* fjord, *firth or fjord;* fjeld, *mountain;* fljot, *river;* foss, *waterfall;* hraun, *lava stream;* heiði, *mountain road;* hreppstiori, *constable, bailiff;* hver, *boiling spring;* landfoged, *steward;* syssel, *sheriffdom;* sysselmand, *sheriff;* sira, *reverend;* surturbrandr, *lignite, mineralized wood;* tûn, *enclosed fields round a farmhouse;* bœr, *house;* vatn, *lake;* jökul, *ice mountain;* skredjökul, *glacier* (N.B.—This word cannot be properly translated into English); holm, *rocky island;* wadmel, *coarse homespun cloth*.

A SUMMER IN ICELAND.

CHAPTER I.

Voyage from Copenhagen to Iceland—Great Auk—Ice-mountains—Reykjavik—Description of Town—Icelandic Officials—Schools—Clergy—Newspapers—Mode of Travelling—An Icelandic House—A Dilemma—Style of Building—A Parsonage—Internal Arrangement of Houses—Strange Fuel—Stables—Agriculture—Mode of Salutation—Mount Esja—National Dress—Everyday Dress—Physical Appearance and the Darwinian Theory—Icelanders warm-blooded—Icelandic Shoemakers.

ICELAND is a country abounding with legends and myths, which tradition and the hand of nature have each done their part in recording. Her people, an offshoot of the Scandinavian family (who have maintained their ancient language and customs, though of course tempered by the influence of Christianity and the long lapse of time, and in whose breast the love of liberty still burns as brightly as of old), though few in number, occupy a place among the enlightened families of the world;

while her Jökulls, or ice mountains, her warm springs, her volcanoes and streams of lava, her sandy plains and rapid rivers—the mighty works of Nature—afford an inexhaustible field for wonderment and for investigation. Iceland is truly a land of reminiscences, where well-nigh every spot has its history, written by the hand of man. But besides this it is an open book of Nature, a country where the formation and transformation of the earth's crust take place on so grand a scale, that the lapse of even a few years is often sufficient to make the effects of this transforming power evident to the attentive observer. And this circumstance is not without importance to the scientific investigator; for that language must needs be far easier to interpret where the same person is enabled to read both its alphabet and its written words, than where one century can only decipher the former, and has to leave it to a succeeding age to arrange the letters in an intelligible form. In the investigation of science, therefore, Iceland is a country of vast importance; while to the inhabitant of Northern Europe she is allied by family ties,—a sister country, with whom one fain would cultivate a more intimate acquaintance.

When I made up my mind to travel in Iceland, in the summer of 1865, my friends at home asked me, why I did not rather bend my steps towards Italy? I was free to choose, and I do not doubt that had I visited the land

"Where the flower of the orange blows,"

I should have returned from my trip with mingled feelings of admiration and regret; but my summer in Iceland afforded me so much enjoyment in the contemplation of its beautiful and instructive scenery, and in the intercourse I had there with so many amiable individuals, that I should have bitterly repented had I permitted the sirens of the south to tempt me, instead of obeying that magnetic impulse that attracted my aspirations and longings towards the north. But still, in a certain respect, a trip to Iceland is an adventurous one; and it is essential to keep one's eyes open to the instructive lessons the rugged soil is capable of imparting, if one would not be wearied by the monotony of its desert tracts, the nakedness of its fjelds and *heiði* (moors or mountain roads), the multiplicity of its foaming rivers, and, not the least, by the difficulties that beset the traveller on his journey. Often and often, during the lonely hours that I have passed in riding over those barren tracts, where not even a blade of grass served to remind one of an animated nature, have I thought of the Arabs of the Desert, with whose mode of life, indeed, the Icelander's bears some resemblance; for, with both of these the horse is their trusty companion. The latter can scarce go a single step without his horse; and, should this fail him, his life is placed in peril. It must carry him over long and barren wastes, where hardly a handful of grass is to be seen wherewith to appease its hunger; and yet the Icelandic horse has one great advantage over its Arabian congener—it never lacks water!

In the following pages it shall be my aim to give the reader a true and faithful sketch of the scenery, the character of the people, their customs and manners, while I shall cursorily touch on the political and mercantile relations of the country.

I may as well mention in this place that my principal object in visiting Iceland was for scientific purposes; and more especially did I desire to cultivate my studies in mineralogy and geology—branches of science in which that country is so rich.

In the month of January, then, 1865, I left home for Copenhagen. This city is, unquestionably, the best resort for any one who purposes travelling in Iceland, and who desires to gain all the information he can previously to setting out on his journey. There he will find several Icelanders, who may be said to represent the intelligence of their country; there, too, he will be able to make the acquaintance of a gentleman who possesses a most intimate acquaintance with the country—I refer to Professor Steenstrup; and, lastly, he will find there a rich collection of natural objects in the University Museum, which will prove of the greatest possible service to him in the pursuance of his scientific researches.

The harbour of Copenhagen had been so blocked up with ice in the spring of this year, that the steamer which ought to have sailed on the 1st of March, and which usually runs six times during the season, to and fro, between Iceland and the Danish capital, could not set out till the beginning of April. It had not, however, been my intention to go by her, as her destination was Reykjavik, on the south-west of the island, for I had purposed taking a passage in a merchant vessel bound for the eastern coast; and my reason was, that this part of the island is the most interesting in a mineralogical point of view, while, as regards its geology, it has been less explored than any other portion of the country. But a few days before this ship was to sail I learnt that a Danish vessel of war was on the point of leaving for Iceland, and I therefore sought and obtained permission to avail myself of this more comfortable and agreeable mode of travelling. The name of the vessel was the *Fylla*, a screw schooner, mounting three guns, and with a crew of seventy men.

We left Copenhagen on the 4th of May, and I fully expected that we should reach our destination in ten or twelve days, as the mail-boat *Arcturus*, though touching at Scotland and the Færoe Islands, usually takes a fortnight on her passage; but fate willed it otherwise, and for three long weeks we were tossed about on the North Sea before setting foot once more upon land. For though the *Fylla* was a screw steamer of 150-horse power, yet her supply of coals was limited, and we therefore had to sail the greater portion of the way, and, as the wind was generally against us, we had to remain longer on the sea than was altogether in accordance with my wishes at least. We encountered our first storm off the Norwegian coast, and many a pale face on board bore witness to the disagreeable feelings of the inner man, caused by the rough usage of the boisterous Skager-rack. Storm number two met us as we were passing a narrow sound between Fair Hill and the Shetlands, and drove us half-way back across the sea towards Norway; and, lastly, after encountering a great deal of rough weather, storm number three — the most violent of all — assailed us on the last day of our passage. I say the last, for I had calculated upon eating my dinner that same evening in Reykjavik. It drove us far to the south; I do not know to what point in the Atlantic. The sea was so heavy that we often went under it as well as over it. I lay in my hammock in a little cabin, which—that is to say the hammock—kept banging up against the sides, and of course dispersed my pleasant dreams about land *à tout prix;* while to add to my comfort, the salt water poured down through the skylight and drenched me as I lay, and wetted all my clothes through and through. It was, indeed, a most uncomfortable night!

I need not say much about life on board ship. It is pretty much the same everywhere, I suppose. Of course the usual degree of excitement was got up when a whale passed close by us, blowing and puffing like a steam-engine; or when one of the hens flew overboard and was fished up again; or when a vessel came in sight, which, I may state, is rather an exceptional occurrence between the Shetlands and Iceland. Certainly a good many vessels, schooners and smacks, go to Iceland every year from Copenhagen, Bornholm, Norway, and England, but they sail mostly at different times, and are bound to different ports. There are about twenty ports and mercantile establishments of different degrees of importance in Iceland; in some of them, especially in Reykjavik and Akureyri, there are a good many resident merchants. Vessels, therefore, have different places of destination, so that although there are annually a good many craft bound to the island—in 1863 there were 148 vessels of 6,850 tons burden—yet, when the large extent of sea they have to traverse, and the different periods at which they sail, are taken into consideration, it will be understood that it is rather a rarity to sight a strange sail.

It was about the eighteenth day of our passage, after we had been driven far to the south, and were again heading our way towards the north, that we first got Iceland in sight. It was one of the lofty rocky islands in Fuglasker, south-west of Reykjanes, the most south-westerly point of Iceland, that our eyes first fell upon. In consequence of this our course was somewhat altered, and we sailed or steamed towards the mainland, which, however, was enveloped by an impervious fog. When it cleared off we were so near land that we could plainly see the surf breaking against the barren rocks which surround the coast. Again, therefore, we had to change our course towards the sound between Eldey, the most northerly of the Fuglasker islands, and Reykjanes; and in the course of the evening our eyes were gladdened by the sight of the looming fjelds and mountain-tops of the peninsula, which juts out in the form of a boot from this corner of Iceland, and thus compels vessels coming from the south to describe three parts of the circumference of a circle, if they wish to reach Reykjavik, which is situated at its northern extremity. This peninsula is remarkable for its numerous lava streams and volcanic craters. The very name—Eldey, or fire island—is an indication that volcanic influence has extended beneath the surface of the sea to this group of islands; in fact, several volcanic eruptions have taken place here, the last of which occurred in 1783, when the surface of the sea was covered so thickly with pumicestone that ships were hindered in their course. In the same year a volcanic crater appeared above the surface of the sea, but the loose slag of which it was composed was speedily washed away by the constant action of the waves, and the newly-formed island disappeared in the course of the same year.

These Fuglasker, or Geirfuglasker, as their southern part is termed, are remarkable as having been the home of the now extinct great auk (*Alca impennis*), a kind of penguin, whose

The Great Auk.

wings are merely swimming flaps. From the fact of there being other Geirfuglasker in several places round the Icelandic coast, there is reason to suppose that this bird was once common there. But the species is supposed to be now quite extinct, owing partly to the persecutions they have undergone at the hands of man or from birds of prey, joined to the little tenacity of life evinced by them. They form thus one of the most valuable ornithological specimens of which a museum can boast.*

On the evening of May 21, when the weather was calm, we passed by Reykjanes, and were struck with the graceful flight of a bird named "Sula" (the gannet), somewhat smaller in size than a goose, and of a beautiful yellowish white colour. They were flying in long rows over the sea. The following day, as we sailed into Faxafjörðr, we passed close by several of them. With their heads under their wings, they were slumbering peacefully on the water, and did not notice our approach till we startled them by clapping our hands.

Faxafjörðr composes one of those broad bays with which the west coast of Iceland is furnished. To the south it is bounded by a peninsula of volcanic formation, and on the north it is separated from Breidifjorðr by a similar tongue of land, which juts out into the sea, and which is crowned by the Snæfell-Jökull, a volcano, 4,577 feet high, whose snow-clad cleft summit, when viewed from Reykjavik, rises up from the sea like a pyramid.

The entrance into Faxafjörðr is very imposing. The chain of mountains that traverse either peninsula to the north and south is continued in the background by a belt of lofty fjelds, of which the majestic Esja, to the north-east of Reykjavik, especially attracted our attention. The mountains, moreover, were rendered more prominent by having their summits and a great part of their sides covered with large masses of snow, which the summer sun had not yet melted; while dark perpen-

* The last known specimen of this species that is known to have existed was killed at Vardö, a Norwegian fortress on the Russian frontier, in 1848.—Tr.

dicular walls of rock, and peaked crags on which the snow could find no resting-place, stood out in bold relief, and presented a most picturesque scene to the eye.

Iceland, as is well known, is a mountainous country, and resembles in this respect the northerly parts of Norway and Sweden.

Some of the loftiest mountains have an altitude varying from 2,000 to 4,000 feet above the sea; while some few volcanic mountains attain to a greater height, such as the above-named Snæfell-Jökull, Herðubreið and Snæfell in the eastern part of the island, of which the first is 5,290 feet, and the other 5,808 feet high. Then there is Hecla, which is 4,961 feet high; Eyafjalla-Jökull, 5,432 feet, on the south coast; and last and highest of all, Öræfa-Jökull, 6,241 feet. The summits of the mountains appear as sharp ridges, and as table-land. The sharp-ridged mountains which are to be found along the coast serve as gigantic partition walls between the numberless fjords that everywhere intersect it; while the table-lands are to be found more in the interior of the country. The volcanoes frequently form solitary and barren crests, rising up from the plains, without any connection with a mountain ridge or plateau; sometimes they spring up from a ridge or plateau, and sometimes the volcanic eruption takes place on the lower table-lands without any apparent connection with the mountains themselves. This lower table-land—which, together with extensive plateaux, constitutes the entire interior of the country—is estimated to reach a height of 1,500 to 2,000 feet above the sea, and it is necessary to cross over it in passing through the island from one shore to the other. The lowlands—which are, in fact, the only habitable portions of the island—consist only of narrow strips, running parallel with the coast, or lying at the bottom of deep valleys. Sometimes, however, though this is exceptional, they appear in the form of a plain or wide valley, which in such cases runs for some distance into the country.

After this trip, let us return once more on board the *Fylla*, and see that she comes safe and sound into port, while we occupy ourselves with some considerations of wider extent. We will only add, that seen from a distance in the fjord, the land which we were approaching seemed to consist only of cold, snow-clad mountains, as the lowlands as a rule are so narrow in extent, that at a distance of even a few miles they are scarcely discernible.

The port of Reykjavik is formed by a little bay on the land side, and is bounded towards the sea by some islands and holms— favourite breeding-places for eider ducks, which may almost be considered a kind of domesticated bird in Iceland. After cruising about for some hours outside these holms, our pilot at length came on board; and then, with all sails set and at full speed, we steered our course into the long-wished-for harbour, and cast anchor on Monday afternoon, the 22nd of May, alongside a French frigate, which, in company with a number of small merchant vessels belonging to different countries, had arrived there before us.

This, then, was Reykjavik that lay before us: a small town with small houses, rather dusky-looking in appearance from seaward, owing, perhaps, to a number of tarred warehouses that shut out from view, in their rear, some painted dwelling-houses; and possibly too because a great many of the neighbouring dwellings were besmeared with the same pitchy covering. This, then, was the far-famed Iceland, on whose soil I purposed to travel many a mile during the course of the summer. The first natives we saw were the pilot and his companions, dressed in a complete suit of dark *wadmel* (home-spun cloth), with round hats furnished with long lappets, and possessed of good-natured intelligent faces withal. Their promise to provide us with fresh fish, however, I must confess, was for the moment the most attractive point about them. As soon as we had cast anchor, I repaired ashore to the Swedish and Norwegian Consul, Herr Siemsen, a merchant of Reykjavik, in order to get him to recommend me a lodging during my stay in the town. I now learnt, during my interview with him, that though the houses in Reykjavik were insignificant to look at, yet that inside I should find them to be replete with all the conveniences and comforts of civilised life; an observation which I found amply confirmed from my subsequent acquaintance with the good people of Reykjavik at whose houses I visited. I lose no time in recording this fact, to prevent the reader who may be unacquainted with the actual relations of the place from thinking that Reykjavik is a semi-barbarous village. On the contrary, Reykjavik corresponds exactly, as far as regards manner of life and comfortably furnished dwellings, to its model, the city of Copenhagen; while it numbers among its inhabitants many intelligent and well-educated persons. The houses in general, however, are small: wooden buildings of one story, with gable roofs, often only painted on the side towards the street, while on the others they are tarred. But as regards their internal arrangements, I can only say that they are all that can be desired. The town is by no means large: it boasts of three principal streets, running parallel with the sea, only two of which, however, are, properly speaking, inhabited; and of three cross streets. Moreover, an irregularly-built suburb adjoins it on both sides, in which the houses are constructed of turf, while a lake bounds it on the rear. On this side are situated the church and the school-house, which, together with the Stiftamtmand's (Lord-Lieutenant) house, compose the public buildings of the town.

Reykjavik, therefore, is a neat little town, with regular streets, which, though they certainly are not paved, are yet at least dry and clean in summer time; for driving is a thing unknown in this country, where a cart is not to be found, and where everything is carried on horseback. Its situation is decidedly picturesque; and the view from the town, with its pretty harbour, and the blue sea outside, and majestic Mount Esja in the background, forms a very charming picture indeed.

The population of Reykjavik is of a mixed character, partly Danish, partly Icelandic. To the first nationality belong the greater proportion of the merchants; while among the last-named may be ranked the officials, a few mechanics, and the fishing population. The number of residents in the town is about 1,500; and counting those living in the country close by, it amounts to about 2,000.

If it be possible to form any opinion from the comfort which prevailed in the houses of the merchants to whom I had the pleasure of being introduced, not in Reykjavik alone, but in other parts of Iceland too, I should certainly be tempted to say that commerce in that country was an exceedingly remunerative business. Only a portion, however, of the merchants who trade in Iceland are settled in the country. The larger number of the mercantile establishments are conducted by paid managers; but as a certain percentage of the yearly profit always falls to their share, their manner of life affords some scale for estimating the state of affairs. And I repeat that I consider these to be in a flourishing state. At all events, they were so till 1854, when a complete system of free trade was introduced into the country, after which time the yearly profit was divided among several competitors. This is the cause why one hears the assertion among the mercantile classes, "Oh!

this business does not pay!" They take care to add—"as well as it did before!"

The public officials receive their salaries direct from the Danish exchequer, since in a financial view Iceland is not yet separated from Denmark; and their position, therefore, corresponds somewhat to that of similar officials in Denmark. The representative of the Danish government in Iceland is the Stiftamtmand in Reykjavik; who, moreover, is Amtmand of one of the three Amts or provinces into which the island is divided in an administrative respect. But the Stiftamtmand is, however, only a kind of intermediate link with regard to the other Amtmænd, who though they receive the resolutions and orders of the government through him, yet occupy an independent position. Under the Amtmænd, moreover, there are officials named Sysselmænd, whose duty it is to collect the revenue, &c., within their respective districts; they act, moreover, as judges in the first instance, and are further tolerably independent in the discharge of their duties; and as everyone only obeys his own Amtmand, and pays no heed to the Stiftamtmand, it will readily be seen that the government of Iceland in the country itself is not of a very centralized form. The point of union is the Icelandic department in Copenhagen, which lies under the Board of Justice; and this point is situated at rather a long distance away. Administrative harmony, therefore, in Iceland, as far as I can ascertain, is in rather an unsound state, as each of the above-named officials is, as it were, a petty king within his own limits; while this strong system of decentralization in a country so thinly inhabited and of comparatively such wide extent cannot but act detrimentally to the proper discharge of duties where a common point of amalgamation is either altogether wanting or else is too far distant.

A good exemplification of this appeared in the treatment of a disease that visited the flocks of Iceland, and which has for some years caused no little panic in the island. In order to improve the breed some Icelandic farmers had imported sheep from abroad; but these new importations introduced a dire disease, which spread in a most alarming manner, and threatened to exterminate all the flocks in the country, which constitute in fact the principal source of revenue. Let us see then how the government acted in an extremity which threatened to become a national calamity. The Amtmand in the north of the island, acting in concert with others, prudently determined on adopting a plan which, under the circumstances, was the only sure way of guarding against the disease spreading; and this was to slaughter all the infected animals, and thus stamp the plague out of the country. But unfortunately the authority of this Amtmand was circumscribed. His proposal, however, was readily embraced, and large sums were raised in the uninfected districts to compensate those who had slaughtered their sheep in the infected parts. Nearly one hundred and fifty thousand sheep were thus actually slaughtered, by which precautions a wide belt was established between the healthy and the infected districts. But the Stiftamtmand in Reykjavik, together with some Icelanders, whose counsel the government in Copenhagen had sought on this occasion, were of opinion that the disease was capable of being cured. The consequence of this determination has been that the plague has secured a footing in certain districts of the island, and thus the people in other parts live in constant dread that it will break out among them, in which case emigration or starvation will be their only resource. In order to guard against either of these evils, a mountain guard has been established under the direction of certain individuals, a standing body of mounted watchmen, whose duty it is to see that no sheep are introduced from the infected parts into those which are free from the plague. The inconvenience and the expense attendant upon such a course of action can readily be understood; and as the expectations of those who hoped to be able to eradicate the parasites which are the cause of the disease, have not hitherto been crowned with success, there is every prospect that the mounted guard will have to be continued, which even then cannot ensure to keep the line of demarcation intact. Up to the present time, however, they have succeeded through a course of years in keeping the plague away from the healthy parts of the island—a happy circumstance, entirely due to that patriotic love which impels the watchmen to be constantly at their post, and on the alert to guard against any infected sheep slipping through their line into those uninhabited and desolate regions whither their duties call them. Only in a few isolated cases has medical science been of any avail in curing the disease. The adherents, therefore, of this method of treatment, amongst whom the apothecary element of course occupies a prominent place, maintain that the disease originated of itself in the country, and that therefore it is purely an accidental circumstance that the slaughter of the diseased animals can be of any benefit. But as it has been ascertained that the disease is caused by parasites which attach themselves firmly to the animals' skin, and as these parasites cannot possibly be self-existent, their opinion is but of little weight. If it had been observed in any part of Iceland that the plague had appeared among sheep which had had no contact with those that were infected, then of course one might have concluded that the germs of the disease had been borne along by the wind. This I say would have been only a reasonable theory, but to suppose that the disease could thus have been propagated from other countries is, to say the least, highly improbable.

This sheep disease, however, affords an instance of the great necessity there is for the existence of a supervisional authority in the country, and of the advantages that would accrue therefrom; for it is only reasonable to conclude that it would be enabled to take better steps to provide for the national interests, than the distant government at Copenhagen can possibly do.

The sheep plague, however, affords a proof of that intense love of country for which the Icelander is so remarkable; for there were individuals, who, without any regard to compensation being made them, slaughtered their entire stocks, and thereby deprived themselves of a very important part of their property, solely for the purpose of setting a good example to others.

The position of the law officers in the country is a good one. Thus the yearly income of a Sysselmand amounts from 1,500 to 2,000 rix-dollars*. Consequently these posts have of late been sought after by many distinguished Danes. The national party in the country, however, look upon this with great antipathy; although Icelanders are entitled to corresponding privileges in Denmark, and can fill similar offices in that country; yet somehow or other this has always been a matter of complaint where a subjected people have received their officials from the superior. Moreover, the principle of nationality is at the present time being strongly developed in Iceland. Still I have met with many eminent Icelanders, who have preferred a competent Danish to an inefficient native official, though such liberal notions are decidedly the exception, and are by no means in harmony with the views of those who would have Icelanders at any price to fill the different posts in their country.

When it is borne in mind that twenty Sysselmænd and three Amtmænd are the only officials in the country appointed by the State, it must be allowed that the administrative government is not of a complicated kind. The first-named, as I have previously stated, act as judges in the first instance, and as such

* Rix dollar = 2s. 3d.

stand nearest in authority to the High Court in Reykjavik, a tribunal that is composed of three members. Added to these officials there is also a Landfoged, who is collector of the revenue for the whole country, and who for the moment unites in his own person the office of Town Foged in Reykjavik.*

Akureyri, which has recently obtained the privileges of a commercial town, also owns its Town Foged, and with this I have enumerated the entire official corps of the country. So much for the political government.

As regards the ecclesiastical establishment there is a bishop in Reykjavik, who together with the Stiftamtmand forms the spiritual magistracy. Below this come twenty archdeaconries, and the extremely high number of a hundred and ninety-six livings, for the filling up of which a pastoral seminary, with a course of instruction lasting over two years, has of late been established in Reykjavik. The only public educational institution in the country consists of an elementary school in Reykjavik, conducted on the same system as the schools in Denmark. It boasts of about forty or fifty pupils, most of whom pass through all the classes of the school, and have to submit to a final examination. It is only within the last ten years that Reykjavik has been made the centre for educational purposes, and for the discharge of high official duties; a circumstance that has undoubtedly caused a great deal of ill-feeling in many parts of the country. Instead, however, of having worked detrimentally, this uniting of the powers and energies of the country for the public weal in one place has produced very beneficial effects. For Reykjavik, which in the beginning of the present century was nothing but a miserable port, can now boast of a most respectable capital of intelligence, whose

* The Landfoged is a superior revenue officer, and is in some instances invested with judicial authority.—TR.

united endeavours will do far more to promote the interests of the country, than when its various bodies were scattered here and there over the face of the land far from each other, and with but little opportunities for reciprocal communion.*

In connection with this, during the last ten years, a library has been formed in Reykjavik, which at the present time boasts of some eight thousand volumes; besides this a public press has been set on foot, represented by two political journals, *Þjóðólfr* or the *National*, which comes out in forty-eight numbers during the course of the year; and the *Islendingur*, which though rather a larger paper than the other comes out less frequently. In Reykjavik too there is a printing-press, or as it is termed, "Iceland's printing smithy," which still maintains the sole right of printing religious books for the country.

There is another printing-press in the country at Akureyri. From this too is issued a weekly paper—*Norðanfari*, the third newspaper of which the country boasts.†

The above-named journals—at least the first and the last—have a tolerably good circulation. In 1864 the entire popula-

---

* Henderson, who travelled in Iceland in 1816 in order to distribute Bibles, speaks of Reykjavik in the most disparaging terms. "The tone of society there," he says, "is the very lowest imaginable. While the town is for the most part only inhabited by a few foreigners devoid of education, and whose sole object is to make money, it affords a mournful spectacle, from a religious point of view, and displays an entire absence of appreciation for anything of a higher nature." But by comparing Reykjavik with what it was to what it is, it is satisfactory to see the progress that has taken place; and, as far as I am able to judge, an opinion pronounced about the town must be of a favourable character. It is true a few complaints may be heard here and there concerning the temptations of the capital, especially with regard to the youth attending the schools. Even the rector of the school himself considers the town, as the seat of the school, to be beneath all criticism. But one may gain some idea of the worthy rector's ideas about education from a remark of his, that he would rather have the school established at Videy, a rocky island or "holm" out in the fjord below Reykjavik. There, he is of opinion, he could educate his pupils after a better model than that which Reykjavik affords.

† The art of printing was introduced into Iceland in 1531, in which year the first printed book was issued in that country.

tion of the country amounted to 66,000, and the *National* numbered 1,200 subscribers. This circumstance is easy of explanation; for not only can every Icelander read, but he enters with interest into everything connected with his country. In this respect they have much in common with their Norwegian brothers; for wherever I came in Norway, even in the poorest peasant-hut, I rarely failed to find a political journal.

The *National* unquestionably fulfils the demands required by any political newspaper. Besides leading articles which bear witness to a lively interest in the weal of the father-isle, it details all the most important political events that have occurred in the world; contains articles from correspondents in Copenhagen and London; gives reviews of the literature of the day, —at least of that which is written in the mother-tongue; besides a host of other matters. As far as regards its external appearance, it is all that can be desired.

I do not know, however, how the *Islendingur* has got on. At the beginning of 1865, it appeared with less regularity than before; and with reference to this an article appeared in the *National*, in which the writer expressed his belief that the *Islendingur* was not dead, but had only gone to sleep. In the autumn, however, as I was leaving the country, the same paper contained another article, in which the writer believed he had made the discovery that the *Islendingur* was no longer asleep, but was really dead.

After these brief pieces of information on Icelandic matters, which will not be without interest, I have to request the reader to lend his attention to the author's person, who is now on the point of quitting the *Fylla*, and has arranged to take up his abode in an unassuming but comfortable little hotel—"The Scandinavian:" the only Scandinavianism, by the way, I could detect any traces of in Iceland.

As soon as I set foot on land, the sight of the snow-covered mountains confirmed the opinion I had already formed, that a long time would have to elapse before I should be able to undertake a journey overland to the east coast, which, it will be remembered, was the goal I had aimed at. The spring this year in Iceland had been extremely cold and backward, owing partly to the large quantity of ice that had accumulated on the northern coast, partly to the heavy snowfall that had taken place during the previous winter. There was therefore too little grass about to render it possible for horses to undertake any lengthened journey; hay, moreover, was an article not to be found at this season of the year, except in some individual farmhouses; and as for oats, the Icelandic horses, from being unused to such fare, will not even touch them. These hardy animals are quite contented if they can manage to pick up a green twig, or a handful of dried grass or moss in winter time from under the snow; or, if they are near the sea-coast, to eat their fill on sea-weed. But during this hungry period they cannot be used, as the Icelander only places a small number of his horses on better fare during the winter time, and these of course are not for sale. The difficulty, therefore, of procuring serviceable horses, and the impossibility of preventing them from starving to death on the road, were the chief hindrances I had to contend with.

Fortunately for me, the neighbourhood of Reykjavik afforded many points of scientific interest; else the delay of three weeks to which I was doomed, and which necessarily formed so large a portion of my short visit to the country, would have proved a great misfortune. Accordingly, I bought a couple of horses, and made short excursions around Reykjavik; and thus acquired a good deal of information respecting the nature of the country and its inhabitants.

The immediate neighbourhood of Reykjavik had a remarkably desolate appearance on my arrival there; and even at any season of the year there is nothing about it calculated to raise one's ideas of its beauty. Both of the long, cold mountain ridges between which Reykjavik lies, appeared at the time of my visit to have a miserable look about them; the more so, as the green, grassy belt which in summer time is formed at their foot, lay at that time still wrapped up in its winter garment. The lowlands presented either a yellowish appearance—caused by the withered blades of grass, which the disappearance of the snow had only recently exposed to view—or else a greyish hue.

Picture of a "melr."

These plains of stone and sand, which are almost entirely destitute of vegetation, are very common in Iceland, and are called by a peculiar name—"melr." But, though desolate wastes, they are not without interest. On examining the surface of one of these wastes, one cannot but observe the regular form the small stones and pebbles assume upon it,—in fact, like land-drains in a field; while the sand between them forms a smooth and even surface. Professor Steenstrup has given the correct explanation of this phenomenon, which may be seen in many places in Iceland. When, for instance, the earth, rendered soft by the melting of the snow in spring, has become dried by the heat of summer, rifts or cracks are formed in it; and when a storm occurs, the small stones that lie on the surface of the "melr" are swept down into them. The accompanying sketch will give some idea of the appearance of these wastes.

That this is the correct explanation of this peculiar phenomenon, is confirmed by the fact that where the sand, as in volcanic districts, lies loose and dry, and where there is no coherence between its particles, no "melr" like that just described is formed on the melting of the snow in spring. For when the heat of summer dries it, the particles of sand fall away from each other, and no cracks are formed in the ground.

The only mode of travelling in Iceland is on horseback. Roads do not exist, and the bridle-paths, though certainly good, are at the same time remarkably simple in their construction, as the reader will presently judge for himself. What a Danish writer, moreover, mentions as being the greatest blessing in other countries, is an actual curse in Iceland; I refer to the numerous and rapid streams, which, though not usually of any great length, coming as they do from the enormous snow-mountains or Jökuls, in the interior of the country, carry down large masses of water; and, occasionally, in the very warmest part of the summer, place insurmountable hindrances in the way of the traveller, while at the same time their passage is not unattended with danger. In most cases it is advisable to let one's horse wade through them, for bridges are a rarity in Iceland; and generally speaking the current is too rapid to admit of a ferry across them. Consequently many a life is lost, either from imprudence, or from causes over which the traveller has no control.

It is therefore essential for the traveller to be provided with a guide, not only on account of the numerous rivers he will meet with in his course, but also because his road has often few if any distinguishing marks; and further, as there are no stations for the entertainment of wayfarers in the country, he will find a guide to be an absolute necessity.

From the short excursions I took in the neighbourhood of Reykjavik, I soon found the desirability of having a guide. One day I took it into my head to follow the road leading to the far-famed Geysir; and could not believe that the narrow, unimportant-looking track I was following could possibly be the right path; and it was not till I had missed my way several times that I became convinced of it. Another day, too, as I was paying a visit to Hafnarfjörðr, about an hour's distance from Reykjavik, I got on all right till I reached a little brook. Here the path disappeared altogether, and I did not discover till after a very long time spent in hunting for it in all directions, that it actually lay at the bottom of the brook in question, where I naturally was unable to see it. This, however, occurred in the spring, before the merchants from the country had begun their journeys down to the capital. In summer-time the roads round Reykjavik at least were more visible; but it was very droll to hear the guide call to one or other of the loose horses in some of the remote parts I had to travel through, in a reproachful tone, "Are you going on the path?" where, to my eyes at least, not the vestige of a path was visible.

The first thing that will excite the curiosity of the traveller in the country, is the style in which an Icelandic house, or "bær," as it is termed, is constructed. They are built partly of earth alone, partly of earth and stone mixed, and have a turf roof. In summer-time, when these are covered with a mantle of green, they can scarcely be distinguished from the surrounding field,

Timber-work is seldom to be found in the fabric of their houses, for in that woodless country timber is a very costly material, and is rendered still more so by the difficulties of transporting it from the seaports up into the interior. Wooden houses, therefore, are a rarity in Iceland; and it is only in the two principal towns, and in the mercantile establishments along the coast, that this luxury is to be found. But yet one must not look upon an Icelandic "bær" as a mere earth hut, and nothing more. Many of them, indeed, are not much better; but many of them possess rather an intricate arrangement, which at first sight is rather difficult of comprehension. Neither is this arrangement the same everywhere, but depends on the taste and the circumstances of the owner. The small number of the clergy in the country who live as gentlemen, and the equally limited number of well-to-do farmers, imitate, as far as they can, the style adopted in wooden houses; for they have rooms with painted or panelled walls, or at least one or two such for the reception of guests, and for their own use, provided with floors, an article of luxury which is not general. But the poorest of the population dwell literally in earthen burrows, though instead of being underground they are above it. I was once in a "bær," in the neighbourhood of Reykjavik, which was constructed of the usual materials. The interior, which was very low and dark, formed only one room, one end of which was occupied by two bedsteads, the two side walls with a small, oblong table, and at the other end of the apartment was a store-room, where provisions, wool, moss, &c., were stored away. The fireplace, which was marked only by a few stones, was in the middle, opposite the entrance. This house possessed no floor, and no other ceiling than the rafters which sustained the roof of turf. Light was admitted through a couple of small apertures in the roof, and the house was so low, that the cross-beams which supported the rafters reached to the middle of my chest as I stood upright. A ceiling, therefore, would evidently have been an impossibility; at least, if there had been one, it would have been necessary to crawl in and out of the room, and to remain in a sitting posture the whole time.

As may be supposed, everything in such a "bœr" is impregnated with smoke, and in a very filthy state; in fact, the filth surpasses description. On the day in question, I had been out on a long and fatiguing expedition. It was evening when I arrived there; and I was almost frozen from the rain and fog, and had a ride of several hours before me before reaching Reykjavik; and, moreover, had had the disagreeable pleasure of riding through an icy-cold brook which came directly from the melting snow on Mount Esja, and had thus, rather against my will, indulged in a foot-bath of Jökul-water. I was glad enough to accept of the peasant's hospitable invite to come in and drink coffee under his roof; for coffee and brandy are, I should state, the national beverages in Iceland.

I have always made it a rule when on my travels to observe that well-known and wise saying, "That which goeth into the mouth defileth not the man." Of course I avoid all filthiness as much as possible; this I consider to be quite as incumbent upon a man as it is to be not too particular. After I had happily succeeded in finding my way through the dark and dirty entrance, and had fortunately avoided breaking my head against the low rafters, I took my seat on one of the above-described bedsteads, and waited for the arrival of the coffee, during which interval I took the opportunity of making the observations which I have already communicated to the reader. The coffee was soon ready, for in an Icelandic "bœr" the coffee-kettle stands upon the fire at all hours of the day; and the coffee was remarkably good, as is universally the case in

Iceland. But I was not a little astounded when I saw my host rummaging about in the foot of the bed, and presently pull out a bag, the colour of which can be better imagined than described, containing some fine sugar. It needed all my stoicism to follow out my principle.

This, of course, was one of the poorest of the Icelandic "bær." In the neighbourhood of fishing stations these "bær" are generally of a very simple kind, but the style of building in the northern and eastern parts is decidedly superior. A well-arranged Icelandic dwelling usually consists of seven houses, six of which at least have only one room; the seventh, in which the inmates usually reside, and which is termed the "baðstofa," is often divided into two or three apartments by means of wooden partitions. Each house stands under its own roof. The walls are composed, as I have already stated, of turf, or of turf and stone, laid on each other in layers, without any further joining, and are usually four or five feet in thickness. The houses are arranged side by side of each other in a row, with their gables to the front, or sometimes behind one another. Besides this, they are constructed in such a way that the two contiguous houses have a common intermediate wall; but, as they are not under the same roof, an open place is formed above the wall where the rain water collects. The roof is covered with turf, which is laid either immediately on laths, or else on flat stones or dried oaten straw, which rests upon them. Neither roof nor walls can keep out the rain, or at least the damp, so that in matter of dryness the Icelandic "bær" is very deficient. The roof and walls, with the exception of the plank-work on the gables, which is either not painted at all, or at best is tarred over as far down as the window-sill, perhaps, are naturally overgrown with grass; and as the whole structure has only a very slight elevation above the ground, and as the quantity of turf used gives it rather a rounded appearance, it really is often a difficult matter to decide whether they are a number of low, grass-grown hillocks one sees before one or an Icelandic "bœr."* The accompanying sketch of a parsonage in the north of the island will give some idea of the Icelandic style of architecture, as I have endeavoured to describe it.

One of the extreme buildings is the cattle-shed, where the

An Icelandic Parsonage.

cows are kept; the house at the other extremity is the smithy. Sometimes, however, both of these, or at least the last named, are detached from the other houses. The remaining houses are used as dwelling-rooms, dairy, store-rooms, kitchen, &c. The first we will speak of is the "skemma;" it has a separate entrance. In the above sketch it is one of the houses lying second from the end. Thus there can be two "skemmas," as is

* Henderson relates that an officer in Iceland told him that one dark night he actually rode on to a "Bœr," and did not find out his mistake till his horse sank into a hole, which proved to be the chimney.

the case here. The other houses communicate with each other by means of passages in the inside of the building. These passages are never floored, neither, indeed, is the kitchen ("eldhuus") or the store-room ("búr"); they have no windows, and are, consequently, pitchy dark, so that even in broad daylight it is necessary to grope one's way along them. The "baðstofa," or dwelling-house, which is generally provided with a floor—at least, amongst well-to-do-people—lies either in the hindmost part of the building or else is situated on the loft; that is to say, under the roof in one of the houses. In Skaptafellsyssel, in the south, this loft is often built over the cow-house, so that the inmates can have the benefit of the warmth arising from the cows below; for fire-places and stoves are unknown there, and the people can only warm themselves by crowding together as much as possible. In addition to the above-named apartments, people in better circumstances have a "stofa," or "gestaskáli," a room specially devoted to the reception of visitors; it is situated either to the right or left of the main entrance, which is termed the "bœardyr," or ante-room: and with this the description of an Icelandic dwelling is complete. The kitchen, as I have stated, is not floored, neither does it possess a brick fire-place; this is formed merely of some flat stones placed on the ground. There is no chimney, but the roof has one or two holes in it, over which a kind of oblong pipe, made of planks, is placed, in order to increase the draught. Of course this arrangement is defective; consequently, the smoke is generally beaten down into the apartment, and as the fuel is not always of the finest description, the odour generated is far from pleasant. Turf and the excrements of cattle form the usual fuel. The contents of the dung-heap are first spread on the field outside, where they lie a little while, and then are collected again; but the droppings of the sheep, which are trodden into a compact mass during the winter, are cut up in spring and dried, and are then burnt. In certain districts, and especially amongst the poor fishermen, even this fuel cannot be procured, therefore fish bones, and especially the backbone of the codfish, sheep bones, dried seaweed, &c., usurp its place.

In the Vestmannöer, a group of islands off the south-west coast, the bodies of two kinds of birds—viz., the sea-parrot and petrel*—are found in great numbers, and are used as fuel. In the first-named bird the breast is salted down for food, and the rest of the body is hung up to dry, wings, entrails, and all, and is afterwards burnt for fuel. In the last-named, head, feet, entrails, and wings are mixed up with cowdung. It is only in a very few places that brushwood is used for burning; and coals, which may be got in the towns, are only used in the smithy, as the cost of transporting them on horseback up into the interior would be too great.

The "stofa," or guest-room, is furnished with a bed, a table, and generally a few chests, which serve as chairs; but in the "baðstofa" the furniture consists only of beds, which are fixed to the wall, and which are so capacious that they will hold two or three persons each. Sometimes, though not often, there is a small table in the room; but everybody eats his meals sitting upon his bedstead, with his plate or porringer before him. Looking-glasses and chests of drawers are a great rarity.

Icelandic houses are low, dark, damp, and unhealthy in every respect; in a word, the style of architecture in vogue there is the most uncomfortable that can possibly exist among

* The sea-parrots dig holes in the sand, like rabbits, and build their nests at the depth of two or three yards below the surface of the ground. They are caught by means of a hook fastened to the end of a stick; and what is singular, when one is dragged out his companions take hold of him and endeavour to detain him, by which means they are often caught to the number of three or four at a time.—ED.

civilised individuals. In addition to this they are always in a most filthy state, and thus help to increase the general mortality in a great degree.

It may be a matter of surprise to the reader to find that in so northerly a country as Iceland houses are built without fire-places; but, though the summer is colder, the winter is milder than under the same degree of latitude in Sweden—a circumstance for which thanks are due to the Gulf Stream, which washes three sides of the Icelandic coast. The inhabitants, therefore, have no need to use fur-coats in the winter time, but are able to walk about in their usual summer dress.

In the above description of their dwellings all the conveniences wherewith an Icelander's house is furnished, be he clergyman or simple peasant, have been enumerated.

For the accommodation of their sheep and cattle, which are allowed to remain under the open sky as long as possible, they have small turf houses, without any windows, erected at some little distance from the "bær." In certain parts of the country, where there is not much snow in the winter time, the stables for the horses have no roof at all, but are only provided with a narrow kind of eaves shooting out from the walls. It would be too warm for the animals were they shut up in a confined place. Naturally in a stable of this description there are no such things as stalls. Icelandic horses are not acquainted with such luxuries; they have their entire liberty, and move about among each other as they list while munching the hay with which they are fed in winter. A "bœr," with its cow-house, sheep-house, and stable, may thus be considered to resemble our farm-houses. They are generally built at the extremity of a hill along the foot of a mountain, or on an eminence on a swamp or fen. Their existence is usually discovered by the green field or two lying around them, rather than by anything else, as they resemble grassy hillocks more than human dwelling-places. Generally speaking they are not built very close to one another, as each farmer requires a large grass walk for his flocks, which sometimes are very numerous, and for hay for the winter store; and as the "tun," as the enclosed land belonging to a "bœr" is termed, is of extremely small dimensions in comparison with the surrounding country, over which the eye, unimpeded by forests or the like hindrances to the sight, can have a free range, these "bœr," with their little patches of land, appear in the distance like diminutive grassy patches, standing out in relief against the gray and sombre *heiði*. In other words, these cultivated patches of land which are scattered very sparsely over the face of the country, would form a remarkably small fractional part of the 1,800 geographical square miles which Iceland contains, if their superficial area could be ascertained.

Much has been said and written about the Icelandic style of building, especially with reference to the dampness of the houses and their consequent unhealthiness. And no doubt there is a great deal of truth in these remarks, for the filth and dirt of the "bœr" is frequently intolerable. But if in order to remedy these defects the motive has been to recommend wood as a building material instead of turf and stone, we cannot think it will have any practical effect; for, however desirable it might be for all classes of society to live in wooden houses, yet as Iceland can never be made a timber-producing country, the necessary materials would be of far too costly a nature. In my opinion it would be a much better plan to instruct the people how to build and arrange their houses of turf after a better model, so that they might be both light and dry. The present style of "bœr" is far from being light; for the thick turf walls through which the passages are made, and which unite the different apartments of which the entire building is composed with each other, make it so pitchy dark, that one might well believe one was entering into a cellar instead of into a human dwelling-place, while the apartments themselves are both uncomfortable and gloomy. A great deal might unquestionably be done to remove these disagreeables, such as by draining, ventilation, &c., whereby the mortality of the country would be not a little diminished. In the present style of houses the damp is so excessive that floors and walls which are panelled rot away in the course of a very few years.

Often when I have looked at the outside of an Icelandic "bær" I have felt astonished at the little taste for colour exhibited by the natives. While our pretty red painted farm-houses present such a pleasing contrast against the green back-ground, the front of an Icelandic house is never of any other colour than a sombre grey, like that of an old rotten paling, or at best of a dark black. Red paint, which is so cheap everywhere, does not seem to have found its way into the country. The furniture of the respective apartments is miserable in the extreme; and should there happen to be a floor in the room it is generally covered with such a mass of filth that one might well believe one was walking on the bare ground instead of on wooden boards. Of course there are a few of the clergy who are better off, and some few farmers who live in a more refined way, who have their rooms floored and indulge in a better description of furniture, and who in matters of cleanliness and good order might well afford a pattern to the people of any country whatever. But unfortunately they are few in number, and are moreover spread here and there over the face of the country. In many places it becomes painfully evident that it is not poverty alone that is the cause of that uncleanliness which is so universally complained of; so that one is almost tempted to believe that the Icelander, though he possesses many good points, has this detestable characteristic, that he cares nothing at all about cleanliness.

As regards agriculture it is well known that cereals cannot be grown with any success in the country. The only native corn that is to be found there is the wild sand-oat, *Elymus arenarius*, from which an eatable kind of bread can be made. In addition to grass, which is the principal vegetable produce of the country, little else is grown besides potatoes and turnips.

From the "Tun" remaining year after year unworked, its original flat surface gets gradually more and more uneven, so that at last it becomes a mass of little hillocks. The cause of this is that the water, especially when the snow melts in the spring of the year, soaks into the ground, and causes it to give way. This depression of the soil increases year by year, till at last it assumes the form of a deep or shallow furrow according to the nature of the soil; and so when these furrows unite and spread over the "Tun" in a net-like form, the ground is broken up into these little hillocks. Certainly there are some among the Icelandic peasantry who say they prefer this hillocky ground, because they thus have a larger surface; just in the same way as some of our country people have a predilection for a farm that has a good deal of hilly ground upon it; but generally speaking this state of things must be attributed to carelessness alone. The labour, however, of restoring one of these neglected fields to its normal state would unquestionably be rather arduous; for in the first place, the turf would have to be carefully removed, the mound of earth underneath levelled, and then the turf replaced on the flattened surface.

Iceland, from its earliest days, for not less than three hundred years, formed an independent republic. Certainly it is a good while since this republic ceased to exist upon paper; for in

1262 she took the oath of allegiance to the King of Norway. But as her isolated position has been the means of preserving the old Norse language in its pure and original form, so also has it tended to keep alive a spirit of republicanism in the country. This may be seen even in the way in which an Icelander salutes one of his countrymen. "Good day, comrade," he says; thus reminding one of the "citoyen" of modern republics. The title "Herre" is almost unknown in the island. In speaking of each other the peasants naturally make use of the Christian name; but they also employ this confidential style in addressing people of superior rank, as for instance a Sysselmand or a merchant. Where there is a family name it of course is most frequently used; but family names are uncommon among the native Icelanders, even amongst those of the upper classes. So that the same custom is in vogue here as we learn to have been the case with exalted personages in the middle ages in our own country, namely that people were usually named by their own Christian names, and their father's name; for instance, Bo Jonson; Carl Knutson; in fact, as is even now customary among the lower classes in Sweden.

The clergy alone possess a handle to their names, "Sira," or Reverend, which is joined to their Christian name, as Sira Jon, Sira Jacob, &c. The above remarks, it should be stated, only refer to their conversational language. In their written language the title Herre is of wider use than with us; thus they allude to a man as "Herr Bonde," or "Herr Repstyrer," which would have the same signification among us if we were to write "Mr. Farmer," or "Mr. Police-constable."

On one of my excursions from Reykjavik in which I made use of a guide, the fellow asked me my name. I told him my surname, but, remembering the custom, I also informed him what my Christian name was. After we had been riding along some distance, and the previous conversation had quite gone out of my head, I presently heard some one calling me by my Christian name from behind. Astounded at hearing myself thus addressed I turned round, but as I did not at once discover whence the voice proceeded, I concluded that I was another Saul who heard voices from the heaven, till at last my eyes fell on my companion, who was mysteriously pointing at a large bird sitting by the roadside. I now recollected the conversation we had held, and regarded the honourable " citoyen " before me with a feeling of satisfaction, remarking to myself that now at least I had come to a country where the people looked on one another as brothers. But though the Icelanders regard each other as brethren, and do not show much respect to rank, I certainly must compliment them on their attentive and polite behaviour both towards strangers and to each other. The Icelander, for instance, always takes his cap off when he salutes anyone, and not content with merely touching the peak, actually bares his head. I have wondered much at this custom, and have thought that possibly it might be the result of the confidential manner in which they kiss each other when they meet, in which operation of course the peak of the cap or the brim of the hat would be in the way. For the Icelandic kiss of welcome and farewell is no empty ceremony; it is given with warmth and expression, and is repeated two or three times, without the least regard to age, sex, or other incompatibilities between the parties concerned. But still as this external politeness appears to me to be only the expression of the feelings, I have abandoned my theory, and have arrived at the conclusion that the Icelanders are naturally polite, at least towards those who are polite to them in turn.

Iceland, however, is not entirely free from that infirmity which is called the title-disease. Still it occurs only sporadically, and where titles are used they have probably been introduced without the wish of the parties principally concerned. There are but few persons in this country who can lay claim to titular rank, for in the whole eastern and in a part of the northern districts of the island everybody knows who is intended when one speaks of the "Cancelliraad" ("Raad," Councillor), and in Skagafjördur the "Kammeraad" is the only person of title, whilst in Reykjavik there is a "Justits-raad," a "Stat-raad," and a "Conferents-raad." I do not think they exist in the plural number.

Whilst staying in Reykjavik I took a trip to the beautiful Mount Esja, which I could see every day from my windows in the town, and which I therefore felt greatly tempted to visit. The first day I rode as far as Moum's Parsonage, at the foot of the Fjeld, a common "bær," surrounded on all sides by soft bogs, to drain which just as little attempts had been made as in other parts of the country. There can be no doubt that it would pay to treat these bogs in this manner, both in an agricultural and a sanitary point of view; for when the summer sun does all in its power to warm the earth, the heat its rays give out during the day is expended in the evaporation of the water in the bog; and the earth, therefore, is as cold in the evening as it was in the morning. In this way the whole summer passes by; for bogs that are not properly ditched are like sponges, which, though the water on their surface may be evaporated, still keep sucking up fresh supplies from underneath. To lay them dry, therefore, is the first essential towards improving the climate; and we all know from experience from other countries what can be done under such circumstances.

The morning after my arrival at Moum, I was anxious to commence the ascent of Esja, and therefore my host, the pastor, asked me whether I had not better ride from his house to the foot of the hill. I looked at him with an air of astonishment, for it seemed to be only a five-minutes' walk. "But," he remarked, "the bog is so soft!" This may serve to give some idea of the rude condition of nature in Iceland, and of the little attempts that have been made to submit it to human agency; indeed, without a horse, one cannot get on at all. The shortest road may be totally impassable, ending, as it may do, in a bog; or else a waterfall or an arm of the sea may suddenly prevent all further progress; so that, without a horse, one's position would be deplorable in the extreme.

The ascent of Esja is very steep, the last portion of it consisting of earth-slips, which present a very precipitous face. The actual top is flat, and was covered with a very deep snow- "Fond," as the large masses of snow which are collected there, and which do not melt till late in the summer or in the early part of the autumn, are termed. My guide pointed out to me a "varde," or stone cairn, which he said had been erected by one of my countrymen many years ago. The Swede in question can have been no other than the famous Archbishop Uno von Troil, who, in company with two English travellers, made the ascent in 1772.

The prospect from Esja is grand in the extreme. Snæfellsjökull can be seen in the north-west, raising its head above the mountain-ridge that forms the back bone of the peninsula bounding Faxafjörðr on the north. To the north, Skarðsheiði rears its snow-clad crown, while, far away to the north-east of this, may be seen the Lángjökull Fjeld, some three miles (Danish) in breadth; and still further eastward, the Hofsjökull, which latter constitute the two principal snowy mountains in the interior of the country. The side of Lángjökull seen from Esja is surrounded by the volcanic mountains, Ok and Skjaldbreið, which are circular in form, and whose summits reach above the limit of eternal snow. To the south the view is bounded by Vifilsfell, one of the most beautiful mountain summits in the neighbourhood of Reykjavik; and by a mountain-chain which runs out to the south-west towards Reykjanes, and thus shuts out the sea from view as far as Eldey Island, which stands prominently out against the horizon. To the south-west the prospect was shut out by a bank of clouds, otherwise I should have been able to see the rocky group of islands, the Vestmanna, off the south-west coast, and most probably the outline of Eyafjalljökull. A country that thus affords such noble and glorious prospects, far surpassing my powers of description, naturally makes the heart beat warmly and the bosom glow; and I left the snowy top of Esja, impressed with feelings of reverence for a nature that can unfold such grand objects to the spectator's eye.

In August, after I had returned to Reykjavik from my trip up the country, Esja was free from snow, and appeared, therefore, of a bluish hue, and presented a more uniform appearance than before. But still I could not refrain from casting a longing gaze upon this, my first love, which first had opened my eyes to the magnificence of nature, and had implanted feelings in my breast which I never forget when viewing other scenes.

During my first visit to Reykjavik,* I had good opportunities of noticing the national costume, and of observing the dress usually worn on high-days and holidays, which I only met with in that city. It is only used on grand occasions, such as a wedding, or other important ceremonies; so that it is but seldom that it sees the light of day. The every-day attire, of course, I continually had occasion to notice. The national costume is only worn by the women, who always adhere to old

---

* Reykjavik is derived from a word "reykr," signifying smoke, on account of the warm springs which are found near the Fjord at no great distance from the town. The same word enters into the composition of the names of many of the towns in Iceland, such as Reykir, Reykholt, Reykjanes.

customs longer than men, or, to express myself in more learned language, constitute the conservative element in the State.

The common dress which is worn every day is extremely simple. It consists of a tight-fitting, woollen-knitted boddice,

An Icelandic woman in her every-day dress.

of a dark colour, with narrow sleeves, buttoned at the wrists, without any decoration; and a wadmel skirt. It has a remarkably pleasing appearance, not only because it is a style of dress well calculated to set off the figure to advantage, but also because it gives one an idea of warmth and of great serviceableness. It is a dress, therefore, that may be well recommended for introduction in other places than Iceland; for it is both unostentatious, and, at the same time, graceful and very serviceable. As a little set-off to this dark-coloured costume, a striped or checked apron, usually either green or red, is worn. But I must not omit to mention the characteristic head-dress— "húfa," as it is termed. It is a small, black cap, fastened across the temples in a coquettish manner, and is furnished with a long, silken tassel, attached by a gold or silver thread. This constitutes the whole costume. Sometimes, of course, a rather extensive and flowing skirt may make one suspect the existence of a little crinoline; but this, of course, is a mystery, and is ground on which one should forbear to tread. I should add that this style of dress is worn by all classes alike—by young misses and servant-girls, as well as by married women. In meeting an Icelandic woman, therefore, it is rather difficult to tell to what class of society she belongs.

In the towns, the higher classes have generally discarded the national costume, and dress as other Europeans; and as there is now a brisk traffic with foreign countries, and a great many of the Icelandic officials have passed a good time in Denmark, added to the fact that French vessels of war come every year to the country, one can see in the streets and *salons* of Reykjavik toilettes as becoming and pleasing to the eye as anyone will meet with in Copenhagen, or, indeed, in any other European capital. In this respect the Icelander is not behind the age.

The state costume is perhaps rather more showy than it need be. The cap is supplanted by a high, white head-dress, something in the shape of a helmet, sitting closely to the forehead, and open behind. The edge is embroidered with gold cord, or is studded with gilt stars, and the apex is enveloped in a white veil of *tulle*, put on in an artistic way. The bodice, which is of black cloth, is richly embroidered with a trimming of gold or silver oak-leaves round the neck, and with a double row of the same down to the waist. Across the shoulder, at the seam, a piece of gold or silver thread is sown on, and the wrists are also decorated in the same way. The dress is of cloth, embroidered below with silk; a velvet band is fastened round the waist, prettily embroidered with gold or silver; or else a silver gilt belt of ingenious workmanship, occasionally set with precious stones. This dress is made exactly in the same way as the every-day costume; but a cloak or mantle of fine cloth, with sleeves, is thrown over it, which is embroidered, like the dress, with silk at the bottom. This cape is often of green velvet trimmed with ermine, and is fastened across the breast with an old-fashioned silver buckle. A heavy silver chain is worn round the neck,—usually an heirloom in the family. Of course, as far as regards trimmings and decorations, some little diversity will be found. Altogether, it is rather an expensive costume, and looks uncommonly well. Over their common dress, the women wear a simple shawl, which the Reykjavik ladies used to wear up so high round their neck and ears, that they looked like nuns afraid of letting their faces be seen.

The Icelandic women have very thick and beautiful hair, and certainly understand how to arrange it in graceful plaits, hanging down from the cap upon their back. Their hair and white teeth cannot but attract attention; though of late years the practice of drinking so much coffee has had an injurious effect upon the latter, while it may, possibly, in course of time affect the former too.

Whilst speaking of their dress, I may as well make a few remarks about their looks, though at the same time it is rather unsatisfactory ground to venture upon; for antipathy and sympathy come so much into play, in matters of this description, that what one person may declare to be absolutely detestable, another may maintain to be incomparably beautiful. Many a dark brown eye and curling lock of hair may be seen peeping forth from beneath the cap; still, the " corn-golden " hair and the azure-blue eye which the old Sagas sing of, is the general type; and thus pink and white are the prevailing hues that nature has laid on their cheeks and foreheads. And should the reader now ask me whether the women of Iceland are pretty or ugly, I cannot give him a better answer than—" Go there, and judge for yourself!" I remember one of the prettiest Icelandic women I met with, asked me, at one of those delightful evening parties which I had the pleasure of attending in Reykjavik, with a very arch look, the treacherous question, " Whether I had not seen a good many pretty girls in the south of the island?" As I knew very well that Reykjavik, though situated on the western coast, is always considered to belong to the southern province of the island, I was sorely tempted to answer—" That I had only seen one!" But I do not mind confessing to the reader, that both in the south, east, and north of the country, I have met with a great many pretty girls. The western parts I have never visited; but I doubt not that they may be found there also.

Having now fulfilled my duty towards the fair sex, I must devote a few words to the men. In general appearance the Icelander bears a great resemblance to the inhabitants of the northern parts of Sweden and Norway, and is well grown and symmetrically formed. As a rule, he cannot be pronounced to be so good-looking, though many a handsome face is to be found among them. They have a peculiarity which is more developed in them than in any other people, and that is the prominence of the eye-ball. The native Icelander is remarkable for the strong build of the lower parts of his person—for his long waist and short legs.

According to Darwin the short-leggedness of the people might be accounted for in the following way :—

Owing to the constant traffic the bridle paths have sunk down, especially where the earth is of a soft nature, while the ground bounding the path on either side, from not having been trampled down, has become elevated, owing to the turf which grows on it; consequently the path runs, as it were, between two walls of earth, and thus persons who had long legs would be very likely to sustain severe injuries, even if a fracture were not the result, should a stone or other impediment come in their way. Hence the necessity of the Icelander's having short legs; and, as nature always furnishes a species with a physical structure suitable to the necessity of the case, the legs of the Icelanders have been getting shorter and shorter during the lapse of ages, in proportion as the traffic of a thousand years has made the paths become deeper and more sunken.

I do not adduce this profound explanation as being my own invention; I am rather inclined to attribute the strong build of the nether parts of the Icelander's person to his descent from his Norwegian ancestors, an heritage which is not the only one which he has received from them, and has preserved intact. Were I to adopt the Darwinian theory I should entertain great fears for the generations yet to come; for since, according to this theory, no bounds or limits can be assigned to the transformation that takes place, and as the bridle paths will in the lapse of another thousand years necessarily sink more and more (at least, unless an entirely new system of road-making be introduced, which, I fear, would overtax the resources of the country too much), it would follow that the Icelander's legs would gradually become shorter and shorter, so that ultimately, at least to us long-legged mortals, or considered from our point of view, they would become a deformed race, with an unproportionately large body and no legs at all. Therefore, in the interest of the Icelanders themselves, and of human nature in general, I trust that the Darwinian theory, at least in this case, may not be the true one, and that my explanation of the phenomenon may be correct.

Dr. Schleisner, who, under the directions of the Danish Government, has established himself in Iceland, has made an interesting observation in reference to the warmth of the Icelander's blood. The temperature of the interior of the human frame, no matter what nation or under what clime, has been estimated to be between $36\cdot5°$ and $37°$ C.; but out of twelve persons in Iceland experimented on by Dr. Schleisner, nine possessed a higher internal temperature than $37°$—the highest was $37\cdot8°$—and only in one of the remaining three did it fall as low as $36\cdot5°$. Consequently the average for these twelve individuals was $37\cdot27°$ C.

In my remarks on Icelandic dress I had nearly forgotten the shoes, but as they appear to me to be very unserviceable arrangements, though they are decidedly peculiar, and as they, moreover, are the immediate causes of bringing in the dirt, my great abomination, into the houses, I will dismiss them with a very few remarks. The top part of the shoe consists of a piece of, generally, varicoloured stocking, whilst the lower is made out of the untanned hide of sheep or other animals, and is shaped like the Laplander's shoe. With such a covering for the feet, of course it is impossible to go a yard in such a damp country as Iceland without getting wet through; consequently, leather socks, with tops coming up over the shoes and legs, are often used—these are very serviceable in riding. Or else they wear leather socks inside the shoe, which cannot be a very healthy thing to do. The only advantage these shoes seem to possess is their cheapness. Whether the Icelandic ladies enclose their small and well-made feet in such shapeless shoes as these I cannot say, but suppose such to be the case.

As it is not essential to be a shoemaker in order to make a pair of Icelandic shoes, this branch of industry is very feebly represented in this country. It is not possible even to get a pair of boots soled except at Reykjavik or Akureyri, where the only two shoemakers the country can boast of reside. A tailor of the male sex is not to be beaten up anywhere, as this trade is carried on exclusively by women. Men of the higher classes, therefore, who do not dress in wadmel, have to import all their clothes, as well as their boots and shoes, from abroad.

An Icelandic shoe.

In Iceland one meets with no little difficulty in taking one's portmanteau or travelling box with one, even though it be not of excessive dimensions. Notes are not taken in exchange, but only silver; consequently all cash has to be taken in the shape of dollars and of smaller coin, which, owing to the limited weight of the *impedimenta*, makes quite a little burden by itself, though, as may be supposed, it gradually gets lighter and lighter.

CHAPTER II.

Leave Reykjavik—Lava Streams—An unpleasant Ride—Thunder and its Effects—Guides—Letters of Recommendation—Fording a River—View of Hecla—A Paradise—Position of Clergy—Their Income—Similarity between Icelandic and Swedish Accent—Hrútshellir—Skógafoss—Sólheima-Jökul—Jökul Floods—Þrasi and Loðmundr—Dyrhólarey or Portland—A Patent Saddle—Víksdalr—Curious Rock Formations—The Volcano Katla—Its Eruptions—The Sea becomes Land—Valleys filled up—View from Mýrdals-Jökul—Mýrdalssandr—Passage over the Kuda—Icelandic Churches—An Epitaph—Strange Incident—A Proselyte—Magnus Eiriksson, the Colenso of Iceland—Icelandic Intolerance—A Man eaten up by Horses.

I MUST leave it to my readers to determine whether, in what I have already said, I have been successful in presenting to their notice in an intelligible form the topics already touched upon. I will now invite them to accompany me in the journey I made along the southern, eastern, and northern coasts of Iceland during the course of the summer. In this trip we shall gain a closer insight into the national customs and the character of the inhabitaants, whilst we shall at the same time become acquainted with those remarkable phenomena of nature which are so intimately connected with the history of the country.

But, before proceeding any further, I must request them, in the ideas they may have formed about Iceland, to prepare for hearing about nature on an exalted scale—of mountains that reach far up into the sky; of "heiði" of immense extent; of boundless sandy plains; of swift and foaming rivers; steep and rocky, ay, often perpendicular, slopes; of deserts of lava, or of snow and ice, of sand and stone; and all this surrounded by the wide, wide sea, which is seldom out of sight! In fine, everything in this country is on a scale of magnificence; only the works of man are little and insignificant; that is to say, the works of his hands, for the works of his intellect are, I take it, as grand in Iceland as elsewhere.

One consequence of this exaggerated scale of nature is that distances are both diminished and increased; diminished, when from some lofty standing-point one can command a prospect of great extent, so that in order to obtain an extensive view over the country it is not necessary to undertake lengthened journeys; but increased, when, for instance, for several days together a mountain summit is in view long before the traveller has reached its base; and increased again because the uneven nature of the ground magnifies the actual distance between point and point when viewed from some lofty eminence.

I left Reykjavik on Monday morning, the 12th of June, in company with a family from Eyrarbakki, named Thorgrimsson. Thorgrimsson was a merchant, a native Icelander, who with his wife and children was returning home after passing the winter in Copenhagen. Eyrarbakki is situated on the south-west of Iceland, on the left bank of one of the largest rivers in the country, the Ölfusá, which rises in Lángjökull, where it is called the Hvíta. In its course it receives the waters of several tributaries, and after joining a river running out of Þingvalla lake, it assumes the name Ölfusá. When the road is in tolerably good condition the journey thither from Reykjavik can be accomplished in ten hours; but as on the present occasion it was in a miserable state, and the caravan, moreover, consisted of some small children, which could not endure a quick pace, it took us much longer. I believe we were fourteen hours on the road, including the passage over the 'Ölfusá. This was one of the most tedious and wearisome journies I encountered in Iceland. The morning shone out bright and promising as we left Reykjavik; but as soon as we had reached Skard, a mountain defile between Vífils and Hengils Fjeld, we became enveloped in a thick fog, which shut out everything from our view for the rest of the day, and by way of variety was accompanied with showers of rain. It was with feelings of great satisfaction, therefore, that I set foot in the hospitable and comfortable house at Eyrarbakki, where the discomforts of the journey were speedily forgotten. The road, however, between Reykjavik and Eyrarbakki is by no means uninteresting, though rather monotonous, as for the greatest portion of the way it goes over old lava streams, or "hraun," as they are called in Icelandic. On seeing these lava streams for the first time one cannot fail to be struck with their varied formations. The outside is formed partly of elongated flattened arches, which are usually burst asunder in the middle, with an elevated and bow-formed surface, or jagged, porous scoria, arranged in fantastic shapes, and jutting out from a tolerably even under-surface of loose shingle, which crackles and churns under the pressure of the foot, and which is almost impassable for equestrians. The first layer of "hraun" was naturally formed when the lava was flowing in a perfectly liquid state, and subsequently became rigid, leaving the upper surface intact; the second when the surface was already beginning to stiffen, but still continued to flow on for some little time in a liquid form, whereby the pieces that had become stiff on the surface were broken up; and finally the third layer when the lava stream burst forth with great impetuosity, so that on cooling the surface was broken up into small pieces. As soon as a stream of lava, which of course always flows in a valley, has left the mouth of the crater, which is often at some considerable elevation and when it is comparatively new, it does not in general exhibit a high ridge, but lies pretty evenly with the valley itself, though it always forms an incline of greater or less steepness with the ground over which it passes. It is not therefore distinguished as a distinct rock, but is recognised principally by the above characteristics, by the nature of its substance, and by the porosity which the stone exhibits, and partly by the absence of vegetable growth; for lava streams, at least those of recent formation, are merely covered with a thin coating of a lichenous growth, with which the bare black lava plains form the only variety of colour. When the "hraun" is of older date the grass begins to grow upon it, first in patches in the moist hollows; and these patches gradually extend till, after the lapse of some centuries, if the conditions are favourable, it is entirely covered under a carpet of green. Lava streams of older formation, however, in Iceland, are very frequently buried under the sand, from which loose scoriæ, or a protruding piece of rock, testify to their existence underneath. Those which I saw on my first day's journey had scarcely any other covering than a lichenous growth or a little moss, and therefore I had an excellent opportunity for noticing the interesting and occasionally eccentric forms they exhibited. These "hraun" are the results of several lava streams which have flowed in and amongst one another at different periods, as may be observed from the meagre and unequal vegetation upon them, and which have therefore formed a comparatively high ridge above the adjoining terrain.

 Their origin is open to question, but must probably be sought for in some of the numerous volcanic caldrons, which are caused by the volcanic fissures extending along the boot-shaped peninsula to the south-west of Reykjanes and Fuglasker, and probably terminating to the north-west in Lángjökul. To the north-east of this latter place no recent volcanic agency has been observed in this direction.

Immediately on the commencement of the above-mentioned "hraun" on the road from Reykjavik, some volcanic craters may be observed at a place which, on account of the reddish hue they assume, is called Raudhólar. The volcano is situated on a lava plain, and, as is the case with many other volcanic craters in Iceland, rises up from the level plain, and not from a mountain.

From what I could make out from the map, I was prepared to meet with a great many rivers on my journey eastward; but certainly I was not prepared to make the passage over the first one I came to—one of the upper arms of the Ellida stream, or as it is called in the neighbourhood of Reykjavik, Laxelv—in the way I did. My horse took it into its head to stumble when it got into the middle of the stream, and as I was quite unprepared for such a movement, I found myself in a moment straddling across its neck; and just as I was about extricating myself from a position which is neither agreeable nor graceful, the good beast rose to his legs again, whereby the reader's humble servant was pitched off into the brook, when the water, though only one or two feet deep, succeeded in finding its way into his boots, and in wetting that part of the author's person which was undermost. As the stream in question came direct from the snowdrifts on Vifil, my bath was rather of an icy nature, and very likely contributed to increase the rather cold impressions which my first day's journey gave me.

Perhaps I ought to have withheld this trivial incident from my reader's knowledge, as it was unattended with further consequences, for he will possibly come to the conclusion that his humble servant is but a poor horseman, and an author ought not to expose his weak side to the reader. In order, therefore, to anticipate him in forming such an unjust conclusion, I will merely remark that during the whole of my extensive journeys in the country I never fell off again—that is to say, into a brook.

After we had passed over the heaps of sand and stone in the neighbourhood of Reykjavik on our first day's journey, and over a large extent of "hraun," where the snow which had not yet melted obliged us to made a considerable *détour* on the soft and untrodden mountain paths, we at last reached the Ölfusá river in the dusk of the evening. The water had overflowed the banks to a considerable extent, owing to the large amount of rain that had fallen in the beginning of the month; consequently we had to made a *détour* down to the sea, where our horses sank deep into the sand. At last we reached the ferry, where we had to wait a whole hour for a boat, during which time, being all the while wet through and nearly frozen with the cold, our only recreation consisted in listening to the surf on the further side of a small tongue of land that separates the Ölfusá from the sea at its mouth, and in comforting ourselves with the prospect of having to wait another hour; for the dense fog prevented us from being seen, and the noise of the surf rendered it an impossibility for any one to hear us from the opposite shore, where the ferry-boat was stationed. Meantime we relieved our horses of their burdens, and took off their saddles. As far as I remember, there were eleven of them, of which three were my property. We then tied them together; and in this condition the poor beasts, which had nothing to eat the whole livelong day, patiently waited till the time should come when they would be driven into the stream to try their powers against the waves and the current of the river. The boat came at last, and after the baggage and the horses had been conveyed over (the latter being towed across after the boat), we reached the opposite shore in due course of time, and, after a short ride, arrived at our destination, a number of swans doing honour to our approach by giving vent to their melodious trumpetings, which, at the time, I remember, I thought bore a great resemblance to the cackling of geese. As the reader will notice from the map, the Ölfusá widens out very much towards its outlet, but contracts again immediately near its mouth. It took our horses, however, ten minutes to cross over.

If my first day's journey in Iceland—of course I except the short trips I took near Reykjavik—did not lead me to anticipate a great deal of pleasure from my proposed tour, the following day, which was ushered in by a storm and an even downpour of rain, appeared as if it would put a stop to my further progress. Towards noon, however, it cleared up; after which I enjoyed the driest and finest weather imaginable during the whole of my travels through the country. One can hardly estimate sufficiently the value and the importance of dry weather to the traveller in Iceland unless after personal experience; for rainy and foggy weather shuts out every prospect from view, and washes out, as it were, the beauty from every object of nature; and not only so, but it makes the paths soft and impassable, the rivers dangerous and unnavigable, and excursions on the mountains an impossibility; so that the traveller's movements are impeded, his energies damped in every conceivable way, and thus the whole pleasure of the journey is marred. I have, therefore, in a great measure, to thank the glorious summer weather I enjoyed for the very favourable impressions I formed of Iceland; for I saw it in its best colours, under a clear and cloudless sky. During a portion of my journey in the autumn from Akureyri to Reykjavik, as well as during my stay of ten days in the former place, the clouds indeed were so low that all the mountains and heights were for a whole week enveloped in an impenetrable fog, so that only the valleys were free from it. During this time, which I occupied partly in resting myself, partly in taking some short excursions, I gained an excellent idea of the monotony of moving about within so circumscribed an horizon. I cannot, therefore, sufficiently congratulate myself on having travelled in Iceland in a summer like this; for there are few which are so sunny as was that of 1865. On returning, however, to Reykjavik, I found that the weather there had not always been so propitious as it had been with me on the eastern coast; and that in the north-western part of the island, a great deal of rain had fallen during the months of June and July.

As an atmospherical phenomenon, I may mention that thunder is very seldom heard in Iceland during the summer, except, of course, when a volcanic eruption is taking place, when the ashes that are thrown out are accompanied with continuous flashes of lightning and peals of thunder. The electricity is probably distributed among the numerous lofty mountains, and thus an explosion is prevented. In the winter, however, thunder is often to be heard. This circumstance is possibly owing to the fact of the sharp-pointed peaks being covered with snow, and thus exposing a rounded surface; or from the snow not being a good conductor. Until of late years, however, but little attention has been paid to this remarkable phenomenon; but a short time ago an occurrence took place which inspired the people with a profounder respect for the thunder-peal. A boat, manned by ten persons, was crossing a fjord, when the people observed a black cloud lowering over the land, and fearing that it was the forerunner of a storm, put back to land, and laid to near a farmhouse close to the shore. The farmer, who had noticed the boat, went down to the shore, and hospitably invited the people to come up to his house and have some warm coffee. He pointed out a little wooden building close to the "bær," which they were to enter while he minded the boat. Accordingly, they went up; but while the farmer was pulling the boat up on to the shore, he saw a flash of lightning, which was instantaneously followed by a terrific peal of thunder, strike the wooden building in question. Hurrying up to the spot, he found all ten of them lying in a state of insensibility outside, for they had not entered the house. The greater number of them recovered, but three were killed on the spot, while some of the others were found to have sustained serious injuries. Those who had been killed wore leathern jackets, which, according to the usual practice, had been steeped in blue vitriol, in order the better to preserve them. Their jackets were literally torn off from their bodies, and split in all parts; but the house, which had sustained great damage, was not set on fire.

Though all journeys in Iceland must be undertaken on horseback, there are, however, two different methods of travelling in the country, I am not alluding to whether one should choose to ride on the horse's neck or on the saddle, but—with reference to guides. One can either engage a guide to accompany one for the whole journey, in which case a double number of horses is requisite; and, in addition to this, when the road is very long and travelling is difficult, it is often necessary to have two or three fellows in addition who are well acquainted with the fording-places, &c.; or, one can engage a guide from house to house, which of course renders it necessary to have to wait a day or two before one can be procured (this, however, did not happen to me more than twice during my whole journey); and further, it may be necessary to pay this chance guide at a higher rate, as the hay-harvest lasts from the middle of July to the end of September. But I did not think I should be able to procure a guide in Reykjavik who knew the route sufficiently well, or who was acquainted with the ferries over the rivers, or with the eastern part of the island, where I intended to stay for some time, and therefore I wished to take as few horses with me as possible; for, by way of parenthesis, there is always a great deal of trouble attendant upon horses,—they are either not to be caught in the morning when one wants to start, or they will not keep in the proper path when they have to be driven forward, or else a shoe comes off, or one of them turns dead lame. So I determined to rely on the general hospitality and kindness of the Icelanders towards strangers, and therefore adopted the second mode of travelling; though, as I afterwards learnt, I was the first foreigner who had ever done so. However, I had no cause to regret my choice.

I had been furnished with letters of recommendation from Reykjavik to the different places on the east coast which I purposed visiting, from the excellent editor of the *National* newspaper, Jon Guðmunsson, to whom I had received an introduction from a friend in Copenhagen. Thus equipped, I did not hesitate to undertake my journey alone through this peaceful land.

After taking leave of the amiable family at Eyrarbakki, whom, in accordance with the usual destiny of travellers, I had no sooner learnt to love than I had to leave, I continued my route along the coast, accompanied by an honest peasant as a guide, across a sandy plain, sparsely overgrown with herbage, and covered with loose blocks of lava that protruded from the sand. I had now, with but few exceptions, a flat and smooth road to the eastern coast; I mean by that, that there were no mountains to cross, but only swamps and sandy wastes, rivers and streams. I believe I traversed the greater number of bogs I had to encounter on this day; but though this were so, by way of requital, they afterwards appeared on a larger scale. It is out of the question for one's horse to follow any definite track across them; for it has to jump from tussock to tussock to prevent sinking. An Icelandic horse, however, goes pretty securely over the swamps, for they are the playing-grounds of his foal-hood, where he is wont to frisk and caper about. But should the bog become too soft, and the horse plump down into the deep mire, so that the rider's feet drag along the surface, the position of the latter is far from being agreeable, especially when the animal sinks down so far as to lie extended with its stomach resting on a tussock, and its hind legs in a deep, muddy hole. Happy for the rider if the good beast has then firm ground under his fore feet, as it will readily recover itself. After riding some distance, I reached the Þjorsá, the second of the important rivers that intersect the large plains, over which the early part of my road lay. This plain is bounded on the east by Eyafjalla-Jökul and Hecla; but to the north it extends up Lángjökul. The Þjorsá derives its principal source from Hofsjökul; it is a rapid river, and has a large body of water. When I crossed it there was a ferry for the conveyance of travellers, while the horses were towed after the boat by means of a rope passing round the under jaw, the end of which was held by a boatman. There was something picturesque in seeing the horses in the deep water, with their lips drawn up so as to show their rows of white teeth, their rolling eyes, and the powerful strokes they took, and in hearing their snorting.

After rowing for a quarter of an hour, during which time one or two shallow places in mid-stream afforded the poor beasts a little rest from their exertions in swimming, we happily reached the opposite shore, and continued our route. I now began to learn what water meant; for a small river,

Rauðalækr, had to be crossed eighteen times; and as my guide had not been very fortunate in his selection of a fording-place the first time, the water came up above our knees, so that the horses almost had to swim for it. The same thing occurred too in crossing another river, the Vestri-Rangú, before reaching Oddi, my night-quarters. The reader, therefore, will imagine that I was rather wet about my nether parts; but at last I became so used to a foot-bath, that I did not notice it. For even if the water did not come down through the tops of my boots, still I was often obliged to let my legs dangle in the stream, to say nothing of the splashing caused by the horses. And as, partly owing to want of fuel, partly to the general dampness in the houses, it was an impossibility to get one's shoes dried during the night, they became like sponges which suck the moisture up; and I thus discovered the utter uselessness of leather boots, at least for a journey along the south-western coast of Iceland.

The Icelanders, as I have already stated, use a kind of socks made of untanned leather, and shaped like bags, which are drawn up over the legs, and tied under the knee. Unfortunately, when I started on my journey, I had not made the acquaintance of this serviceable arrangement, and had therefore been unable to furnish myself with a pair.

After a hearty reception by the excellent pastor, Sira Asmundr Jónsson, in Oddi—a classical ground in Iceland, as it formerly was the seat of Sæmundr Fróði, or the Wise, and of his grandson, Jon Loptssón, Snorre Sturlason's foster-father—I continued my journey on the following day, for I did not wish to make any important stay till I had reached the east coast. That day I had the most glorious weather, the clouds which had been lowering and threatening on the previous days had now lifted, and I was thus enabled to look about me, and I had a magnificent prospect before me. In front was the Eyafjalla-Jökul and the snow-clad summit of the Tindfall-Jökul; farther in the distance Torfa-Jökul was visible, one of the snowy giants of those parts; and in the north-east, Hecla majestically reared its crown, which, seen from this side, forms a perfect cone, and at this period of the year was entirely covered with snow. Behind me lay Ingólfsfell, and other mountain tops, which I had already passed; and somewhat to the north, in the same direction as that in which my road lay, was another fjeld, named Þrihyrningr, looking like an obtruncated cone. In comparison with these mountains the lowlands over which I was riding, and which were about nine geographical miles in length by half that number in width, seemed to form one enormous plain, the low and diminutive eminences of which scarcely struck the eye. After having passed three large arms of the Markarfljót river, which has its source in the above-named Jökuls, I rode along under the perpendicular walls of the Eyafjalla-Jökul, which for the two following days continued to be my steadfast companion.

As we were crossing one of the arms of this river I met two men and a woman, each on horseback, and each holding a sheep in front, a ewe with its lambs, that had probably strayed. As soon as they had got over with them they set the sheep down on the ground, and, while the woman held it, the man began to flay it from head to foot, an operation which he seemed to perform with great satisfaction and alacrity; that is to say, he flayed the wool off, for in Iceland sheep are not clipped, but the wool is allowed to remain on the whole year, till it becomes loose of itself, when it is pulled off. If the sheep are in good condition, and well kept, all the wool comes off at the same time; in other cases it is no little trouble to pluck it, first in one place, then in another.

That angle of Eyafjalla-Jökul that juts out towards the Markarfljót possesses a most interesting spectacle in a little foss,* called Seljalandsfoss, which falls over a perpendicular wall of 300 feet in height, separating the stream which comes from the snowy mountain from the plain below. To see this foss, as I did, illumined by the rays of a south-westerly sun, with a clear blue sky overhead, and in perfectly calm weather, is to imagine oneself in a little paradise, where by the way no forbidden fruit is to be found. Everything there was clear, pure, transparent, and perfumed; the water fell in graceful festoons, or descended from the imposing height above like a fine, transparent, gauzy veil. The sun's rays fell directly on the foaming water at the foot of the fall, and the spectator could enjoy the rare sight of an entire rainbow, whose lower hemisphere stood scarce a fathom's distance away, whilst the circle took a slanting direction upwards, only two or three fathoms in diameter, surrounded on all sides by the glittering foam. Near the little basin at the foot of the fall the grass grew of a luxuriant emerald hue, watered by the nourishing moisture which a brisk wind threw around. After having feasted one's eyes on the sight from this side, it is possible to walk in under the foss, and go entirely round it. Standing thus under the protruding rocky arch one can hear the roar of the foss overhead, like the din of many carriages on a stony road or street. Masses of rock that had recently fallen down showed plainly that the rock is being gradually hollowed out—a warning to the intruder, maybe, behind the boiling foss. The herds of sheep that were grazing up the green-clad mountain slopes surrounding the foss contributed not a little to render the scene a perfect idyl.

After leaving Seljalandsfoss I rode over a verdant plain, where the balmy perfume of spring for the first time made

* Waterfall—in Cumberland, &c., "Force."

itself apparent—for it will be remembered that the spring that year had been a late and cold one—and came to another little foss which fell in graceful festoons over a lofty and precipitous wall of rock more than 1,000 feet in height, and after gazing with admiration at the noble fjeld lying to the east of Holt, a spur of the Jökul itself, which in form put me in mind of a house with a slanting roof and perpendicular walls, or rather of a church, whose chancel, contrary to all the rules of ecclesiastical architecture, was turned towards the west—a church, whose roof-ridge lay 2,618 feet above its basement, and whose builder had not considered himself bound by human prejudices —I arrived at Holt parsonage, where I purposed asking for night quarters.

Any one accustomed to Swedish parsonages and Swedish pastors cannot fail to be struck with the great difference he will observe in these respects in Iceland; for the Icelandic pastor is neither so plump nor so venerable-looking an individual as one of ours. With but very few exceptions he is nothing but a farmer, dwelling in his own farm-house, mowing his own grass, carrying his wool to market himself, and, in a word, performing all the customary duties of a regular farmer. With this he unites the nature and habits of a farmer, so that while our clergy belong to, or aim at belonging to, the class of gentry, the Icelandic pastor nearly always continues to be the farmer, both in his habits and in all the relations of life.

This is a natural consequence of the small value of the livings, which thus compels him to turn farmer, and to work with his own hands. Of course the Swedish pastors cultivate their glebe, but they usually do so in the capacity of gentlemen farmers; but the small incomes of the Icelandic clergy compel them to perform all those duties which are attached to a farmer's calling, for there are parishes in Iceland where the number of souls does not amount to more than two hundred—the average is, perhaps, three hundred—and as the greater proportion of these are in needy circumstances, it can readily be conceived that the clergyman's official income cannot be a large one. Three hundred rix dollars, I believe, is considered to be a good income! But although this disproportion exists between the pastor's income and the responsibility and importance of his office, it is astonishing to mark the pertinacity with which the Icelander clings to the existing state of affairs. The pastor says, "that he would have so far to ride, if his cure were of larger dimensions;" and the peasant objects, because "he would have such a long distance to go to church." Now both of these objections are undoubtedly valid, but still they are only relatively so; for there are parishes in Iceland which are pretty good ones, where both pastor and peasant have a longer distance to go than in poorer ones. And further, these two objections must undoubtedly in part give way to the better position the clergyman would thus occupy, partly owing to the fact that the population of the country is too small to be able to provide all the hundred and ninety-six parishes with perfectly efficient pastors. The advantage would thus be twofold, for it would obviate the necessity of so many of Iceland's sons entering upon a profession to which only a minority are suited, and would render it unnecessary for the pastor to be under any pecuniary obligation to his more wealthy parishioners, as is often the case now, and which cannot but impair the respect and esteem due to his sacred office. Moreover, he would then be able to set his parishioners a good example, which his better education would enable him to afford them, and at the same time have more opportunities for the cultivation and development of his intellectual attainments.

It is by no means my intention to say that the Icelandic

clergy do not fulfil their duties to the best of their power; on the contrary, it must be a matter of astonishment that with their needy circumstances they are able to discharge them as well as they do.

One of the objections that has been made against limiting the number of the clergy is, that they are the only teachers the people possess. For there are no national schools in Iceland: the children are taught at home; and it is the duty of the clergyman to superintend the instruction they receive, which he does by examining them at home and in church. But with respect to this the question arises whether it would not be beneficial to set on foot a special scholastic establishment, at least, in places where there is a necessity for it, and at the same time to make a better division of the parishes. In a country like Iceland, we are of opinion that the clergyman ought to occupy such a position as to enable him to set the peasantry a better example in practical matters, such as the adoption of a better style of building, a more comfortable system of housekeeping, cleanliness, &c. For as concerns this latter desirability, a great reformation is needed not only in their dwellings, but in the preparation of their daily food; and it requires good spokesmen to bring about such a happy state of things. But precept is of little avail here: it is the example that is needed, and this it ought to be in the power of the clergy to give. I have visited more than one parsonage house, where the dust had never been swept off the floor of the keeping-room for a length of time; where butter, milk, and cream, have been so full of hairs and dust, that it was impossible to relish them; and where the state of the house was in strict harmony with this uncomfortable state of things.

At Holt, where I passed the night on the third day of my journey, a better state of things than that which I have above described existed; for my host, the cheery Sira Björn, was a man who held his house in great esteem, though in other respects he lived as a farmer. After leaving Oddi, I did not meet with a single parsonage house suitable for the occupation of a gentleman, before arriving at the eastern parts of the island; for the district I was now travelling through is one of the poorest in the whole country. Far be it from me, however, to say anything depreciatory of my hosts along the southern coasts of Iceland; on the contrary, I cannot sufficiently praise them for all the hospitality and attention they showed me. The above remarks, therefore, do not refer to individuals, but to the existing state of things. Doubtless, it would be a great boon for Iceland if more of her sons, who are destined for holy orders, were to study at the University of Copenhagen; but owing to the poorness of the livings in the country, a university education in Denmark would entail too great a sacrifice. By far the greater number of candidates for holy orders, therefore, undergo a course of instruction at the "Pastoral Seminary" in Reykjavik, which, though doubtless an excellent institution, cannot possibly confer all the advantages of a regular university education. Before this seminary was established, the young men used to go straight from school to fulfil the sacred and responsible duties of a pastor.

The guest-room at Holt had been recently built. It was not painted, and was without paper on the walls, as is usually customary. The furniture consisted of a bed, a chest, and a table; but they were all scrupulously clean, and the bowl of porridge, with which I was treated at twelve o'clock at night, was both free from dirt and grateful to the palate. Sira Björn, like his neighbour in Skógur, could not express himself in Danish, and as far as I could ascertain, did not understand the language; I had, therefore, for the first time, to test my knowledge of Icelandic. This, unfortunately, was not very extensive; but I was complimented the following day on my acquaintance with the language; and, indeed, whenever I spoke the vernacular in any part of Iceland, the people regarded me with feelings of admiration and surprise. I do not mention this circumstance in order to bestow any praise upon myself, for my knowledge of Icelandic is very meagre; besides, what praise is due for having learnt a language whose literature contains such rich sources of enjoyment and pleasure? My only motive is to show that a great similarity exists between the accent of the Swedish and Icelandic languages: for what I did pronounce, I pronounced correctly; and I was often told that if I only remained a year in the country, I should speak the language like a native. And just as the Icelanders were astonished at my Icelandic, so was I surprised to hear their Swedish accent; for often when I have heard short Icelandic sentences pronounced, I have been tempted to believe that it was a Swede who was speaking to me.

I had a message to Sira Björn from his daughter Frida, in Reykjavik; but I am quite certain that neither this nor any other introduction was necessary to induce that hospitable man to entertain the stranger who visited him. In the morning when I set out, he saddled his horses, and together with his little boy, accompanied me to Skógur, my next night quarters, showing me, too, the additional attention of placing one of his own horses at my disposal, so as to give mine a little rest. It was his daughter's horse—Frida's chestnut—that I rode; and we set out at a brisk trot on our road to Skógur. There were several objects of interest to be noticed in the grottoes hollowed out in the fjeld. In my opinion, these grottoes had been formed by the action of the surf at a time when the land was submerged, or before the now existing plain below the fjeld had become land. They are called "hellir" in Iceland, and are very useful both as houses for the sheep and as places for storing hay in. The first of them was in the form of a semi-dome, and was about forty feet in radius, and fourteen feet in height; the outer arch was covered with the most lovely matting of delicate but luxuriant ferns of a bright, pure green. Another consisted of a transverse cave under the mountain; but there was nothing of especial interest about it. A third had been partially formed by human hands; it was semi-cylindrical in appearance, about seventy feet in length, twenty-four feet in width, and about twelve feet high. It had also a lateral arch leading into a grotto above the first one; but it communicated directly with it by a round hole in the roof, about as large as a man's girth. This grotto is named Hrútshellir, and there is a history attached to it. A giant named Hrútr lived there with his slaves; but as he was a hard master, they made use of this hole for ushering the tyrant into another world; while at the same time they rendered him immortal in this.

Among other notabilities on this road may be seen a hill called Drangshlið, the western side of which forms a perfectly smooth rocky wall of considerable altitude. Riding immediately under it one looks like a pigmy; and while the eyes are occupied in admiring the glorious scenery under the magnificent Eyafjalla-Jökul, a sudden bend in the mountain wall presents the noble Skógafoss to view, one of Iceland's most beautiful fosses. It falls perpendicularly from a height of about two hundred feet, and has a large mass of water. Seen from where I was standing it looked like a broad belt of white as it dashed over the precipice.

As Sira Björn had given me to understand that it was the proper thing to pay our respects to the clergyman in Skógar,

F

who would then act as our guide to any objects of interest in the neighbourhood, we directed our course to the neighbouring "bær." Whether it was merely out of regard to the duties of politeness, or whether Sira Björn adopted it as a *ruse* for getting the cup of coffee which always awaits the traveller's arrival at a "bær," I cannot say. So we set off home, as they say in Iceland on going to a house, even if they be total strangers there; and with my former host's help I soon made the acquaintance of my new one.

Sira Kjartan received us with great hospitality, and afterwards went with us to see the foss in a shower of rain, which, perhaps, was the reason why I was not so much struck with its beauty as I had been with Seljalandsfoss; but certainly its environs were not quite so pleasing, though the body of water in it was greater.

In this foss the wizard Þrasi, about whom I shall have more to say presently, is said to have sunk a chest containing gold and other valuables. Formerly people could see the rim of the chest, and after the middle of the seventeenth century some persons tried to get hold of it; but on their first attempt it seemed to them as if their houses were in flames, and accordingly they desisted from their purpose. Another time they succeeded in getting hold of the ring attached to the end of the chest; but as they were in the act of dragging it up, it gave way, so that they only secured the ring, which, as the story goes, may be seen on the church door in Skógar at the present day.

The following day I again set out, after changing Sira Björn's company for that of Sira Kjartan. I expected to enjoy much pleasure by the sight of Eyafjalla-Jökul's glacier, which goes by the name of Sólheima-Jökul, and its Jökul river, the renowned Fúlilækr, or stinking river, and one of the most dangerous in the country. After following the usual path to the river, over a barren waste, by name Skógasand, I rode up to the end of the glacier, where one of the numerous streams from which the river takes its source lept out from under the Jökul or glacier. I scarcely think that this was the principal arm, but the foggy weather, and the vapour that arose from the water, prevented me from gaining a clear view. The edge of the glacier was perfectly black, and the ice lay hid under the slimy mud that had come up to the surface on the melting of the mass of ice; for here there was certainly no "moraine" at the extremity, or piles of *débris*, as is usually the case on the ridge of a glacier. Most of the stones, too, bore evident traces of having been carried along under the glacier, for they were generally of a rounded and polished form, and marked with fine scratches. This rounded appearance, for they were as round as shingle on the sea-coast, was naturally the work of the becks or streamlets issuing on all sides from under the extremity of the glacier. I followed the course of one of these streams a short distance into the glacier; it flowed under a niche-formed arch, so narrow that a man could scarcely pass through it, but it was about seven or eight feet in height, and between twenty and thirty feet in length. When I had come in under this arch I feasted my eyes with the sight of the emerald green ice that formed the thin roof, through which the daylight shone, and which was rendered more striking by the darker colour of the walls of ice. A shingly ridge shot out from the end of the glacier, at the foot of which my guide informed me a river had run about a century back. A glacier river does not, I should state, always run in the same channel, but changes its course in lapse of time, owing to the large masses of water which, under the name of "Jökulhlaup," or "Jökellöb," issue from the glaciers, and which have committed such great devastations in Iceland. These "Jökellöb" occur periodically at longer or shorter intervals. In the latter case they originate from masses of water collected in the glaciers, which make a way for themselves at a certain moment of time, and discharge sand, *débris*, and pieces of ice, with which they overflow the lowlands beneath the glacier. It is from these causes that the glacier stream under Sólheima-Jökul has gained its importance; for when these masses of water burst forth, they make the river unnavigable, or at all events highly dangerous to cross. As the bed of the river, which is bounded by lofty walls of sand and stone, is of tolerable breadth, and the distance from the end of the glacier is but trifling, a "Jökellöb" can take place at the very time a person may happen to be in the bed of the river, so that his position may be extremely precarious. The end of the glacier, however, is not broken up, but the swollen mass of water, carrying pieces of ice and *débris* along with it, breaks out from under the glacier, so that there is probably an arch of ice in the current of the river, at least some distance up under the glacier. From what Sira Gisli, in Fell, told me, however, the reservoir or lake, the filling up of which is the cause of the "Jökellöb," is easy of access; so that the Solheima peasants in their wanderings over the mountains are able to judge from the mass of water it contains whether there is any danger of a "Jökellöb." If this tale be true, and if such a lake really does exist and is easy of access, the exploration of the surrounding terrain would certainly help to remove the mystery that rests over the cause of these "Jökellöb." Unfortunately, I was not at this time prepared to undertake such a journey of exploration.

A pastor in the eastern coast, Sira Bjarni, of Stafafell, in Lón, told me that he knew a point—it was in Heínabergs-Jökul, a part of the immense Vatna or Klofa-Jökul, which covers a surface of one hundred and fifty geographical square miles (Danish), in the south-east of the country, with its snow and ice—where the "Jökellöb" originates in this way, namely, that two glaciers coming from unequal valleys block up a third valley, where there is no glacier, but where there is running water. The mass of water which thereby accumulates at last bursts the glacier, and the "Jökellöb" takes place. He was of opinion that the "Jökellöb," which usually takes place every seventh or tenth year under Skeiðarar-Jökul, a glacier about three miles distant from Vatna-Jökul, and which changes an extent of country some forty-three miles in length, and fourteen and a quarter in breadth, into a frightful wilderness, was caused by some warm springs up in the glacier, because when the "Jökellöb" took place, columns of vapour could be seen ascending in the glacier from the plain below.

The "Jökellöb" that occur less seldom, but are accompanied with more terrible results, and which have changed a large portion of the lowlands along the south coast of Iceland into a sandy plain, must be attributed more immediately to volcanic agency, of which we shall soon hear some striking proofs.

When I crossed over the glacier stream under Sólheima-Jökul there was not a very large body of water in it, but it formed a most repulsive mixture of clay and particles of sand, like mud porridge. There was a peculiar smell of rotten eggs rising up from the seething water which was almost unendurable. The cause of this probably is that the stones which are ground by the glacier contain sundry grains of iron pyrites or sulphate of iron, and coming in a pulverised state into contact with the water, the iron becomes oxidated as it absorbs the oxygen, which constitutes one of the component parts of water; the other part, hydrogen, then unites with the sulphur, and becomes sulphuretted hydrogen gas, which, as is well known, gives forth the well-known savour of rotten eggs. When in addition to this I have to remark that the ground adjoining the bed of the river consisted of barren land quite devoid of vegetation, the reader will not, I am sure, think that the neighbourhood of Sólheima-Jökul was a paradise. It struck me, I remember, as very strange, on finding a pair of eider ducks that had established themselves on a bare "holm," surrounded by the muddy water. The poor duck had got one of her wings broken, so that she could have only reached the sea, some three miles distant, by swimming; and it occurred to me that this circumstance was a strong confirmation of the opinion that the female does not go to seek for food during the time she is sitting on her eggs; for it would have been absolutely impossible that she could have swum up this rapid river back to her nest. From finding this pair of eider ducks in the middle of the stinking Fúlilækr, I arrived at the conclusion that amongst birds the eider duck must represent the chemical element, for the smell resembled that of a chemist's laboratory.

The following tale is told concerning the origin of Sólheimasandr, and of Skogasandr, two barren wastes lying east and west, in the Landnamabok, an ancient MS., in which the colonization of Iceland by the Northmen in 874 and in the succeeding years is mentioned, when a number of the most illustrious families left their fatherland on account of Harald the Fair Hair's despotic rule.

Two wizards, Þrasi and Loðmundr, dwelt, the one in Skógar, the other in Sólheimar. One morning Þrasi discovered that a flood from the glacier was approaching. By his magic arts he diverted its course in the direction of Sólheimar, where Loðmundr lived; but Loðmundr's slaves saw it coming, and declared that the sea was breaking in from the north. Loðmundr, who was blind, ordered his slave to bring him a little water in a vessel, and when he had come with it, Loðmundr said, "This does not appear to me to be sea-water." Thereupon he made

DYRHÓLAREY, OR PORTLAND.

the slave conduct him to the water, and ordered him to put the end of his staff into the water; a ring was fastened to the staff, and Loðmundr held the staff with both his hands, but he bit the ring with his teeth. The water then began to fall in the direction of Skógar. After which they each of them kept making the waters recede from themselves, till they met in a crevice (the actual bed of the river), where they agreed that the river should flow by the shortest route to the sea. On the banks of this river are two hills, which even to this day bear witness of the magical arts these two wizards displayed, and which are called Loðmundarsæti and Þrasahals.

After these remarks we will continue our journey, and introduce the reader to the talented Sira Gisli, Thorarensen in Fell, pastor in Sólheimar, and one of Iceland's poets. He was an amusing man, and talked Danish fluently. After staying with him some hours he accompanied me to Dyrhólar, where I expected to meet a Sysselmand from the eastern part of the country, who was to hold a court here, and from whom I wished to obtain some information. We now left the glacier in our rear, and passed over a verdant plain, on which some barren rocks reared themselves up. The name of one of these was Pétrsey or Petersö, and Dyrhólarey (Dyr, door), or, as it is called by travellers, Portland. This rock rises up from the sea to a height of 392 feet. They have obtained the name of islands, probably, owing to their isolated position on the level land.

The last-named, Dyrhólarey, has an arched opening in the form of a gateway, in the side that juts out into the sea, nearly large enough to admit of sailing vessels passing through it, as the accompanying sketch may suffice to show.

At Dyrhólar the "Thing," or Court, is held. The temple of justice consists of a large and spacious grotto, named Loptsalahellir, lying high up on the extremity of a rock in the vicinity of the town.

I had purchased at a saddle-maker's in Copenhagen the very worst article a traveller bound to Iceland can possibly possess —an inferior saddle. The saddle-maker averred that the saddle in question had been made expressly for the Exhibition, but had not been sold; from which circumstance, I might have concluded that it had not been considered an efficient one. But as he, of course, assured me that it was the very best saddle conceivable, I let my credulity silence my doubts, and was, therefore, taken in. One can readily imagine the position I found myself in on my arrival at Dyrhólar, with all my horses saddle-galled. It is pretty much the same thing as breaking an axle in other countries, where it is impossible to get a smith to weld it together again, for in this place I could not get any good saddle instead of my own. For the moment I was at a loss what to do; but the good people there were as kind as it was possible to be. They placed wool under the saddle, and Sira Magnus Hákonarson, who happened to arrive at Dyrhólar, in order to attend the Thing the following day, lent me his own saddle, and turned back with me to his home in Vík, a good two hours' ride, where I was to remain the night, though he had to return to Dyrhólar himself on the morrow.

I mention these trifling incidents in order to show the courteous and self-sacrificing manner in which a stranger is received in this country, and also to dissuade every traveller who purposes visiting Iceland from buying a saddle at the corner of Store Kongensgade and Gothersgade, especially when he is informed that it is a patent saddle, as the inconveniences he may have to submit to are incredible; for although my saddle was now repaired as well as it could be, I had to make use of galled horses the whole way to Berufjörðr.

The road from Dyrhólar to Vík lay partly over a flat plain, partly twisted itself in sinuous bends over Reynisfell, on whose summit a dark cloud enveloped me and my travelling companion in its misty veil. The farther side of the fjeld was very steep, so that we were obliged to dismount and make a portion of the descent on foot. In such cases the horses have to take care of themselves; the reins are thrown over their necks, and they are driven in front down the narrow and precipitous mountain path. Indeed, whenever one dismounts in Iceland, it is quite requisite to let the reins fall, for the horse then never runs away, and is thus easily caught again. The guides, therefore, always impress this precaution on travellers, for otherwise the horses might give some trouble in being caught. The path, as I have said, was steep and precipitous, but very picturesque; huge masses of rock hung over it in a very threatening manner. A horseman that we met was working his way up the steep path, and the next minute we saw his misty form immediately over our heads; but below, a green and smiling valley invited us to repose and refreshment. Many of the valleys in this country are completely devastated in their lower parts by floods, arising either from the above-named "Jökellöb" or from the melting of the snow in spring; consequently they present the appearance of a stony river-bed of sombre hue; so that it was an unexpected pleasure to see the deep and narrow valley between Reynisfell and another fjeld, named Víkshamrar, to the east of this, covered with a luxuriant crop of grass.

After a short but agreeable stay with Sira Magnus, at Vik—who, in speaking of his domestic occupations, told me that in the long winter evenings, when the time hung heavily on his hands, he would take up his Cicero or Horace—I continued my journey, accompanied by my host and his little son and a guide, along the shore, purposing to reach the deanery of Mýrar, in the western district of Skaptafell, which is called "Álptaver,"* or the home of the swans. The road ran along the sandy beach. Behind us three perpendicular rocks of fantastic forms reared their heads above the sea. They are called Reynísdrángar: the foremost of them has a three-cleft summit, and there is a popular legend attached to them. This rock, it is said, is a ship, on board of which is a young Trold or magician; the rock behind it is the Trold's sweetheart, who is endeavouring to hinder the vessel's progress; and the hinder-

Reynisdrángar.

most of the three is—well—the Trold's son. Just, however, as the giantess is in the act of overturning the ship, the sun rises, and three pillars of rock occupy the place of love and hate.

In front of us, to the left, the precipitous wall of Víkshamrar rose up from a rocky ravine. It is a bird rock, and myriads of a snowy white bird, *Procellaria glacialis*, are hatched there. These birds eject a stinking fluid, resembling train oil, over

* Álpt in Icelandic signifies a swan.

their pursuers—the ravens, or human beings. They are much sought after, and every autumn about three thousand young ones are taken. Víkshamrar lies close to the sea, and is green all the year round—at least, when the winter is not extremely severe; and when its surface is besprinkled with white patches of birds, as they are sitting in repose, or else brooding over their eggs, it presents a most picturesque appearance. At its base the fjeld is hollowed out, from the action of the surf and the waves, into grotto-shaped arches; for the coast land along which we now were riding was sea at no very ancient date. Its transformation is due to an eruption of Katla, or Mýrdals-Jökul as it is called, a volcanic mountain, in the eastern part of Eyafjalla-Jökul, which in the lapse of ages has discharged fearful "Jökellöb" over the adjacent plain, whereby incredible quantities of sand and masses of *débris* were washed down. The first of these eruptions took place in 874, contemporaneously with the colonization of the country, which I will presently describe. Since that period sixteen eruptions have taken place, the last happening in 1860. In 900 there was one; in 1000 one; in 1200 and the three following centuries one each; three took place in 1600, and the same number in the two following centuries. At neither of these eruptions did any flow of lava take place; but they were characterized by masses of volcanic ashes, and streams of water, which carried with them an incredible quantity of sand and *débris*. The volcano is situate in the middle of a snowy fjeld, where large quantities of snow and ice are massed together during the time the volcano is at rest, and these are melted and overflow the lowlands when an eruption takes place. Katla is not, as might be supposed, a rock lowering above and distinct from the Jökul; it is a large mountain fissure running from south-west to north-east, and from south-east to north-west, with several smaller fissures issuing from it.

It is, therefore, called Kötlu-gjá* as well as Katla. The Katla volcano has only once been visited, namely in 1823. I will now give an account of two of its most destructive eruptions. One of these occurred in 1625, and was distinguished by the huge masses of water which it discharged over Mýrdalssandr as far as the other side of Þykkvibær, near Mýrar, when the houses in the neighbourhood were nearly washed away. Large quantities of ashes, moreover, were thrown out from the volcano, which being carried along by the wind, rendered it so dark that day was changed into night; and people who were out of doors had to take hold of each other's hands for fear of being lost. Flashes of lightning, however, occasionally illumined the pervading darkness, and caused great pain to those who were struck by them. The lightning was succeeded by such terrific detonations that the people thought their heads would split open. These phenomena, however, disappeared after a short interval; and the ashes were carried by the wind in another direction. The eruption was not of long duration; it began on the morning of the second of September and ended on the evening of the thirteenth. Immense quantities of sand fell on the lowlands, and in some places the sand and ashes lay so deep, that they reached up to the knees of a full-grown man.

The next eruption, in 1660, began on the evening of November 3rd, and was preceded by an earthquake which lasted a whole hour. At midnight an alarming mass of water was discharged into Kerlingardalsa, in the valley east of Víkshamrar; it rose forty-nine feet higher than any previous "Jökellöb," and lasted till the 5th. This flood discharged the greater quantity of the masses of ice it carried down with it into the sea, and overflowed the whole of Mýrdalssandr, as far as the eye could reach, from Höfðabrekka, a house on the fjeld of the same

* Gjá signifies a fissure.

name, to the east of Kerlingardalsa. On the seventh the flood reached the farmhouse and destroyed a portion of the home fields; the next day the inmates were awakened by the roaring of the water, which reached up to the house itself, and carried away a gable of the church and half filled the houses with water, so that the people had to fly for refuge to some neighbouring heights. A shower of ashes fell during the whole time. On the ninth the water had abated, and as the weather became fine, the people determined to repair to the farmhouse; but just as they were on the point of doing so they heard the terrific sound of an approaching flood, which dashed along with such impetuosity, that the very ground shook beneath them. In an instant the water washed away the remainder of the church, and all the houses attached to the farm, so that scarce a vestige of them was left, though they had been almost entirely buried in sand and rubbish. Earthquakes, thunders, explosions and detonations in the air accompanied this eruption. On the twelfth there was another flood, surpassing all the former ones in violence. Besides masses of ice these floods carried down such enormous masses of *débris*, sand and mud, that the sea was driven back; for according to the accounts, in a single night, where people had formerly fished in twenty fathoms of water, it was now dry land. On this occasion the eruption lasted till late in the winter, though no mention is made of any more floods having occurred.

In the eruption of 1721, fearful floods again took place over Mýrdalssandr. At the commencement of the eruption a stream burst forth, consisting principally of half-melted snow and large masses of ice, which tumbled about in the sea like floating islands; while, simultaneously, another stream issued in a south-easterly direction, and inflicted great injury on the land. The first of these two streams filled the sea with ice to such an extent that even from the highest mountains it was impossible to see open water till it was broken up by the action of the waves. It then drifted westward as far as Reykjanes, and up into the rivers along the coast, so that large icebergs were left standing on the bed of the river in the Ölfusá. The greater portion, however, of the ice that had been washed down from the glacier, remained fixed aground at the distance of about seven miles from land, in a hundred fathoms of water. It formed, moreover, a high ridge over the land from the sea as far as Hafrsey, a fjeld on Mýrdalssandr. The lashing of the waves against this barrier was felt in Vík, where it committed some damage upon the houses; and extended westward along the south coast by Eyafjalla-Jökul, and even as far as Grindavík, near Reykjanes, where it reached high up on to the land; and also at the Vestmanna islands, where it also inflicted injury. A stream of a similar terrific character broke out on the following day, and submerged the masses of ice that had been previously discharged into the sea, as far as the eye could reach. Further, it made its way through Kerlingar valley, and dammed up the stream there. The deluge, or, more properly speaking, the ice, carried, moreover, immense masses of rock with it; and in the vicinity of Hjörleifshöfði, a mountain on Mýrdalssandr, a rock of twenty fathoms in height, entirely disappeared; not to speak of other instances. One can form some idea of the altitude of this barrier of ice, when it is mentioned that from Höfðabrekka farm, which, as I have stated, lies high up in a fjeld of the same name, one could not see Höjrleifshöfði opposite, which is a fell 640 feet in height; but, in order to do so, had to clamber up a mountain-slope east of Höfðabrekka, 1,200 feet high. The distance between Höfðabrekka and Hjörleifshöfði is one geographical mile, or the fifteenth part of a degree.

The third eruption of Katla took place in 1755,—the same year as the memorable earthquake at Lisbon; when several other volcanoes on this side of the globe were also in a state of activity. The eruption was accompanied again by large floods. The same, too, was the case in the eruption of 1823, which lasted for three weeks; during which time it was calculated that eighteen distinct floods washed over Álptaver and Mýrdalssandr. Large quantities of ashes were at the same time discharged from Katla, and fell so thickly in the neighbourhood of Sólheimar, under Eyafjalla-Jökul, that the grass fields were buried on the second day after the eruption had taken place. This eruption, which began on June 26th—that is, just at the commencement of the summer—brought with it very cold weather. It was ushered in with snow, whereby a quantity of the ashes that fell were mixed with hail; so that the stones consisted of two-thirds ice and one-third ashes. Symptoms of this eruption had been noticed in the summer of the preceding year, when the glacier near Katla decreased in magnitude to such an extent, that several mountain-peaks that had formerly not been visible now towered over the glacier's surface. This phenomenon could not have been caused by the melting of the ice, for the rivers which come from the glacier simultaneously diminished in volume, but was rather due to evaporation. During this eruption, Mýrdalssandr was raised considerably above its former level, whereby fissures and clefts were filled up, so that the road over the sand could be accomplished in a shorter time.

And lastly—only briefly to allude to the eruption in 1860, which lasted from the 8th to the 27th of May—we will merely remark, that, as in former instances, it was accompanied by rumbling noises, showers of ashes, and floods; and that it was one of the least destructive of all the eruptions of this volcano.

The reader will remember that the author, accompanied by Sira Magnús, was journeying along the road to the coast below Víkshamrar, which became land after the eruption of Katla. After passing this we turned northwards, and rode along Kerlingardalr, which was filled with *débris*, and which had formerly been a fjord, and then directed our course towards Höfðabrekka. It was a lovely day, and the neighbourhood was very inviting, owing partly to the historical associations connected with it, partly to the striking contrast between the grass-covered fjeld sides, and the grey, shingly bottom of the valley, through which Kerlingardalsá discharged its muddy, glacier stream. I sat on my horse, and was looking with surprise at the contrast before me, the fleecy clouds floating over my head, and behind, the sea, when, at a bend of the road, the round, shining, and snow-covered crown of Katla suddenly struck my eyes. It was such a surprise to me, for I had not expected to get a view of the mountain, that I jumped up in my saddle for joy at the sight. We now rode up Höfðabrekka fjeld, where everything was green and bright in the sunlight; we also rode a little distance down it, when almost as suddenly as the snowy mountain had appeared in view, a boundless, dark plain of driving sand exposed itself to my sight. This was Mýrdalssandr, which I have alluded to before. Again I jumped up in my saddle, but this time not from emotions of pleasure, for along this black, barren, and drifting sand, to which no bounds could be seen, my actual route lay. I took leave of Sira Magnús at the foot of the mountain, where the sandy plain began, and set out on my lonely journey over the barren waste, some upright posts, at short distances from each other marking out the proper course to take, rejoicing that the wind lay behind us as we began our voyage across this sandy sea. The sand was very loose, and our horses sank deep in over their hoofs at every step. Three rivers which take their rise in Mýrdalsjökul, but which do not contain a great body of water, intersect it. Naturally, the wet sand at the bottom of these rivers was of a darker colour than the dry sand of the plain. Múlakvísl, as one of these rivers is named, which, moreover, conveyed the muddy waters of the glacier, had, from these joint causes, a colour resembling ink, or at least of coffee with a very little cream in it. The banks of these rivers, from having been hollowed out by the water, were occasionally so steep that the horses had to slide down them almost in a sitting posture. An Icelandic horse, however, is not afraid of such precipitous places; neither are they disinclined to jump over small streams, especially when their instinct tells them that there is soft ground at the bottom. When they are loose, one can often see them execute regular summersaults—when, for instance, they have to go down a perpendicular height which is higher than the horse itself.

On the western part of Mýrdalssandr, that is, on the side from which I approached it, two isolated fjelds rise up; the one to the north, the other to the south of the usual bridle-path. The last of these, the above-mentioned Hjörleifshöfði, possesses an ancient and historical celebrity. It was here, namely, that Hjörleifr, one of Iceland's earliest colonists, landed in 874. In the following spring he was enticed by his Irish serfs into a neighbouring wood, who had told him that there was a bear there, and, together with his followers, was murdered by them. After this the serfs fled away to the Vestmanna, a rocky group of islands about a mile from land, to the south-west of Eyafjaka-Jökul, but were discovered and slain by Ingólfr, Hjörleifr's friend and comrade. On leaving Norway, Hjörleifr, probably because he was a Christian, would not sacrifice to the gods; and now Ingólfr lamented his death—" Here a noble man fell ignominiously, for worthless serfs were his destroyers; but thus it happens to all who will not sacrifice to the gods."

To judge from its name, Mýrdalssandr, which now forms a barren and hideous sandy waste, was probably, at the time when Iceland was first discovered, a swampy tract overgrown with grass. On its eastern side the remains of an ancient lava stream, probably the first one which laid these districts waste, protrude from the soil; for, according to the Landnámabók, a Viking, named Rafn Hafnarlykell, is said to have fled away from this place, the first he settled in, as far as can be ascertained about the year 874, owing to a volcanic eruption. The names of two farmers, Hraunbœr and Hraungerdi, are standing memorials of this lava stream, now partly hidden from view by the floods and drifting sand from Mount Katla; for the eruption of 894 is attributed to this volcano. The fjeld Hjörleifshöfði, where Hjörleifr landed, lies a short distance from land. There is no wood in the neighbourhood. As may be supposed, Mýrdalssandr is a long, barren waste; and my guide from Vík was scarcely more entertaining than the above-named guide-posts.

On entering the parsonage in Mýrar, which was my immediate goal, I was nearly turning back, as I thought that the door of the "bœr" which I first entered led into the stable; but I was soon discovered by the little dean—whose name I have forgotten—who gave me a hearty welcome into this caricature of a parsonage-house. The day following I had to cross the Kúðafljót, a broad and important river, remarkable for its soft bed, owing to which no regular ford can be maintained. It was Sunday, and quite a caravan of men and women, many of them with little children in their arms, crossed over with me. The passage over took about twenty minutes, and the water frequently came up to the knees of the riders. In crossing a river, one rides in single file, so that the first horse may trample a path for the others, and because the fording place naturally lies in a direct line across the river, outside of which it would be unadvisable to go. After a short ride from the river over a sandy plain, I reached a clean-looking farmhouse, near Lángholt church, where I changed guides, and therefore had to stay some little time. The churches in this district were the first I had seen since leaving Oddi that had any approach to an ecclesiastical-looking exterior. Usually they consist of a little, square-shaped, tar-covered barn, made out of planks; or else an earthen structure of the same style of architecture as the "bœr," with two small windows in the gable to admit the light, and a little aperture in the roof. Externally, with but very few exceptions, they are destitute of every kind of adornment that might be supposed to refer to religious purposes; and one would be able to form no idea of the nature of the building before one, did not the materials of which it was composed, together with its size, and still more its isolated position, mark the difference between a church and a "bœr." The churchyards are just as unostentatious; for a tombstone is a rarity. A cross is scarcely to be found upon a grave in Iceland, and the green mounds are soon levelled to the ground. With reference to size, I remember to have seen a church in course of building, in Þingmuli, in the east, which was twenty-four feet long inside, fourteen feet wide, and at most seven feet in height. This certainly was smaller than usual—in fact, it was no bigger than a moderate-sized room; but at all events it serves to give an idea of the dimensions of the rest. The church at Lángholt was certainly a small one, but it was ornamented with a cross on one end of the roof, over the entrance, and had moreover window-sills painted white, which was something quite out of the common course of events. The church, which usually lies close to the parsonage, is made use of during the week time as a store-room for the clergyman's wool, or similar articles; and it is used also as night-quarters for guests. The clergyman can almost regard the church as his own property; for according to the antiquated institutions of the Icelandic church establishment it is generally incumbent on the pastor, instead of on the community, to build a new church when the old one falls into decay; and as this is a pretty heavy drag upon him in proportion to his income—he collects, however, a certain tithe for this purpose—pastors not unfrequently adopt the precaution of looking out for another cure when the church in their own parish begins to get out of repair.

The interior of the churches in Iceland is usually as unpretentious as the outside. They contain benches which are unpainted, boarded walls, a simple altar and altar stool, and an equally simple pulpit; and the floor is boarded. Sometimes, owing to the lowness of the building, the pulpit is arranged in such a manner that its upper edge reaches up to the cross beams in the roof. Occasionally a little altar-piece may be found; and some memorial tablets hanging on the walls to the memory of persons of distinction. Besides the necessary information concerning the deceased, one of these memorial tablets contains a few verses giving a sketch of his virtues. In the church at Holt, under Eyafjalla-Jökul, a memorial tablet with an inscription, set in a simple frame and glazed, was found, of which the following is a literal translation:—

> "Here are preserved
> the mortal remains—
> the spirit lives
> with the Father of spirits;
> only the precious memory
> of Arni Sveinsson remains behind.
> He was born 1 Nov., 1780;
> married 7 June, 1821, with
> maiden Jórunn Sighvatsdatter,
> who still survives him here below.
> God blessed them with three sons,
> one of whom fell asleep at an early age;
> the other, followed by three children,
> inters his father, who
> departed this life 25 June, 1853,
> (during the absence of his beloved eldest son),
> after having been Mediator of the
> 'Arbitration Court' for twenty-four years.
> He was
>
> | | |
> |---|---|
> | Calm in mind, | Therefore will many |
> | firm in counsel, | sorely miss him, |
> | watchful, active, | in the society of men; |
> | his friends' friend, | but among blessed spirits |
> | hospitable, bountiful, | will the gracious God |
> | upright towards all, | always gladden his spirit |
> | the affectionate father | with pleasant occupations. |
> | of his house and children. | |
>
> Thus a beloved brother is remembered
> in the family and in society.
> E. . . ."

Though the churches in Iceland are thus of a very unimposing appearance, the people are none the less devout; just as they are not more religiously disposed when worshipping under arches and aisles of Gothic architecture. There is a strong belief in authority existent in Iceland, which, among other things, is evident from the fact that though the Roman Catholic mission has a chapel and two priests in Reykjavik, it has not succeeded in perverting a single individual from the Lutheran faith.

That this belief in authority sometimes verges upon superstition is only natural. I will adduce an instance:—

Once, by some mistake, the Communion wine in a church up

in the country had been changed for Cognac, which, it must be allowed, was an unfortunate circumstance. The men, however, being used to strong drink and to their favourite corn brandy, swallowed the Cognac without taking any notice of the mistake; but a poor woman, who found it too strong, could not restrain her feelings, but muttered so loud that those next her could hear—" *Beiskur er þú nú, drotinn minn!* " (" Thou art angry to-day, O Lord! ").

As I have already had occasion to remark, the Icelandic clergy are generally noted for their attainments, especially in the Classics, which, considering their poor circumstances, is the more remarkable. I never dreamt, therefore, to meet with an incident, which I will now narrate. I was sitting one day at the dinner table with a worthy, but rather simple-minded pastor in the eastern districts of the island, when the conversation turned upon the subject of the foreign mission to Iceland. Wishing to pay the good pastor a compliment, I stated that I thought the Icelandic clergy must be very zealous and excellent pastors, as the foreigners had not succeeded in making a single proselyte. " Proselyte! what is that?" said my reverend companion, interrupting me; "we—we generally call it orthodox." And I had great difficulty in convincing the worthy pastor that his interpretation of the word was incorrect; but when at last he perceived his error, he naïvely remarked— " Proselyte! Well, I never heard that word before!"

There has been some little stir of late among religious circles in Iceland, owing to the appearance of a critical work on the genuineness of St. John's Gospel, by an Icelander, named Magnus Eiriksson, a candidate in theology, residing in Copenhagen. This book goes by the name of " the great book " in Iceland, and has excited a great deal of attention among the author's orthodox countrymen. The book was first published in Danish, but has recently appeared in Icelandic, and is looked upon as forbidden fruit in that country. When it was known that it had, moreover, been translated into Swedish—for the author had taken care to make his countrymen aware of the fact—I was perpetually being assailed with questions both from pastors and peasants concerning it; and as I had not read the book, their questions very often put me in a dilemma; for while I naturally could not deny the privilege of free investigation, I was unable to speak in favour of a book which I knew only by name. Still, as I knew something about the tendency of the work in question, I used to get out of my difficulty by answering—"that as far as I was concerned, it was a matter of indifference whether John or Luke had written the Gospel; for it was a good book, and that was the main point;" and although they would shake their heads at my remark, they were not sufficiently good theologians to be able to refute it. Meantime, poor Eiriksson is being treated very badly in Iceland, both in the journals and in common conversation. Some people would like to burn him; others would hang him, if not bodily, at least, figuratively; others, again, express their surprise that he has not been banished from Denmark, "as an example to Iceland," and so on. I cannot deny myself the pleasure of laying one of the numerous articles that have appeared on this subject before my readers. It appeared in the *Islendingur*, and the following is a literal translation :—

"In the last series of the *Skirnir* journal, it is stated that our countryman, Candidate Magnus Eiriksson, in Copenhagen, has published a large work on the Gospel of St. John, in which, according to the writer of the article in the *Skirnir*, the author proves with great acuteness and depth of argument, that the Apostle was not the author of the Gospel; and he further states that the clergy and theologians in general receive so many severe rubs in this work, that it cannot but be a sign of their weakness, if they make no attempt at refutation. Although I have seen the work in question, and the loan of it has been offered to me, I acknowledge, without blushing, that I refused to read it, certainly not from any fear that my childlike and simple faith in Christ would thereby become the weaker, but because I remembered the prayer, 'Lead us not into temptation!' and the warning, 'Thou that thinkest thou standest, take heed lest thou fall;' and, therefore, I would not rush blindly into temptation. Moreover, I said to myself, 'If the devil has been able so fearfully to seduce Magnus, whom I once knew to be an orthodox man, how can I feel sure, if I read the book, that he will not seek, when I am least aware, to shake my faith in God through Christ who reconciled the world to himself?' a belief which is more precious to me than aught else. Hence, it is not my purpose in these lines to allude to any particular passages in this blasphemous book, or to seek to refute the arguments which Magnus has adduced; for this would be too prolix a subject for a newspaper article; and I know, moreover, that there are many who are more capable of doing so than I am, and who will doubtless in good time speak forth words which, through the power of the Holy Ghost, will crush Magnus's serpent-head. I will, therefore, merely express my surprise and sorrow that the spiritual heads of the Church of Christ in Denmark have for the moment been lulled to sleep on the pillow of indifference, and have permitted such a book as Magnus Eiriksson's to be printed and disseminated—a book whose object evidently is to break down the most sacred, the most comforting, and the most saving of Divine truths. Oh! that the burning spirit of our forefathers is quenched! Oh! that this new Arius has not been driven into exile! that this Servetus has not been burnt at the stake! Nay, this open blasphemer, this tool of Satan, goes still unmolested—ay, even honoured for his work—in the very midst of those who ought to watch the flock of Christ. Whence comes it?"

After the author, who subscribes himself "An Old Pastor," has thus given vent to his feelings in carefully-selected expressions against "this devil in the shape of an angel of light," "this wolf in sheep's clothing;" against "the dark and corrupted spirit," "of which a whole legion has entered into Magnus Eiriksson, to use him as a blind instrument against that Gospel which they (the devils) hate the most;" against "this worst Antichrist that has ever appeared," and thereon has addressed himself with fervent prayers "to the spiritual shepherds who have been appointed by God to watch over Christ's lambs," "lest they too should allow themselves to be over-reached by this cruel wolf," he continues:—

"I charge you, who are called the strong corner-pillars of the Church of Christ in Denmark, in God's name, to resist with power this onslaught of Satan; do not use merely half your strength, but with glowing spirits, as the true soldiers of Christ, first refute, with those incontrovertible proofs which are so plentifully at hand, this lying book; and then seek in the spirit of love to lead poor Magnus Eiriksson to renounce his artfully-concocted lie, and publicly to acknowledge his repentance; and if he cannot be induced to do this—which would be of the greatest benefit to himself—then never rest till he has been driven out of the kingdom, and every copy of his book has been confiscated and burned on the pile. This is the very mildest sentence possible; for in olden days such open endeavours to destroy God's husbandry were not endured: then would Magnus himself have been placed in the midst of his books, and have been burnt together with them."

Another contributor in the *Islendingur*, who, in the main

agrees with the first one, will not, however, believe that Magnus Eiriksson is Antichrist, "for that old Satan does not make his choice from among the class of minor devils" when he attacks the Church of Christ. This writer further suggests "that as Magnus is our neighbour and countryman, we ought to pray for him in every church in the country, that the unclean spirit may depart out of him." This last article smacks rather of irony, for it is difficult to imagine that a drunken Sysselmand in the west should mean it seriously; but in Iceland they are of a different opinion.

After this rather long stay at Lángholt—for I have long since finished the unavoidable cup of coffee which is always offered on entering a "bær"—we now direct our course a little more to the north, over soft meadows, probably belonging to the farmer at Lángholt. He is a well-to-do man; for he owns eighty sheep, two cows, and ten horses, a number which may possibly sound strange in many an English ear, but which is quite in keeping in this country. For it is impossible to scrape together sufficient hay during the summer to feed a larger number of cows during the winter, especially as provision has also to be made for the ewes. "But are all those horses necessary?" Yes; and the farmer at Lángholt ought to have had at least fourteen horses to be well provided; for he would rather not have to make more than one journey to Eyrarbakki in the course of the year, which occupies about a fortnight; on which occasion he has to bring all his stock of coffee, seed, sugar, iron, &c., enough for a whole year's consumption on horseback home with him; and, further, he has a long way to go to bring the hay home from where it is mown, and this can only be done on horseback. But as this number of horses is quite out of proportion to the rest of his farming stock, and as it is, of course, impossible to let them go quite uncared for during the winter, it may be said with truth of him, and of many like him in Iceland, that he is eaten up by his horses.

After passing the soft meadow which gave rise to the above remarks, our route lay by the side of a deep river, which bears the anomalous name of "Eldvatn" (fire-water), though it is composed of nothing but pure water, without the smallest admixture of the elixir of life, flowing along the edge of a large loose stream, of which, in the next chapter, I will give the reader some account.

CHAPTER III.

Skaptar Volcano—Eruption in 1783—A River dried up—Enormous Lava Stream—Fearful Devastations—Consequences of the Eruption—Pestilence among Animals and Men—New Rivers formed—Bread and Butter—A Fairy Tale—Icelandic Fare—The Meaning of the word "Beg"—Snuff Horns and Powder Flasks—Remarks on Brandy Imports—Strange Advertisement—Articles of Import—Reppstyrer or Constable—A Farmhouse in the Eastern Districts—Fording Places—Skeidarar-jökul—Progressive Motion of Glaciers—Iceland formerly a Wooded Country—Skeidararsandr—Svinafells-Jökul—Crevices—Danger of falling into them—Glaciers melting on the Surface—Öræfu-Jökul and Volcano—Eruption in 1727 described—Terrific Results—Great Mortality—Continue Journey—Bird Rocks—Bird-catching in the Færoe Islands—Great Dimon—Insect Powder—Its Blessings—Mercantile Caravans—Icelandic Whip.

KAPTÁRFELLSHRAUN derives its name from a volcano, of whose activity in bygone ages nothing is known. It consists of two lava streams, the largest that have ever been known to flow within the memory of man. The craters from which these streams have flowed lie at the foot of Skaptárfells-Jökul, or on the western side of Vatna-Jökul, in the angle which is formed by the Skapta and Hverfisfljót. From these, one of the streams must have flowed in a south-westerly direction, and subsequently have turned towards the south along the valley of the Skaptá; while the other flowed towards the south in the bed of the Hverfisfljót. An account of the volcanic eruption, to which these streams owe their origin, has been given by Magnus Stephensen, who examined the ground the year after the eruption had taken place, at the request of the Danish Government. The following extract must suffice:—

"The unusually mild winter of 1782-83 was followed by an equally mild and agreeable spring; the weather was calm and warm, with southerly winds and a fertilising rain. At a very early period the fields assumed their green and odoriferous spring garb; and the month of May decked the earth with many flowers and herbs of the most luxuriant growth. After the mild winter, all the cattle were found to be in excellent condition when spring came round, and everything contributed to lead the people to expect a favourable summer and good crop; but these hopes vanished with the month of May.

"Towards the end of that month, a thin, bluish smoke, or vapour, which is sometimes to be seen spread over the surface of the earth, attracted the attention of persons conversant with such matters; but nobody had any idea of their real import till sundry severe shocks of earthquake (which were first observed on the 1st of June over the whole district of Skaptárfell, and which increased in violence each day, especially in the mornings and evenings, and continued throughout the week till the 8th, which happened to be Whit Sunday) announced that some violent commotions were taking place within the interior of the earth.

"Whit Sunday was ushered in by a clear and beautiful morning, but towards nine o'clock in the forenoon, a black wall was seen to rise to the north, over the Síða fjelds. From the houses situated on the southern slope this wall could not be seen till it stood right over Síða, but from Landbrot, immediately to the south, it was observed that columns of smoke emanated from the mountain tracts to the north, and subsequently joined the black wall. As it approached nearer and nearer, Síða gradually became darker; and when the wall, or dark cloud, stood immediately over it, a great quantity of sand and ashes fell, to the depth of one inch. They resembled coal cinders, mixed with a curious, grey, shining mass of lava, which, by the force of the explosion, had assumed the appearance of delicate threads as fine as hairs. A strong breeze, however, kept this wall of sand or ashes from advancing; but the shocks of earthquake, together with violent peals of thunder and subterranean detonations and reports, increased; and for the whole of this and the succeeding days noises could be heard in the mountains on the north resembling the sound of a multitude of waterfalls, or of a kettle that is boiling over.

"On the 10th of June sundry columns of fire were first observed to issue from the northern slope, and each day the wall became higher and higher, while the shocks of earthquake and the thunder peals increased in violence every hour.

"On the following day (June 11th) a circumstance occurred which astounded the inhabitants in the greatest degree; for the Skaptá, a river of some importance, that rises on the Skaptar-Jökul north of Síða, and runs first in a south-westerly, and then in a southerly, direction till it joins the Kúdafljót, and which, in the winter and spring of 1783, had had a large body of water in it, and even on the 9th and 10th was still rapid and fretting and chafing in its course, became completely dried up, so that people could cross over at places where formerly they had the greatest difficulty of putting over in a boat. The cause of this remarkable phenomenon soon made itself apparent, for a terrific lava stream burst forth, like a foaming sea, from between the mountains along the valley of the Skaptá. This stream lay partly in a channel of 400, 500, or even 600 feet in depth, and 200 feet in width; but it was completely filled up with lava, which actually flowed over the sides of the valley and flooded a large extent of land on either side. Only in a very few places were the tops of the rocks which formed the channel visible, as they jutted upwards above the lava. The terrible phenomena that accompanied this first eruption of lava served to make this day a fearful one indeed: a dark wall towered up in the north-west, and discharged a large quantity of ashes, sand, and sulphureous particles, together with this hair-formed larva, while a deadly vapour brooded over the earth, and shut the sun out from view, which occasionally peeped forth from the smoke and sulphureous mist, like a blood-red globe. Constant shocks of earthquake, too, and concussions, pillars of fire in the north, together with the seething lava stream in the valley of Skaptá, subterranean noises, accompanied with incessant flashes of lightning and the most terrific peals of thunder, caused such a panic in the breasts of the inhabitants that they thought every minute that heaven and earth would perish, and themselves be doomed to instantaneous destruction.

"The lava stream meanwhile rolled along in its channel with a steady and ever-increasing force, and, as I have already said, overflowed the sides. In a single day, on the evening of the 12th, it had reached the farm at Ás, which lies at the angle the Skaptá forms, as it turns eastwards, and overwhelmed the house and farm in its devouring flood.

"Fears were now entertained that this fearful lava stream, which flowed along like molten metal, would overwhelm Meðalland, which lay below, but fortunately its course was arrested by a deep hollow in the valley into which it poured; but when this chasm was filled up, and the lava, in consequence of fresh streams from above, had reached up to a towering height, it again burst forth with a terrific crash, resembling the roar of an avalanche, so that the whole country round literally trembled, accompanied with vivid flashes of lightning and deafening peals of thunder. The glowing mass now extended towards the east and south, and on the night of the 14th and 15th overwhelmed another farm, with all its meadows and grass walls. During its continued course to the south and south-west, on the 16th and 17th, it spread over older lava streams, filling up the fissures in them, and producing a rushing sound, like that caused by an innumerable quantity of bellows, in consequence of the air in the fissures being compressed by the liquid mass that poured into them, after which it forced a way through the narrow openings on the surface of the older stream. Moreover, it forced its way down into subterraneous caverns, and cast up the overlying crust high into the air or on the sides; and, after thus undermining hills and mounds, through which the hot vapour could scarcely find an outlet, it overthrew rocks and cliffs of 120 to 180 feet in height.

"On the 18th another terrible eruption took place. The lava stream now dashed along over tracts that had already been devastated, where the former stream had somewhat cooled down and become solid. The new stream, therefore, flowed over the older one, whereby the height of the whole mass was considerably increased. In its midst, large, glowing masses of rock could be seen floating about, while the water that had been dammed up on both sides of its course was thrown into a violent state of ebullition.

"On the following day the lava stream divided into two branches; one of which pursued its course towards the south, over Meðalland, where, on the following day, it overwhelmed and destroyed several farms, till at last its progress was arrested, north of the farm Hnausar, about the middle of July; the other arm penetrated further to the east, where it destroyed several houses, and found its way into a valley where the farm Skál and a church of the same name lay, completely blocking it up. On the two following days it rained heavily, so that the mountain streams filled up the valley which had been dammed up by the lava, and submerged the church and farm. This occurred on June 21st, and on the following morning this water was boiling fiercely. Subsequently other lava streams followed, flowing over the old stream, and, on the 2nd of July, overwhelmed the same houses that a few days before had been boiled.

"Meanwhile a new eruption of lava had taken place, and had forced a way for itself along the bottom of Hverfisfljót, a river lying on the east side of Síða, where the same fearful scenes were enacted. This outbreak had been announced beforehand on the 14th, but especially on the 28th of June, by a thick black wall of ashes that rose up from the mountains to the north, and caused it to be so dark, that even at mid-day it was almost impossible to see a sheet of white paper when held up against the window of the house. From this wall a fearful quantity of ashes, sand, and large red-hot masses of stone, were hurled over the whole western portion of Fljótshverfi, which scorched all the grass in the fields, spoilt the drinking water for man and beast, and moreover threatened to set the houses on fire. On the 3rd of August, smoke was noticed to emanate from Hverfisfljót, and the temperature of the water in the river kept constantly rising, when after the lapse of some few days the river was entirely dried up and disappeared. Naturally, therefore, the inhabitants were terribly alarmed lest the same calamities should befall them as had overtaken their neighbours in Skaptárdal. The result showed that their fears were well grounded; for on the morning of the 9th August, numerous columns of smoke were again seen to rise up between the mountains, and presently to form themselves into a thick wall, from which a seething lava stream burst forth into the old river-bed in Hverfishfljót, accompanied with incessant flashes of lightning and peals of thunder. This stream was succeeded by others, which piled themselves up in the valley in the same manner as has been described above, overflowing and destroying two farms in their course, besides injuring others."

From what Stephensen says in his work, the general impression in the district with reference to the origin of the lava streams was, that they had been formed by the joint action of several craters—the western arm is from forty-three to forty-seven and a half miles long, and the eastern about nineteen miles; their width varies according to the nature of the ground, but at its lowest end, the west stream is nine and a half miles broad,—or that one point of eruption existed for the western stream, and another for the eastern stream. Though the above-named author is not unwilling to favour this opinion, he yet totally rejects it after the attempts he made in the summer of 1784 to reach the volcano. Stephensen undertook this expedition from the neighbourhood north of Kirkjubær, where he was staying, across Kaldbakr, to a fjeld named Blængr, lying further to the north. On this trip, as well as on his return journey, he was enabled to see over the eastern and western lava streams, along which clouds of sand and steam were even then rising up. The reader will remember that both of the lava streams flowed in the beds of large rivers, the water of which was converted into steam by the glowing masses of rock, and was mingled with the gases that emanated from the lava. The smoke that ascended from the lava plain, north of Blængr, and which is said to have been as indescribable as it was terrific, shut out the prospect from this fjeld, which otherwise would command a good view over the scene of the eruption. At a long distance off in the lava, however, Stephensen saw a large hill, like a small mountain, broader than it was high, from which a very thick, dark-coloured smoke was rising up. There, he supposed, and naturally not without good reasons, lay the crater; and accordingly determined to continue his journey thither, which, however, seemed to be attended by insurmountable obstacles; for when he had gone about a couple of hundred steps on the lava stream, he found it so burning hot, that he could not possibly stand upon it, while the incessant columns of smoke that rose up on all sides caused him to lose his way. After repeated attempts at other places, which always met with the same unsuccessful results, he found it impossible to penetrate farther towards the north; and when an experiment was made with a boring instrument, it became so hot after reaching the depth of only a few feet, that it was with difficulty they could pull it out again, even though they had thick gloves on. As the reader, therefore, will observe, Stephensen was unable to reach the crater he had discovered from Blængr; but as he did not notice any other, he felt convinced that this crater was the only one.

From a personal interview which I had with Procurator Jón Guðmundsson in Reykjavik, who had visited Blængr a year or two previously, Stephensen's views—which it will be remembered had been formed through smoke and steam—must undergo some alteration. For from Blængr the two different points of eruption of both the lava streams can be plainly discerned; that of the first stream lying to the north-east of this fjeld, and that of the other to the north; for in these two diverse directions several volcanic craters are found in both places. Further, Herr Guðmundsson is of opinion that the easternmost lava stream first flowed in the same direction as the one to the west, but its progress being obstructed, it thereupon took a turn to the east and south, in the bed of the Hverfisfljót.

These observations thus explain the cause of the stream first taking this direction on August 9th, or long after the first commencement of the eruption.*

The lava discharged from Skaptár volcano is distinct in its composition from other known specimens of lava in Iceland, in that it contains copper,—at least according to an analysis which Stephensen made. The height of the streams is reckoned to be 100 feet in the open plain; but in the Skaptár ravine it attained a height of 600 feet, as the reader will remember.

We will now give some account of the devastation this volcanic eruption committed in the western districts of Skaptárfell; and this made itself manifest in several ways. In the first place, it put a stop to the fisheries; for, from the thick smoke that enveloped the district, but few trips could be made out to sea. In the next place, the *débris* and ashes that fell into the lakes destroyed the trout; but on the other hand, the residents derived some advantage from the drying up of the Skaptár in the beginning of the summer, as quantities of salmon, which happened to be at that time in the river, were caught, as it were, on dry land, or in holes in the river that had been dammed up. But in return for this, they lost all their egg-harvest, as the birds that used to breed on the mountains were driven away by the eruption; and the swans, too, that used generally to be caught in great numbers up in the mountains during the month of August, when the moulting

* The author had intended to visit these volcanic craters, but was obliged to relinquish the idea, owing to the mountains being still covered with snow. It is remarkable that this volcano, which has discharged the largest known lava stream, has never yet been visited; at least, not by any one who has had a special interest in the subject.

season comes on, at which time they can be killed with a blow from a stick, were driven away by the sulphureous vapours; and the few eggs that were found were so saturated with smoke as to be unfit for food. The grass, moreover, suffered beyond description, not only in the immediate neighbourhood of the volcano, where sand and ashes had fallen so thickly, that when Stephensen went over Siða, they lay from four to six inches in thickness on the ground, but farther away; and as the ashes had been distributed over the whole country in minute particles, the mis-growth was general. Wild plants which are used as articles of food—as the angelica and the Icelandic moss—were completely buried under the ashes. Neither did the animals go unscathed, owing to the inferior quality of the grass. But the symptoms of disease among them became more apparent during the following winter, when their only fodder consisted of the wretched hay that had been made during the summer. The sheep, however, suffered most. As early as the autumn, several of them were attacked with a disease that had never been heard of before. They could neither stand nor walk; their teeth became so loose that they could not chew their food; while their jaws became full of lumps, and their joints were swollen. Towards Christmas the epidemic increased in severity, and attacked the cattle also. When the animals were slaughtered, it was observed that the inside of their carcases was attacked in the same way as the outside; for sometimes the heart, liver, and kidneys would be covered with hundreds of boils, or swollen up; or else be wasted away or inflamed; or else one kidney would be greatly inflated, while the other had wasted away in a similar degree. The jaws became terribly inflamed, the ribs covered with hard lumps, the bones of the consistency of gristle, and the hardest vertebræ became so soft after being boiled, that they could be picked to pieces with the fingers; and when the entrails were boiled, they crumbled away, so that they could readily be ground into powder. This epidemic raged in many parts of the country, mostly among the sheep; but still it visited the cattle and horses with great severity.

Neither did human beings escape. The unhealthy and fœtid state of the atmosphere caused by the eruption, the impure condition of the water and of the necessary means of subsistence, produced a fearful dearth, which was felt with tremendous severity in the immediate neighbourhood of the catastrophe. The epidemic attacked individuals in much the same way as it had visited the animals. The symptoms made themselves apparent by a fearful swelling in the feet, loins, hips, and arms, as well as in the neck and head. A painful cramp contracted the sinews to such a degree, that the body assumed a bent form. The teeth became loose, and disappeared from sight under the swollen gums, and ultimately rotted away and fell out. The neck and throat were attacked both on the inside and outside with putrid sores, and in many instances the tongue became rotten and dropped out of the mouth. The epidemic, therefore, resembled scurvy; and in the first half of 1784, about 150 persons fell victims to its ravages in the western parts of Skaptárfell alone. In one farm, Núpstaðr, all the inmates were attacked, so that there was not literally a single person left to nurse and succour the infected; and the dead had to lie as they were struck down, till news of the disaster was conveyed by travellers to other places. Those who suffered from hunger and privation were naturally the first who were attacked; and there were many whose only means of subsistence were the flesh and milk of the diseased animals, or old hides that had been boiled down. These misfortunes, too, came upon the country at a time when it was oppressed by an unwise and destructive system of commerce, which served to raise the price of the necessaries of life, while the native produce of the country had to be sold almost for nothing. Consequently, when an unexpected dearth like this fell upon the country under such circumstances, the consequences it entailed, among the poorer classes especially, were disastrous in the extreme. Of late years the entire commercial system in Iceland has been placed on a better footing; and it is to be hoped that human beings, at least in Iceland, will never have to undergo such horrors as this eruption caused. The days of monopoly are gone by, and we can only trust that the disasters which visited Iceland towards the close of the last century, and which form a dark page in the history of human suffering, can never be repeated.

We will now resume the thread of our narrative. The author had first to travel along the lower edge of the western lava-stream and the river Eldvatn, which first became a river owing to the partial damming up of the Skaptá valley. This river had already begun to be formed when Stephensen visited these regions; at least, so it appears from his description. For he mentions that a large mass of dammed-up water, which oozed forth from under the lava over the bog in the neighbourhood of the farm Hnausar, had forced itself a way into a brook that passed by the house, and then flowed gently down towards the sea. This tiny stream has now become an important river, and has cut out a deep bed in the sand by the side of the lava-stream. The bridle-path runs along the edge that separates the lava-stream from the river, and is so narrow that there is scarcely sufficient room for a horse; and should the animal stumble, the rider could scarcely avoid making a summersault over the steep bank down into the river below; or if he happily avoided this, he would in all probability severely injure himself against the sharp wall of lava on the other side. From Eldvatn the route lies over an even plain, which reaches down to the sea-shore; after which it passes over an old "hraun," or slaggy eminence, which proves that volcanic agency has been in full activity in these regions long before the Skaptár volcano poured forth its fiery streams.

The ash and slag heaps are from twenty to thirty feet in height, and their shape reminds one of the old barrows. They cover the terrain as far as the eye can reach, and their number has been computed at from two to three thousand. There is but little grass growing on them.

After fording the Skaptá and Geirlandrá, both of them deep rivers, the author found comfortable quarters at Hörgsdalr, under Kaldbaksfell. The first half of the journey to the east coast was now completed, and the Oræfa-Jökul loomed in the distance.

The usual food with which the traveller is entertained during the middle of the summer in this part of the country consists of smoked or dried mutton, or, as it is called, "hangi." When not too old or dry it is not an unpleasant dish. It has a gamey taste about it, for the sheep in Iceland live in a state of semi-wildness. Possibly this peculiar flavour may be caused from letting the fresh meat acquire just a "suspicion" of being high before boiling. Very little bread is eaten in Iceland, in proportion to other countries. The bread which was generally before me resembled that which is usually met with in Scandinavian countries. It is not, however, made so well in Iceland, for there are no ovens there, and it has, therefore, to be baked in iron pots.

The common sort of bread in Iceland consists of thin, flat cakes, resembling those we have in Sweden; the only difference is that it is never dry and crisp, a defect which is doubtless owing to the absence of baking ovens, and to the universal dampness of the Icelandic houses. This bread, which is considered to be of a simpler kind, is seldom offered to travellers, if there is any other sort in the house. I remember perfectly rejoicing the heart of Sira Björn, in Holt, when I told him that the Icelandic bread was very like what we had at home; and when my worthy host apologised for offering me the simpler kind of bread, he used the same words that the Icelandic pastor, Sira Lafranz, once used to King Erik Magnusson in Norway, when he asked him how it was that he, a priest, went about in a red garment. "Því," answered Sira Lafranz, "at eg hefi engi önnur til" ("Because I have none other"); "otherwise," said Sira Björn, "my wife would not have offered our guest this bread."

Bread, therefore, is not an article of daily consumption in Icelandic houses; the poorer classes eat dried fish instead, plentifully smeared over with butter. During my travels through the country I seldom had dried fish offered me as a substitute for bread, though, when the butter is good, it has a very agreeable flavour. It is not considered *comme il faut* to do so in Iceland, for the butter is often unendurable, owing to the dirty way in which it is prepared; and, moreover, the so-called "sour" butter is generally used. This sour butter is prepared as follows:—the butter is allowed to remain in its unsalted state till it becomes sour, and then, as Eggert Olafsen observes, it has this advantage over salt butter, that while this latter becomes rancid after the lapse of half a year, the sour butter remains the same as it was at first, even though it be kept for seven, eight, or even for twenty years. It is also said that this sour butter, when used with the dried fish, is a better "digester" than the salt butter; or, as the above-named author expresses himself, "it diffuses such an agreeable warmth over the stomach."

Butter, therefore, usurps the place of seasoning and of salt, which, indeed, are seldom used. The poorer classes among the fishermen, however, according to Schleisner, have to be contented with a mixture of tallow and oil in lieu of butter. Sometimes a little oil is put into the churn to make the butter go further. In the Vestmanna isles the poor fishermen use the fat which is skimmed off the pot on boiling sea-fowl instead of butter. As a rule, Icelanders are very fond of fat; and this predilection of theirs is alluded to in the popular Sagas in the following story :—

A man named Fusi seated himself one Christmas-eve at a cross-road to wait for the elves, who come at this time with their riches. It is only necessary not to speak to them or take anything from them during the whole of the night, otherwise they will vanish, and all their riches are turned into stones. But when the sun rises, one must say, "God be praised, now it is morning in the heavens!" and the elves vanish, leaving their stores behind them. Fusi, then, was sitting by the cross-road, and an elf came to him and asked him if he would not partake of a piece of fat. The temptation was too great to be resisted, and he replied, "Fat have I never refused!" But, alas! elves fat, and all, vanished from sight.

In summer, when they begin to milk the goats, they prepare a dish, which is extremely good, and is called "skyr." It is made by allowing the boiled milk to become cool, and then, by the means of rennet, it is curdled. The whey is then strained off, and the curds are eaten with cream or milk, together with a little sugar. This dish ought to have a rather sour taste about it, and be quite free from lumps, to be considered first-rate; it requires no little skill in its preparation. The curds are kept through the winter in the same way as the thick milk is kept in the north of Sweden.

On the coast the people eat a great quantity of fresh fish; a capital halibut may be bought at about a penny per pound; and in some parts of the interior a large quantity of trout are taken, which, together with salmon, are the only fresh-water fish.

In the autumn the surplus stock of lambs is slaughtered, and their meat is sold to the merchants at the rate of threepence or fourpence per pound. It is then salted, and fit for market.

Thus it will be seen that though there may not be a great variety in articles of food, yet it is possible to live very well up in the interior of the country; and this, indeed, would be much more the case if the food were always prepared with due regard to cleanliness. At Hörgsdalr I had the satisfaction of finding things entirely to my taste, for the landlady, a wealthy pastor's widow, kept her house in good order.

The Icelandic language possesses a word which sounds somewhat strangely on our ears. I mean the word to beg. It is not used in its active, but in a passive sense, and means to take, to receive. On coming to a house one is often asked the question, "Will you beg coffee?" or, "Will you beg some food?" To which one must, of course, answer in the affirmative if one wishes to have anything. At first, I must confess, it seemed rather strange to go about begging a meal.

My next night-quarters were at a farm-house named Mariubakki, on the road to which I passed by the end of the easternmost lava stream. This farm was owned by an old, staid peasant, named Runólfr, on whose lips it was difficult to provoke a smile. I succeeded, however, in doing so; but "thereby hangs a tale."

Travellers who have visited Iceland have often expressed their astonishment not only at the quantity of snuff the natives take—in which, however, I cannot participate, for my own dear fatherland is extremely snuffy — but at the shape of the snuff-boxes, which resemble a powder flask, and which are usually ornamented with silver, for silversmiths are tolerably abundant in Iceland. When I first read this remark in some traveller's book it did not particularly strike me, as I did not understand how the shape of a snuff-box was the necessary consequence of the national mode of living. But so it really is; for when a person is riding on horseback, and has to hold the bridle in one hand, he would find it extremely difficult, if not downright impossible, to open the lid of his snuff-box with

A Snuff-horn.

the other, in order to take a pinch; but it is by no means so difficult to pull the stopper out of the snuff-horn, put it up the nose, and turn it up and down, first into one nostril and then into the other. Well, when I was at Mariubakki, I began to speak about these snuff-horns; and Runólfr showed me one of them, likewise a brandy-horn, which had both the same shape and appearance. I remember I asked him whether he never by mistake put the snuff-horn to his mouth, and the brandy-horn to his nose; and, if so, what had been the result. At this Runólfr laughed, stroked his chin, and put by snuff and brandy horn.

As I have already hinted, the contents of these horns— namely, snuff and corn brandy, together with coffee—serve to exhilarate the Icelander in his joyous hours, and console him in time of sorrow. Well do we know that this people are not singular in this respect; and, if a "consoler" is necessary, one, perhaps, is as good as the other. Brandy, tobacco, and coffee are poisons, which do not, however, kill immediately when judiciously used. But the great thing is, here as well as everywhere else in this "vale of tears," to use moderation; but, unfortunately, as far as the brandy is concerned, the Icelanders have not cultivated this desirable quality. When brandy can be bought at the rate of sixpence per quart, it is not to be expected that people will be contented with a thimbleful. There is, therefore, no limit to drunkenness in Iceland, except the duty which each individual owes himself; and this, alas! is too easily stepped over in northern climes.

A well-disposed Hamburgh merchant, who traded with Iceland, and who, therefore, had ample opportunities of knowing the deleterious effects brandy-drinking produced among the Icelanders, presented a petition a few years ago to the Danish Government, signed by all the merchants of the country, praying that the importation of brandy into the country might be entirely discontinued; but, whether the Government was of opinion that it would be unwise to stop this outlet for Danish brandy; or whether, if it acceded, it would encourage smuggling, for which the extensive seaboard of Iceland affords such numberless opportunities; or whether it was considered to be contrary to the principles of humanity to deprive the Icelander of his "comfort," it is enough to say that the petition was rejected. The worthy merchant whose name appeared at the head of this petition was the means, however, of sowing good seed, for from that time forth but one opinion has prevailed amongst the educated classes in Iceland (provided they are not addicted to drink themselves, which, unfortunately, is not unfrequently the case), that the importation of brandy ought to be restricted. But, as yet, the opinion is expressed merely as a pious wish; for the Althing, the representative assembly of Iceland, on whom it is incumbent to take the first steps in the brandy question, will have nothing to do with it from the reason that it is merely a deliberative council, which certainly has the power to propose to the Government the expediency of levying a tax on brandy, but has no voice in the way in which such tax should be employed. Hence arises a little hitch; for they are afraid that if the tax were to be levied it would flow into the Danish exchequer, whither all the other revenues of Iceland find their way; and thus Denmark would very possibly be induced to circumscribe her annual contribution of 30,000—40,000 rix dollars, which she gives to Iceland, or else would employ the tax for other purposes. It is difficult to say whether these apprehensions are well grounded or not; but it is quite certain that so long as the question of finance continues to be in an unsettled state, there will be no new taxes levied in Iceland; so that boon companions may for the present drink in peace.

The author, who is no disciple of the brandy-loving Bacchus, or of the tobacco plant, in its powdered or pressed state, has often created no little astonishment in Iceland with respect to these articles of consumption. "He does not use tobacco, and he drinks no brandy;" or, by way of variety, he has often heard people say of him, "He does not drink brandy, and takes nothing between his fingers;" expressions which, among other things, have afforded him a proof of the striking resemblance that exists between Swedes and Icelanders in their train of thought, for the very same expressions are standing subjects of conversation in Sweden. I am of opinion, moreover, that the traveller in Iceland who has no predilection for the alcoholic nectar, has good cause to thank his good fortune, else the temptations that will constantly assail him in that country would be too enticing. One can hardly pull up at a house, and still less meet a comrade on the road, without being addressed with the words—"Just a little dram!" And even if the invitation be not clothed in words, a knowing wink, and a movement of the hand towards the brandy-flask in the breast-pocket is equally significant. But especially when a farmer has returned from market he is almost, as it were, obliged to offer everybody he meets a little of the brandy store he has purchased, unless he wishes to be set down as a niggardly fellow. The probable cause of this profuseness is that in this thinly-peopled land, everybody knows everybody else in his own district, and therefore feels it obligatory on himself to ask him to drink.

Brandy imports, however, are steadily on the increase in Iceland. From 1849 to 1862, they have increased 79 per cent. From the following advertisement, which appeared in the *Pjoðolfr* of September 16th, 1865, it seems almost as if some of the habitual drinkers were beginning to see their degradation. The advertisement in question was subscribed by a farmer in the south, and ran as follows:—

"As each and all of my friends know that I have, hitherto, been addicted to strong drink; I now give notice, once for all, that from this day forth I will abstain from the use of intoxicating liquors of any kind whatsoever."

Some malicious persons, however, insisted that the man was paying his addresses to a rich widow; and that as he had been known to be a tippler, he wished it to be generally known that he had entered upon a new course of life.

Brandy imports in Iceland in the year 1862 amounted to 6·7 pots* for each person. By comparing this with the state of things in Sweden, where 38,000,000 pots are annually produced, of which, perhaps, 6,000,000 are used in manufactures and the arts, the advantage appears to be on the side of Iceland, especially as a large quantity of other intoxicating liquors are consumed in Sweden besides. The difference consists in this, that every individual in Iceland drinks more brandy at one time—

* The Danish pot is, I believe, rather more than an English quart.

namely, during the time when the people frequent the trading establishments of the country; while with us, the consumption is more evenly spread over the whole year. It is a matter of complaint that those Sysselmænd who are native Icelanders, and whose number is predominant, are for the most part addicted to the vice of drunkenness, as well as a great many of the clergy, an evil which is greatly owing to the absence of any efficient system of supervision in the country; otherwise such pernicious customs could not have gained such a firm foothold.

In 1862, the imports of coffee amounted to 6·5* pounds for each person; of tobacco, principally in the form of snuff, 2 pounds; while the corn imports amounted to 0·6 barrels† for each person. These statistics show that an increase has taken place in the consumption since 1849 and 1855. The consumption of tobacco and coffee, however, has somewhat decreased since 1855, possibly owing to the pressure occasioned by hard times during the last few years.

Runólfr, of Mariubakki, was the " Reppstyrer," or chief person in his municipality, or "Repp."‡ The "Repp" is not synonymous with parish or cure, but depends upon a different system of classification. The office of a " Reppstyrer " is a post of confidence, which no one under a certain age can refuse to fill. He is appointed by the Amtmand, on the nomination of the Sysselmand and Pastor, after previous election at a meeting in the municipality. The appointment holds good for three years, but can be renewed after the lapse of that term, though only with the consent of the party concerned. There is no remuneration attached to this office, except the dignity it confers and a few occasional fees. The " Reppstyrer " has the sole

---

* The Danish pound is 10 per cent. heavier than the English.

† One barrel—four Winchester bushels.

‡ We have Rape of Bamber in Sussex, and I believe in other places. The word is, I believe, synonymous with a "hundred."—Tr.

juridical control over his municipality; but at the same time he must consult with the other municipal authorities at the "Reppsthing," or assembly, which is convoked every spring and autumn. His principal duty is the supervision of the poor, and the levying of poor-rates (the poor are boarded by one of the members of the municipality, for there is no such institution as a poor-house in Iceland*). He also has to assist the Sysselmand in his official duties,—such as the drawing up of summonses, the conveying of criminals, &c., for there are no prisons in Iceland; and therefore when a thief, for instance, is brought before the Sysselmand to receive sentence, he appears before him as any other individual, although he is accompanied by the "Reppstyrer." Rather curious rencontres occasionally result from this usage. One fine morning, when a Sysselmand of my acquaintance had just stepped out of his house, he saw a person standing in the yard who was an entire stranger to him. Accordingly, he went up to him and saluted him (no doubt kissed him) and asked "what the news was;" for this is generally the first question put to a stranger. But shortly afterwards he met his "Reppstyrer," who informed him that the person in question was a thief, on whose tracks he had been for a long time, and whom he had at last discovered. The following day the Sysselmand had the thief brought up before him. After the examination was over, he turned to him, and said,—"Yes, you may go now; but you must not go far away." That was the whole of his imprisonment. Subsequently I learnt that the thief in question had not felt inclined to obey his

* "To prevent the parishes from being overburdened, the greatest care is taken that none be allowed to settle in any other than that in which he was born, except he can give security that neither he nor any of his family shall ever be burdensome to the public. When any family happens to be so reduced that it can no longer maintain itself, it is separated, and the members placed out in different households; and if the husband or wife belong to different parts of the island, he is passed on to his native parish, perhaps never more to behold the wife of his youth."—HENDERSON.

orders, but had "gone far away," in other words, "skedaddled."

The same Sysselmand also had an adventure with two other thieves, who had been sentenced to be flogged, and who had accordingly been conveyed by the "Reppstyrer," to the "Thing,"* to receive their punishment. When the judge had arrived who was to superintend the execution of the sentence, it was found that the "Reppstyrer," whose office it was to administer the punishment, was unable to attend on account of illness, and that the person who had conveyed the prisoners to the spot was lame, and therefore incompetent to discharge his duty. Upon this the Sysselmand tried to persuade a farming man to flog the fellows, promising to pay him for doing so. But as he refused, and no one could be found willing to take upon himself the task of flogging them, and as it further appeared cruel to keep them waiting in suspense any longer, the Sysselmand took hold of the "cat," and administered a sound drubbing on the backs of the delinquents with his own hands.

As the "Reppstyrer" possesses independent power within the limits of his own municipality, and as no questions—such as about schools or public buildings, &c.—arise, it follows that the duties of a public official are not of a complicated nature. The "Reppstyrer" governs his "Repp;" the "Sysselmand" his "Syssel;" and the "Amtmand" his province, or "Amt." Still, this somewhat absolute executive power, at least as far as the "Reppstyrer" is concerned, appears to be quite to the taste of Icelanders; for they know that the chief of their municipality is always ready to counsel with them, and that he can by his authority coerce the stubborn; and they are not disposed to favour minorities, or acknowledge their rights. In a word,

* Thing—sessions.

they are somewhat despotic in their views. I was informed that when some question or other came before the "Althing" in the previous summer, some of the members refused to vote; whereupon the President was requested to compel them to do so. It was deemed to be a dangerous precedent if every one were not compelled to give his adherence to a party in the questions that might be brought before them.

After first traversing a "hraun," and afterwards passing close under the nearly perpendicular wall of Lómagnúpr, a fjeld

Núpstaðr.

about 2,400 feet high, my route lay over Skeiðarársanðr, a sandy plain some six miles in width, which, as I have already stated, has to thank a "Jokellöb" from a Jökul of the same name for its large extent. At the edge of the above "hraun," below Lómaguúpr, lies the farmhouse Núpstaðr. As the reader will perceive from its appearance, it is built in a similar way to the usual "bær." The fjeld above it, which is separated by a valley from Lómagnúpr, cannot be seen in the picture, but its gigantic, craggy peaks shoot far up into the sky. Its base is washed by the sea. In front of the window of the dwelling-room the farmer may be seen speaking to his wife, while their little girl is standing by them.

Below Lómagnúpr the ground is covered far and wide with the *débris* of a mountain slip, which has evidently fallen from the beetling heights above. This slip has formed a number of small hills on the plain below the mountain, and has covered an extent of 1,000 feet diameter in all directions.

Skeiðarár-Jökul is one of the largest glaciers in Iceland, and the Jökul rivers which flow from it—the Núpsvötn and Skeiðará—are two of the most dangerous and rapid water-courses in Iceland. When I was in the Núpsvötn, I scarcely knew whether my horse was advancing or receding; for the foaming rapid carried away every sound which my horse's hoofs made, and the swiftly-running water rendered it difficult to decide the position I was in at any given moment. It requires a practised eye to find a way across water-courses like these, where no regular fording-place exists. The secret is, always to ride above the "Foss," or rather at its extreme edge, where the water is shallowest; for below it the water hollows out a deep channel in the river-bed, where the horse can find no footing. A point, moreover, should be selected where the river is divided into several branches, for of course the water is lower in these than when they are united in one main stream. Very often the water in the main stream is two or three feet higher than it is in one of these branches, at least when there is a large body of it in the river. When the river is shallow and the water is clear, it is naturally easy to decide where the "Foss" begins, and to steer one's course accordingly; but should it be rapid and deep, and consist of muddy water from the glacier, it is not so easy to determine.

After one has ridden over one of the two or three arms into which rivers which flow over level plains are usually divided, and the right fording-place in this has been ascertained, it by no means follows as a matter of course that the fording-places over the other arms lie in the same direction. On the contrary, it is almost always necessary to ride some distance into the water either up or down the flooded river-bank to find the next fording-place.

Most glaciers have a river issuing from their centre, besides a smaller one on either side. The first is probably in consequence of the defile along which they glide being deepest in the middle; the others are the result of the running water produced by the melting of the glaciers against either wall of the defile. But these conditions are not apparent in Skeiðarár-Jökul, which shoots down on an almost level plain. It has two Jökul rivers, one on each side—the above-named Núpsvötn and Skeiðará; but there is no main river issuing from its protruding extremity. But almost immediately under it are found a number of small streams, which have to be crossed one after the other in one's passage over the plain. The constant splashing from these and the two large rivers makes it a wet day's journey. The brooks* carry along with them and deposit a mixture of fine sand and clay, and produce a singular formation at the foot of the Jökul; for this clay is deposited between and covers the pebbles, which are carried down by the Jökul rivers; so that the same natural causes produce two totally different formations in the same place, viz., a stratum of pebbles, and a stratum of clay. And a person who was not aware of the circumstances of the case would naturally be very

---

* It is worthy of remark that salmon do not seem to object to this turbid water. They will run up the Jökul rivers, and thence into the clear side streams.

much astounded at this remarkable phenomenon; for it often happens that these Jökul rivers change their course; so that where at one time a rapid stream has flowed, at another it may be found to be only trickling gently along, or even be entirely dried up.

Skeiðarár-Jökul was as black on its surface as Sólheima-Jökul. The cause of this can be ascertained from our acquaintance with white glaciers. These carry along on their ridge dark masses of *débris* or moraine, at the end of which a Jökul river may always be found; but, from the first named, small streams issue everywhere from under the edge of the Jökul, and this is naturally the negative cause of the dark colour of the Jökul. In other words, the moraines lie evenly spread over the surface of the Jökul, caused by the fact of these Jökuls shooting down on to flat plains, along which the ice cannot have so definite a course as when they project into a valley. It is well known that the masses of ice in a glacier are incessantly advancing, partly owing to the weight of the ice, when it rests on a slanting substratum—these glaciers are sometimes 2,000 to 3,000 feet high, or even more;—partly from the elasticity of the ice itself; partly from the melting that takes place in its mass, and from other causes. In Iceland this progressive motion is a well-known fact, though it has only been observed at the edges of the Jökuls; and, consequently, the erroneous idea has been formed that the mass of ice in the Jökul is steadily on the increase, so that a glacial period may be anticipated. True enough, the mass of ice is in a state of augmentation when the edge of the Jökul extends beyond its former boundary; but the cause of this is that this edge, which is naturally always in a melting state, as it gradually slips down between walls of rock covered with herbage, and which is thus exposed to the influence of the warmer temperature that prevails there, thaws less in some years than in others, either because a larger quantity of snow has fallen on the mountains during the winter, or because the summer has been colder. The advance, therefore, and retrogression of the edge of the Jökuls are thus periodical, and do not necessarily infer the existence of a severer climate; though, on the other hand, it is quite possible that the climate of Iceland may have become colder subsequently to the colonisation of the country, when the forests were well-nigh exterminated—a proceeding which would naturally have the effect of rendering the climate colder.

We will now offer a few remarks with reference to the former extent of forests in Iceland. It is stated in the "Landnáma" book that "there was forest over the whole country, from the sea to the mountains," when the land was first colonised. Now, in my opinion, rather an exaggerated notion of the extent of the forests in Iceland has been inferred from this rather high-sounding statement. By the way, the same work alludes to cattle which had strayed into the forests, where they had become quite wild. There can be no doubt that the mountain tracts were as extensive at the period when the country was colonised as they are now. Many of these mountains reach up above the limit of snow, which is situated at 2,700 to 3,000 feet above the surface of the sea; and, besides this, the greater portion of the island consists of table-land, the elevation of which ranges from 1,500 to 2,000 feet; and, when the relations that exist in other parts of the north are taken into account, it is evident that no forest can possibly grow upon it; for as the forest limit, for example, in the interior of Scandinavia is estimated to lie about 2,500 feet under the limit of snow, it cannot in a country like Iceland, where the summers are much colder, be placed any higher. Consequently it will be seen that forests cannot exist on this table-land. There are, therefore, only the lower slopes and the bottoms of the valleys left, where these are not occupied by soft swamps and bogs; but these only cover a limited portion of the surface of the country. That forests have grown there, and further, that they were considerably larger than is now the case when they were primitive forests, we are quite willing to allow. And, when we read the passage quoted above, we cannot deduce any other meaning from it. It should be borne in mind that the colonists, who were Northmen, and were therefore well acquainted with mountains and forests, were naturally of opinion that the mountains took their beginning where the forests ended; and the expression, therefore, can only be taken in its literal sense, that the lowlands—that is, the land between the sea and the mountains—were overgrown with forests at that time. The trunks of trees which have been found in the bogs prove that they were forests of birch which grew there. Hence we are entitled to draw the conclusion that the coast of Iceland is the limit for pine and fir in this part of the world; or, in other words, that the region of birch in Iceland reaches down to the surface of the sea. It is a known fact that in forest lands the spruce fir is the first tree to disappear, and that the Scotch fir extends some few hundred feet higher up; and that, finally, the birch, which is the most hardy, reaches some hundred feet higher still. That Iceland, in consequence of its climate, lies above the region of fir, is moreover evident from the fact that neither fir nor pine grow there, but only the common birch and dwarf birch (*Betula alba* and *nana*), and also from its flora, which is almost exclusively alpine; and, finally, from the low altitude of the limit of snow above the sea. By comparing the statements in the Sagas with the actual state of the case at the present day, it is found that on several places where forests formerly grew there are now bogs. Thus, in this northerly climate the forests, after having once been destroyed through excessive abuse, have never been able to recover their former state. But once more we must bear in mind that, with reference to climate, the country lies above the region of fir, and that the experience which Iceland furnishes in this respect cannot be applied to places which are not situate within the limits of this region.

The edge of Skeiðarúr-Jökul was as ragged and as full of fissures as Sólheima-Jökul; and was, therefore, with the exception of a small portion, impossible of ascent. The *débris* that covered the low ground underneath, where it was not intersected with rills and covered with clay and fine sand, consisted almost entirely of pebbles of a round form, like those found on the sea-shore; but sometimes bearing traces of fine scratches in all directions, which showed that the glacier had moved over them after they had first assumed their round form in the Jökul river. No remains of moraine were found on the plain below the Jökul; but there were two banks of pebbles lying evenly with the edge of the Jökul, which occupied the position assumed by the moraines that had been left behind on the retrogression of the glacier; but in these the *débris* consisted of pebbles. There is no grass growing on Skeiðarársandr except on a little spot in its middle, below one of these little pebble-banks, where it is fertilized by the water which the pebble-banks have dammed up. The ride over this sandy waste, or rather over this waste of earth and stones (for occasionally these last are as large as a man's head or hand), is very tiring for the horse; and the rider feels more comfortable when, after having waded through the water, and having ridden over the barren tract, he reaches a more lively scene. The last "Jökel-lob" over Skeiðarársandr took place three years ago, that is to say, in 1862; and as the floods from this Jökul do not usually occur oftener than every seventh year—the last had been expected for ten years—I could now traverse it without apprehension. The evening of the day I crossed Skeiðarársandr, I reached the farm Svínafell, a place which is well known from the old Sagas, and took up my quarters for the night there, where I found good accommodation.

Svínafells-Jökul is one of the most important of the minor glaciers that descend into the valleys from the snow-clad summit of Öræfa-Jökul. It is very conveniently situated for observing the phenomena attached to glaciers, as it comes down into the plain close to a farmhouse of the same name; it is scarcely a five-minutes' walk from thence to the ice-wall of the glacier. On surmounting the edge of the valley-slope which bounds the field of ice on the south-east, and which is overgrown with a luxuriant green sward—luxuriant at least for Iceland— and beautifully decked with white *Dryas*, one can see over the ridge of the enormous mass of Jökul ice, which is perhaps, two hundred feet high. It is of a white and bluish-green hue. The moraines are not so evenly distributed over it as over Sólheima and Skeidarár Jökuls, but appear here and there in thin stripes in the fissures that succeed each other in regular order on the sloping side of the glacier. A little side moraine is formed here, and occupies the valley-formed or channel-shaped bottom that is made by the sloping side of the valley and the wall of the glacier. This moraine is of a sharp and coarse nature, proving, therefore, that it is composed of sand and stone that have fallen down on the surface of the Jökul from the heights above. It is carried down towards the end by the constantly-advancing glacier, and is at last precipitated into the raging stream coming from under the ice at the end of the above-named channel-shaped chasm, to be mingled with the *débris* which is being carried along under the glacier, and which is polished and rounded in form from the action of the advancing superincumbent mass, to be itself twisted round in the violent whirlpools, and then is carried down into the plain.

One can hardly form a right estimate of the enormous power of one of these Jökul rivers, which seem to be no larger than that one could leap over them in two springs. But after standing for a few moments on the edge, a man would pause before making the attempt; for down in its depths can be heard terrific crashings and rumblings, caused by the huge masses of rock which are being dashed along by the impetuous current, and hurled against each other. It certainly evokes a feeling of respect!

The side of the glacier with an acute angle makes the slope of the valley; and the fissures, which are partly formed by the small streams on its surface, caused by the moraines, and which appear when the ice melts, partly by deep marginal chasms which descend as far as one can see, make this side a sharp and steep ridge, which it is rather dangerous to clamber up in order to get upon the glacier.

As all the men in Svínafell had gone to Papós, a commercial village, and I could get no guide, I was unable to undertake any long excursion on the glacier. In such excursions it is impossible to go alone. There should at least be two or three in company, who should keep at some distance from each other, and should have a rope secured round their waists, so that, if one of the party should chance to fall into a fissure, he can be hoisted up by the others. It is not, however, necessary to climb high up on Svínafells-Jökul in order to enjoy the sight of the beautiful green colour of the ice in the fissures of the glacier, or to look down into their profound depths.

Some of the sheep that roam about the mountains during the summer occasionally fall down into these fissures, and, by their subsequent history, give rise to various superstitious beliefs, and sundry strange theories. For instance, although a sheep may have fallen down into a fissure of 50, 60, or even 100 feet in depth, whence it was impossible to extricate it, after the lapse of a year or two it may be found lying on the surface of the glacier quite unscathed, with its wool on, and without a single broken bone, while its flesh is so fresh that it can be readily eaten, though it is said to have rather a salt taste. Sometimes, after the ravens have paid it a visit, nothing but the skeleton will be found; but then it is always entire, not a bone will have been crushed or broken, provided it was not broken in the fall. In Iceland the belief is entertained that the appearance of the sheep on the surface of the glacier is caused by some violent convulsion, whereby the bottom of the glacier comes to the top, and that this is occasioned by a Jökellöb. But that this is an impossibility is quite plain; and the belief, therefore, rests upon an erroneous supposition. But as the carcass comes up to the surface of the glacier so quietly and peacefully, that it looks as it lies there as if it had only been recently slaughtered, this strange phenomenon can, in my opinion, only take place in the following way:—that the ice of the glacier melts on the surface, till the melting reaches the place where the fallen object lies. The people, moreover, express their surprise that though the object in question has fallen down into a fissure, it is yet found lying on the solid ice. But this admits of the following explanation:—the sheep has sunk down to the bottom of the fissure, but under the process of the melting of the ice it has naturally advanced more and more forwards, till at length the solid ice, on which the carcass has been lying, has reached to the surface of the glacier.

It has long been a matter of observation that objects which have fallen down into the fissure of a glacier have been found on its surface after the lapse of a certain time. Agassiz, who has devoted so much time to the study of glaciers, has explained this phenomenon as being produced by the pressure which he assumes the superincumbent mass of ice to produce. According to his theory the object "freezes upwards," so to speak. It is known that a stone can freeze up from a soft soil. This takes place from the water in a thaw penetrating between the lower surface of the stone and the ground; and when this water freezes it expands, and thus exercises a pressure on the frozen ground underneath, and on the lower surface of the stone. Of course the substance which offers the least resistance must give way; and this, naturally, is the stone, for the frozen ground is as firm as a rock. But that this should be the cause why an object that has fallen into the fissure of a glacier should reappear on the surface seems incredible on theoretical grounds, while, practically, it is impossible. If, for instance, the action of pressure in the mass of ice were to lift the sheep up, it is quite inconceivable that the animal would be unscathed or uninjured in any way; but, as this is never the case, no other explanation can be offered for its re-appearance than the melting of the glacier on the surface. Many people may, perhaps, look on the whole affair as an exaggeration, and may think it an impossibility that the dead sheep could make the excursion; and the author begs to state that he by no means guarantees the authenticity of the phenomenon, as he has only had the statements of other people to rely on. But he thinks it probable that the warm winds blowing from the Gulf Stream, and which sweep over the glaciers that are but a little distance from the sea, in connection with the heat of the sun, may exert a powerful influence on the surface of the ice, at least in the lower parts. He did not, therefore, wish to pass by in silence the tales he heard in Öræfa about the glaciers, as the subject is of itself worthy of the best attention. The scientific world, and all persons who interest themselves in such matters, have recently received great encouragement to give their close attention to the phenomena attendant upon glaciers, in the interesting remarks made by Professor Sexe, of Norway, in 1864, about the glacier of the Folge-Fond. The Professor informs us that in August, 1860, he buried three thermometers in the above-named glacier, or Jökul, purposing to ascertain what had been the lowest temperature after the lapse of a year. The lowest thermometer was buried 12 feet deep, the next 8 feet, and the last only 4 feet deep. After the lapse of a year, the thermometer which had been buried at a depth of 4 feet was found lying on the surface of the Jökul, the second one in the surface, and the lowest one only 2 feet underneath. Whence Sexe naturally concludes that the ice which lay above had thawed in the interior, and that this thawing process had not only shown its influence on the surface of the ice, but had extended underneath it, as the distance between the two lowest thermometers had been diminished from 4 feet to 2 feet.

With reference to the sheep reappearing in a salted form, it must certainly be allowed that this sounds a little improbable at first sight. But when it is remembered how the water in the Jökul brook from Sólheima-Jökul smelt, and that it possessed in a measure the same qualities as the refuse water from a chemical laboratory, perhaps the above statement may not be quite so unreasonable. At all events, it shows that a glacier does not make a very good ice-cellar if it salts fresh meat. It has not occurred to any one to make any practical use of this property it possesses of salting. It must further be remembered with reference to the transformations that take place in Jökuls, that the glacier-ice during its advance actually displays a close resemblance to the motion of water in a river, and that the ice can thus sometimes shoot up from the bottom to the surface, though at the same time this occurs very slowly, and cannot be assumed to take place without a certain amount of pressure being exerted by the rest of the ice on the parts which are pushed up. The above account of the vagaries of glaciers was given me by a peasant in Fáerholtsmýri, south of Breiðamerkr-Jökul. To the above-named farmhouse it was but a short day's journey from Svínafell, past Sandfell parsonage, where, with the reader's permission, I will make a pause in my narrative, though in reality I passed by it rather quickly.

Here lived, in 1727, Pastor Jón Thorláksson, who was a witness of the volcanic eruption and accompanying "Jökellöb" which took place that year in Öræfa-Jökul from Mount Flaga, which lies between Sandfell and a farm, Hof, to the south-east. The following narrative, which was given fifty years after the occurrence, appears in the Pastor's name:—

"On the 7th August, 1727, which was the tenth Sunday after Trinity, when divine service had begun in the church at Sandfell, I was standing by the altar, and perceived a tremulous movement under my feet, to which at first I did not pay much attention; but in the middle of my sermon it increased so much that everybody became alarmed. Still it was said that it was of no uncommon occurrence. A decrepit old man went to a spring below the house, where he knelt down, which caused much laughter. But when he returned I asked him 'what he had been doing?' and he replied, 'Take care, Herr Pastor, the earth is on fire!' At the same moment I looked towards the church-door, when it seemed to me, as it also did to the other bystanders, that the whole building looked as if it were bent together. Thereon I rode away from the church, and could not but help thinking on the old man's words. When I had reached the middle of the base of Flaga, and looked up to its summit, it seemed to me as if it rose and fell in turns. Neither was I wrong in my supposition, as the results showed.

"On the following morning, which was Monday, the 8th, alarming shocks of earthquake were constantly heard, and terrible reports, scarcely inferior to thunder-claps. Everything in the houses was thrown about in all directions, and we fully expected that mountains and houses would collapse; but the alarm of the people became more intense, as it was impossible to hazard a conjecture from what quarter the disaster would appear, or what direction it would take. The same morning, three terrific reports were heard, and shortly after several eruptions of water followed, of which the last was the largest, for it carried away any horses or cattle that came in its way. After these had passed, the ice-mountain itself slid down on to the open plain, like molten metal from a crucible; and when it had thus slid down on to the plain, its height was so great, that I could only just see a portion of the far-famed Lómagnúpr, about as large as the size of a bird. Thereupon the water broke loose on the east side, and destroyed and laid waste the little pasture that remained.

"I was most concerned to see the women crying, and my neighbours frightened out of their wits, and destitute of spirit. But as I perceived that the flood was taking the direction of my house, I removed my people and children on to a high ledge on a mountain named Dalskarðstorfa, where I had a tent erected, and had all the church furniture, together with clothes and provisions and other necessaries, conveyed; for I thought we should be safer there.

"Affairs now assumed a different aspect, for the Jökul itself burst, and a large quantity of fragments of ice were discharged into the sea; the largest pieces, however, congregated a short distance from the foot of the mountain. Fire and ashes flew about in the air, with continuous detonations and reports, so that one could hardly distinguish between day and night, owing to the darkness that ensued, and which was only illumined by the gleaming of the fire that issued from five or six fissures in the mountain. Thus for three successive days the parish of Öræfa was visited with fire, water, and clouds of ashes.

"But the scene almost surpasses description; for the whole surface of the earth appeared black with pumice-sand, and it was impossible to move a step from fear of the hot, burning stones which fell from the sky; so that many people, by way of protection, went about with pails and other vessels on their heads.

"On the 11th it cleared up a little, but the ice-mountain still continued to discharge fire and smoke. On this day I went with three others to see how it fared with the church at Sandfell, for there the danger was most imminent. The journey thither was a very dangerous one, as it was impossible to advance except between the mountain and the Jökul river, and the water was so hot that the horses were nearly wild. Just then I happened to look behind, and noticed a fresh deluge of hot water coming towards us, and which would certainly have carried us away had it reached us. It, therefore, occurred to me to get on to the ice, and I called to the others to follow me as quickly as possible. Thus we escaped, and finally reached Sandfell, where the whole farm, together with two of the buildings belonging to it, had been destroyed. The dwelling-house was saved, and one or two small patches of land had escaped. The people were standing in the church weeping; but the cows there, as well as at other places, had escaped, contrary to everybody's expectation, and were standing, lowing, by some haystacks that had been damaged during the eruption. Half of the male occupants of the Parsonage during the breaking out of the "Jökellöb" took refuge in four recently-erected Sæters (*châlets*); while two women and a boy got on to the roof of the house. But soon after, the flood carried the whole of this house away; and as far as one could see, those three wretched persons were standing on its roof. One of the women was subsequently discovered in the mud of the Jökul, but so scorched, or rather boiled, that the flesh could scarcely bear to be touched. Everything was in the most piteous condition; the sheep were all lost, and some of them were washed up by the sea a long distance off from the scene of the disaster; moreover there was no hay for the cows, so that not more than one-fifth of them could be fed. Fire issued from the mountain night and day from August 8th till the beginning of summer in the month of April. The stones gave out smoke till late on in the summer; at the beginning of the summer, indeed, one could not even touch them. Some of them were calcined; some were black, and full of holes; and others one could blow through. The greater number of the horses which were not driven out to sea, were found perfectly crushed. The eastern parts of the parish of Siða were completely laid bare with pumicestone sand, so that owing to this cause a great many cattle had to be slain. On the first day of summer* in the following year (1728), I got a trustworthy man to explore the mountain fissures with me, most of which were so large that we could creep into them. I found a quantity of saltpetre there, which, had I wished to collect, would have been impossible, owing to the great heat. At one place a heavy calcined rock lay just above a large

---

* According to the old Icelandic system, which was made about the year 900 by a man named Þorsteinn Surtur, the year was divided into twelve months and four days, which was afterwards increased so as to agree with the new style. The year, moreover, was divided into two parts; namely, into "summer weeks" and "winter weeks," a mode of reckoning still used in the country. According to this method summer began between the 13th and 19th of April, between which days therefore the first day of summer occurs.

fissure, into which we managed to topple it over, but could not hear it strike the bottom. These are the principal events I have to relate concerning this mountain. . . . . Thus God has carried me through fire and water and many a misfortune into my eightieth year. To Him be praise and honour to all eternity!"

After a perusal of this account, one will not be surprised to find that the terrain to the south of Svínafell down to the sea consists chiefly of a homogeneous, stony plain, similar to Skeiðarársandr. Two rapid Jökul rivers, which dashed forth from the blue glaciers which hung down from the mountain, and which were of a dirty-grey colour, formed but a slight contrast against the dark-coloured plain, and thus occasioned me to make several *détours*, especially as my guide, a little lad of twelve or thirteen years, was no better acquainted with the fording-places than I was myself. On this account I was obliged to ride up to Sandfell, and apply to the clergyman there, to whom I had a letter of introduction from the Sysselmand in Skúptarfell-syssel, requesting him to assist me by procuring a guide for the rest of the journey to Fáerholtsmýri, about an hour-and-a-half's ride; and further over Breiðamerkrsandr, which I was to cross the following day. The Pastor, who had already gone to bed, as it was late in the evening when I reached Sandfell, was soon on his feet again, and, saddling his horse, rode with me to Fáerholtsmýri. The good people there had to be knocked up, as it was eleven o'clock when we arrived; and after due introduction, I was shown into a tolerably clean room, which had been recently constructed out of drift-timber. Coffee was soon brought in, and discussed after about an hour's interval, during which time my eyes had been directed partly towards the bed, for I was very sleepy, partly towards the door, through which I was in hopes of seeing the farmer's wife enter with food of a more solid nature. Meantime the Pastor amused me very much, for he read out my "meðmæli," *i.e.*, my letter of introduction from Reykjavik, in a loud voice to the two peasants, one of whom rejoiced in the classical name of Skarphèdinn; while he especially dwelt on those parts of the letter wherein the duties of Icelanders towards my honourable person were set forth. Neither did the peasants themselves afford me less amusement, as they sat and listened with folded hands to this important despatch. "Sjálfsagt"—"they would assist me to the best of their power." It was plain to see that I had before me, if I may so express myself, primitive natives, of genuine honour and extreme simplicity; qualities which it is generally touching to witness, even though in particular points they may strike the children of the great world as a trifle comical or strange. At length, at midnight, there arrived two plates of the "standing" dish, rice milk,— one for the Pastor, and one for me. They seemed to find favour with both of us; and after the pastor had taken his leave, without receiving aught but sincere thanks for the inconvenience to which I had put him, I undressed myself, as it is occasionally the custom, in the presence of the family, and then turned into bed, where I slept soundly till the coffee was brought in the following morning.

I had now a day's journey of from thirty-three to thirty-eight miles before me, more than half of which lay over the stony waste Breiðamerkrsandr, in whose midst runs a Jökul stream, which, though only a quarter of a mile in length from its source in the Jökul to the sea, is still considered to be one of the very worst watercourses in Iceland over which one can take a horse. In summer-time, when the snow and ice on the mountains are melting, it rises to a considerable height, and has a very rapid current; it is then, at times, impossible to cross over, in which case one must either attempt to cross the Jökul itself, which can sometimes be accomplished, or else turn back, for, as there is no herbage to be found in the neighbourhood, it does not do to wait for the falling of the water, which generally does not take place before a change in the weather occurs. Generally, however, one rides through it, and it often happens that the rapid stream washes over the horse's shoulder, and thus, without taking into account the icy cold nature of the glacier water, it gives one a bath far from being peculiarly grateful. When I crossed it, it was comparatively shallow, as is generally the case in the spring and early summer.

It might be supposed that a ride across a stony waste of over twenty miles, where no beaten track exists, and where it is impossible to travel quickly, must needs be monotonous and wearisome; but to a person with any perception for the peculiarities and the magnificence of nature, a ride across Breiðamerkrsandr, provided the weather be favourable, is really of a very agreeable character. In the first place one rides by the end of a small, snowy-white and ice-green glacier, which descends on to the plain between two lofty fjelds, one of which, Staðarfell, is 3,782 feet above the surface of the sea, and which is environed by two symmetrical moraines, which form themselves into a rampart before its bow-shaped, protruding end. Next comes Breiðamerkr-Jökul, which is more than fourteen miles in width at its end; the first half of which was full of fissures and crevices, as far as a fjeld summit named Breiðamerkrmúli, which towers aloft near the edge of the Jökul; but the other half, which was even and smooth, had on its surface three very regularly-shaped "middle" moraines, which lay, like black ribbons, along the white icy mass. This proves that the Jökul has been formed by the union of four glaciers in the fjeld above; for a "middle" moraine is caused from two glaciers uniting so as to form but one, while the banks of earth and stones, which they each have along their sides, are brought together to the centre of the united mass. It was a glorious sight to look back from the plain towards Öræfa-Jökul, from whence the ice and snow seemed as if they were dashing down like a cascade into the field of ice at its foot, whilst its mighty peaks, more than 6,000 feet in height, were lost to sight in the clouds. On the right the waves of the sea could be plainly heard dashing against the coast.

The *débris* on this plain was of the same nature as on Skeiðarársandr, round and smooth; but sometimes bearing traces of fine scratches in all directions, as memorials of the action of the glacier. High up on the ice, on the end of the Jökul, lay a quantity of similarly looking *débris*, which, from its appearance, had probably come up from the bottom of the Jökul. A similar pebbly bank to that found at Skeiðarár-Jökul lay by the northern side of the Jökul near its end. This bank, or ridge, was formed four years ago, when the glacier, after having descended a certain distance, and having buried itself in the sand, had heaped up the pebbles at its base into a ridge of 30 or 40 feet in height, and had subsequently receded. On the same occasion, most probably, the pebbles at the foot of the Jökul had become scratched by friction against one another under the advancing ice. On the same side of the Jökul, somewhat further to the north, there appeared under it a substance resembling dark cakes, which, on closer inspection, was found to be turf. Thus in former days the Jökul covered a moss the contents of which are now brought to the light of day. The *débris* that the great glaciers from Vatna-Jökul have brought with them contains specimens of nearly all the minerals that are found in Iceland—lava, pumicestone, pearlstone, basalt, trachyte, dolerit, tufa, &c.

The origin of the southern part of Breiðamerkrsandr is historical. Accounts from the middle of the thirteenth century state that this district, which had formerly been a fertile and inhabited tract, was about that time completely devastated by eruptions from the Jökul. A solitary farmhouse, named Kvisker, still remains in this waste.

Although, owing to the absence of vegetation, these sandy plains are waste and barren tracts, they are not quite devoid of life, for a great many birds resort thither in spring for breeding purposes. Thus, on its north side, Breiðamerkrsandr affords a home to flocks of terns or "kríur," as they are called in Iceland, owing to their peculiar cry. On approaching their breeding-ground they flew up in a body from their nests (or rather from their eggs, for they deposit them anywhere among the stones, and, as they are of a greyish brown colour, they do not readily strike the eye), and swarmed in the air like clouds of gnats. Presently I saw them swoop down in a compact mass on a certain spot—I can only compare their appearance to a swarm of bees—and when I rode up to see what it was that had attracted them, I found a little tern lying there dead.

Among other birds that lay their eggs on the sand or among the stones is a species of gull, of a brown colour, and rather greyish about the neck; they are very hideous-looking birds as they go hopping about with their wings outstretched, and occasionally are very impudent, especially when the traveller is accompanied by a dog. Every now and then they came flying towards me, so that I involuntarily ducked my head down on to my horse's neck; and so close did they approach that I could have struck several down with my whip. The dog seemed quite nonplussed at their attacks, and stuck close to me, thus making me a butt for their bold onslaughts.

The Icelanders derive a good harvest from collecting the eggs of several kinds of wild fowl; and the birds themselves are also captured in large numbers where the bird-rocks, which I have already alluded to, are found. There is a bird-rock named Ingolfshöfði, which is 260 feet high, to the south of Fúerholtsmyri; it descends almost perpendicularly into the sea. It owes its name to Ingólfr, whom I have before spoken of, who landed here on his second visit to the country. The bird-catcher is lowered down by means of a rope 240 feet long, with a pole of 14 feet in his hand, and collects what he can find. At the parsonage house at Sandfell, in Öræfa, I saw a large quantity of birds of various kinds that had been taken on this rock. On the Færoe islands bird-catching is more generally practised, and is more remunerative than in Iceland; and the islanders there are known for their daring hardihood in catching birds. They allow themselves to be lowered down perpendicular walls of rock to a depth sometimes of seventy fathoms, with nothing but the foaming sea beneath them. In order to guard against the rope twisting, they have constantly to push out with their feet against the face of the rock, or else they would become dizzy. When they want to enter any holes and crevices in the face of the rock, they have to swing themselves more violently; they accordingly take with them a hook, which they manage to strike firmly into the rock during one of these swinging movements, and thus reach the desired crevice. The birds are then caught in nets. A skilful bird-catcher will catch 300 birds a day in this manner. Thus the birds are not terrified, but continue flying backwards and forwards along the face of the rock, and pay very little attention to the individual who is dangling at the end of the rope.

Some of the bird-rocks on the Færoe islands are so steep on all sides that it is impossible to get to the top of them in the usual way, in order to let a rope down, so the bird-catchers adopt the following stratagem. Three men meet at the foot of the rock, bringing with them a pole several feet in length, the end of which is furnished with a spike and a small piece of board. They fasten the spike through the seat of the breeches of one of their number, who is thus seated on the board, and in this position he is hoisted up by the other two to a ledge on the face of the rock; for the rocks of the Færoe islands, like a great proportion of the Icelandic rocks, belong to the so-named basaltic formation, and sometimes slope down in the form of stairs to their base. When he has thus gained a firm foothold he lets down a line, and hoists up his companions, who assist him by pushing with their feet against the face of the rock. After all three have thus reached the ledge the same operation is repeated from ledge to ledge, till at last the top is gained. Here a line is made fast, which remains stationary the whole summer, and by which the bird-catchers ascend and descend; but in the autumn this line has to be taken down. The last person, who must be a clever climber, accordingly fastens the line by a pin into the ground, so that it will just bear his weight, and no more, and then carefully lets himself down; and when he has reached the bottom, by jerking the line, he pulls the pin out of the ground above, and the rope falls down.

As may be supposed, the employment of a bird-catcher is a very hazardous one, and many an accident occurs through imprudence and foolhardiness, for, should he miss his footing, he must be irretrievably lost.

The Færoe islands look like mountains or large rocks rising out of the sea. There is but little low ground on any of the islands, and on some of them none at all. One of the islands named Dimon belongs to this class. It is owned by a farmer who is in a position to feed so many head of cattle, that he enjoys a certain degree of respect among his neighbours; but none of the inhabitants of this island can quit it without help from outside, for the rocks descend perpendicularly down on all sides into the sea. There is therefore no creek for a boat; but when the farmer wants a boat in order to get to Thorshavn, a commercial town of the Færoe isles, he has to telegraph to Sandö island, close by; that is to say, he has to hoist a signal, whereon, weather permitting, a boat sets out. But this is not all. The lowest part of the coast is about 200 feet above the sea; consequently persons and goods have to be hoisted up and down the face of the rock to and from the boat. Of course such a proceeding is attended with no little hazard, and a former proprietor of the island is said to have lost his life on one such occasion. One autumn or winter a few years ago, another calamity occurred on this island. The inhabitants, for instance, were in the habit of keeping in the fire, from one day to the other, heaping turf on to the embers at night time, and covering them with ashes; but one night it happened that the fire went out. There were no lucifers on the island, and the poor people were at a loss how to kindle a fire by any other means, so that they were obliged to go the whole winter without a fire, for at that season of the year no boat could lay to by the island. In order to guard against the cold of winter (which is never very severe in these islands, as they lie in the middle of the Gulf Stream) the poor people had to huddle together as well as they could, and as they were unable to cook any food, they were obliged to live on milk, dried fish, and similar articles of food. No wonder if they found that winter a long one!

My companion over Breiðamerkrsandr, who in the early part of the day had appeared to me to be a brisk fellow, had made too intimate an acquaintance with the brandy flask in the afternoon, and towards night began to be rather merry. An amiable childishness displayed itself in him; but whether it was a consequence of his too intimate acquaintance with the brandy horn, or whether it was natural to him, I cannot say. But when we arrived at Kálfafellsstaðr, a parsonage house, where I begged for a night's lodging (which, owing to the unpleasant circumstances that resulted, I ought not to have done), Þorvarðr, for so the fellow was called, asked me my name; whereupon I gave him my card so that he could the better remember it. At this he evinced such boisterous joy, that he took a mark out of his pocket, in order to pay me for it: "Sjálfsagt"—"I must be paid for the fine card;" and it was all I could do to make him keep his money.

As I have just hinted, I ought not to have gone to bed at Kálfafellsstaðr, for the company there was of rather a mixed nature, and my insect powder which had hitherto been my protection against unbidden guests, had unfortunately become wet on crossing one of the numerous fords, and was therefore useless.

On journeys in general, and in Iceland in particular, there is every reason to prize the blessings which the Persian insect powder confers. Strangely enough, it can only be bought at one place in Iceland, namely, in Akureyri, and therefore unfortunately it is but little known in the country. For many a native, as well as many a foreigner, has, at a pinch, to seek night quarters in places which are not over cleanly. Memorial pillars ought to be erected to the inventor of the insect powder in all lands, if he be a single individual; or should the discovery be due to an entire nation, eternal peace ought to be pronounced over it. A less recompense could hardly be awarded to a people who have secured the blessings of so many peaceful and happy hours to such numbers of their fellow beings.

On my road over Breiðamerkrsandr I met the first trading caravan of the year; it consisted of persons from Öræfa who were returning from Papós. These caravans present a singular spectacle. In front, one or two of the men ride, according as the width of the road permits; and each holds a led horse, which is tied by a rope to its tail to another horse, and so on, till there are eight horses in a row. Each horse has a pack-saddle, and is laden with goods of a varied nature ; here a couple of sacks of corn, there a few bundles of dried fish, there a sack of coffee or sugar, all of which have to be placed high up on the animal on account of the many fords that have to be crossed; while here a coffee pan, or a piece of iron may be seen. Of course the brandy kegs are not forgotten! But the timber loads look the strangest. On each side of the horse three planks or a small bit of timber are fastened, the top end of which projects into the air, while the lower end draggles on the ground, and thus gets rather chafed on the long journey home. Very little timber, however, is carried to Öræfa, for enough drift wood is cast up by the sea to supply the wants of the people. People who have a long distance to go to the towns, only visit them once a year; but those who live nearer make two or three journeys during the spring and summer. In dealing everything is carried on on the bartering principle, and the credit system is very extensively developed. Almost everything is bought on a year's, or six months', or three months' credit. But we shall have occasion by and by to discuss the commercial system of Iceland, which, owing to monopolies through a long course of years, inflicted so much injury upon the country, till the introduction of free trade a few years ago.

It is scarcely necessary to say that the Icelanders must needs be an equestrian people, as it is impossible to travel any distance except on horseback. The Icelander, therefore, is as intimately acquainted with his bit, as the boatman with his oars, or the sportsman with his gun. No little care is devoted to their riding whips; the one here given is made of rattan with silver fittings. The thong is attached to a ring on the stock, and can administer a hearty blow.

A whip.

CHAPTER IV.

Volcanic Systems—Basaltic Formations—Tufa—Geological Age of Iceland—A Dog on Horseback—Remarks on Dogs—Tape-worms—Mountain Passes—Dangerous Mountain Excursions—Roadside Flowers—Sira Bjarni and his Eider Ducks—Fishery and Frenchmen—Icelanders not a race of Sailors—French Companies—Eider Down—A Wooden House—Lonsheiði—Absence of Woodland not depressing—A Natural Crinoline—Wages of Guides—Price of Horses—Hippophagy—Recipe for a good Complexion—A Bishop with Nine Hundred Children—Remarks on Birds—Plants.

IN the composition of that portion of the crust of the earth constituting the main bulk of the country above the level of the sea, three different geological formations may be noticed, which, however, possess this in common, that they have arisen from ebullitions or eruptions of a molten mass in the interior of the earth, and whose mutual boundaries can therefore now be ascertained with perfect accuracy

The youngest of these is the lava formation, under which may be classed all the formations ascribed to recent volcanic action. Amongst these, lava occupies the first rank; it usually appears under the form of lava streams, which generally speaking cover the lower parts of the country, as the liquid masses discharged from the volcanoes naturally seek the valleys. But it appears also under the form of loose pieces of slag, heaped upon each other, of which sundry of the volcanic craters in the country are composed, as, for instance, Rauðhólar, in the neighbourhood of Reykjavik. To this class also belong the loose, heaped-up masses of volcanic sand, which, especially in the neighbourhood of the large volcanoes, form the upper stratum of earth, which is black, and for the most part destitute of vegetation. To this also we must add those real companions of the volcanoes, the warm springs, which are of two kinds, or as they are termed in the language of the country, "hverir" or "laugar," and "námar." The first of these are boiling or hot springs with clear water; the last named are formed from gaseous exhalations from the ground, which deposit sulphur; or from boiling mud springs, the so-called mud volcanoes, or "Makkaluber." The lava formation appears distributed over large portions of the country; but is not found, I believe, on the eastern or northern coast, west of Skúlfandafljót river, neither is it found in the north-west peninsula, or if found, is represented only by "hverir," or hot springs. It is most developed along the volcanic fissures, which have already been referred to, and which extend in a north-easterly and north-westerly direction. One of these, as far as we remember, extends from Eldey and Reykjanes up to Láng-Jökul, and may be denominated the Skjaldbreið system; while the other, which has Hekla for its central point, may be termed the Hekla system. Further along the peninsula which it will be remembered bounds Faxafjörðr on the north, and where the volcanic fissure, judging by the craters and lava streams, runs east and west, is what we will term the Snæfell system; and finally along the fissure, or rather the system of fissures which, with Leirhnúkr as a central point, extends in a direction north and south from the neighbourhood of Mývatn in the north-eastern district of the country down to the large Vatna-Jökul, is the Leirhnúkr system.

In descriptions of Iceland the usual direction which the

volcanic agency assumes is stated to be from the north-east to the south-west, as is the case with Hekla and the south-westerly peninsula. But that this is not in every case the direction assumed appears, among other instances, from the above named Leirhnúkr, where the volcanic craters, and, therefore, also the fissures, lie almost north and south. The older volcanic craters, too, on the eastern side of Mývatn have the same direction. The direction, moreover, in which the large rivers run on the north coast is also north and south; which, together with the mountain ridges running in the same direction, give the general line of elevation in the country. If the volcanic fissure, therefore, of the Hekla system is continued to the north-east, it takes a turn, at least, by Mývatn, towards the north; just as the fissure of the Skjaldbreið system turns a little to the west. However, it is just as probable that the volcanic fissure of the Leirhnúkr system goes more in a southerly direction through Vatna-Jökul; as, for instance, through the Skaptár volcano, which appeared in 1783. The necessary observations, however, to settle this point are wanting. Skaptár volcano has never been visited, and therefore the direction of its fissure is unknown. Neither is much known about Katla's fissure; it is supposed, however, to turn from north-west, to south-east, and then again towards the north-east.

The Katla volcano must, however, be considered to form an independent system; in which eruptions have taken place both from Katla itself, as well as from the neighbourhood north of Sólheimar. This therefore forms the fifth, or the Katla system.

The other volcanic eruptions in Iceland range themselves round the large Vatna-Jökul; but no distinct direction of the volcanic fissures of these has yet been found. Along the south side of Vatna-Jökul eruptions have taken place in all the large

Jökuls, Skaptár-Jökul, Skeidara, Öræfa, and Breiðamerkr-Jökul, though from the last three no lava streams have been known to flow. Eruptions have also occurred on the north side of Vatna-Jökul. We may therefore class this volcanic agency under the head of the Vatna-Jökul system; a term which, however, must not be supposed to assume the direction of any distinct volcanic fissure, but merely to imply a central point, round which the volcanoes that do not belong to any of the above named systems are situate.

The next oldest geological formation consists of several strata of palagonite tufa, or tufa of palagonite, intersected by numberless "dikes," of distinct columnar basalts, and thus appears in strata with this last-named mineral, in which, however, tufa is most prominent. By tufa is generally understood a mineral of a loose consistency, composed of a fine cement, which either forms the principal component, in which case the stone resembles hardened clay or fine sandstone; or else it contains larger or smaller grains or fragments of different minerals, when it bears a resemblance to a coarse sandstone or a conglomerate; and "palagonite tufa" is a tufa which is composed mainly of a mineral named "Palagonite," and which externally bears a close resemblance to a piece of brown or yellow resin. By basalts, however, is understood, a firm, crystalline mineral of a dark blue colour, so fine-grained that the minerals which form its component parts cannot be discerned plainly with the naked eye, or even with the aid of a magnifying glass. The composition therefore of these minerals is not yet properly known; and under the name of basalts accordingly, distinct kinds of minerals, though nearly allied to each other, come to be classed. The cooled rock occupying a fissure is termed a "dike"; and this formation, which we may conveniently term the Palagonite formation, consists therefore of several strata of tufa of palagonite, with

L

"dikes" of basalts, also with subordinate strata of this rock. Palagonite tufa is either fine-grained and close, cement therefore being prominent, or else it contains in larger or smaller quantities fragments of basalts, which are sometimes of a rounded form, sometimes sharp-edged, when it becomes "Conglomerate" or "Breccia." Palagonite tufa is the true companion of a volcano. Most of the volcanic fissures, for instance, in Iceland lie in palagonite tufa; but this mineral, with the enclosed "dikes" of basalts, covers a large portion of the country which the younger lava has left untouched, as in the terrain between the systems of Hekla and Skjaldbreið, as well as to the north and north-east of these. In the neighbourhood of Leirhnúkr there are large mountain ridges that belong to this formation; and that this is the case with the large Jökuls, both along the southern portion of the country and in the interior, may be seen from the steep walls of Eyafjalla-Jökul, as well as from the stones which the glaciers and Jökul rivers carry with them from the interior of these mountains. During my journey to the east I could observe the steady appearance of palagonite tufa in the mountains till I had passed by Breiða-merkr-jökul, where it began to decrease, and where the third and oldest mineral formation almost exclusively appeared in the mountains on the coast. The material which constitutes palagonite tufa in all probability consists of old volcanic ashes and sand; and where the tufa is of a conglomerate character, of scoriæ, which have been ejected from the interior of the earth, while the land still lay submerged under the surface of the sea, and which under the action of the waves and currents were arranged in strata, like sandbanks, whereby the fine volcanic ash passed over into palagonite, and the whole was formed into a hard stony mass. The "dikes" of basalts which intersect these strata penetrated in a molten state into the fissures, as may be observed from their slaggy appearance and from their composition. In a "dike" which intersects a stratum of palagonite, north of the farm Herdisarvík, near Krísuvík, on the south coast of Iceland, this may plainly be noticed; and in a conglomerate stratum belonging to this formation near the parsonage of Stórinúpr, northwest of Hekla, I have found several pieces of basalts of perfect lava construction, and with bubbles or fused with edges; wherefore there can be no doubt that this basalt proceeded from a molten mass in the interior of the earth. It can thus easily be understood how it happens that basalts appear in alternate strata with palagonite tufa, for when the mass had filled up the fissure, it flowed over its edges, in the same way as a lava stream is formed.

That the Palagonite formation is the next oldest formation to the lava, or the younger volcanic formation, can be ascertained from its near connection with it, as above alluded to; for palagonite tufa is the substratum of the lava streams.

The oldest or basaltic formation lies, as may be inferred from what has already been said, like a belt round the last-named mineral, at least along the northern part of the country. Thus it appears on the fjelds north of Reykjavik by Faxafjörðr, on the north-west peninsula, and on the mountains that enclose the large fjords and deep valleys in the northern and eastern parts of the country; but it appears also in many mountain tracts in other parts of the country; and it may therefore be called the principal formation of the country, the more especially as it forms, as it were, the substratum for the others. This formation consists partly of dark-blue, fine-grained minerals, which, as we have stated, is called by the common name of "trap" or basalts (the word itself is derived from the fact of these minerals frequently forming layers one above the other, in the shape of stair-formed ledges,—"trappe," a step), partly of a mineral named dolerit. Further, tufa appears in this formation in strata with basalts, and in several places light coloured minerals belonging to the Trachyte class appear, but not so prominently as the strata of basalts and tufa. Basaltic strata are the most prominent in this formation. These strata are of various thicknesses, but seldom attain to a hundred feet. On the other hand many of these strata follow each other in such order, that mountains of basaltic formation look like featherbeds or mattresses, laid on each other, in such a way that the lowest stratum juts out farther than the one above it, and so on, whereby the stair-formed ledges on the mountain sides appear. Between the firmer strata of basalts there are strata of a looser kind of tufa (not always palagonite tufa), or of vitrified minerals, which are of less coherency than basalts. The consequence, therefore, is that between every stratum of basalts, a slip of loose stones is formed; on which account the basaltic strata and the basaltic formation are more prominent. In the upper divisions of the basaltic mountains I have found some few unimportant strata of palagonite tufa, wherefore the change to this formation begins here. The three formations are not perfectly or sharply separated from one another. But the whole stamp of the country is entirely different where the basaltic formation is the prevailing one, to what is the case where palagonite or the lava formation is more prominent. And the above distribution is therefore correct, though it cannot be carried out quite in all its singularities.

These general features of the mountain-system of Iceland we may possibly have occasion to exemplify; and I have, therefore, deemed it expedient to lay them before the reader now.

The geological antiquity of the formations of which Iceland consists is, comparatively, not very great. Geologists, as is known, divide the rocks in which fossil remains of extinct plants and animals occur into three great periods, for the duration of which, reckoned by years, no measure has hitherto been found, but concerning which it is only known that it must have been immeasurably great. It is among the youngest of these three periods of the development of the earth that the oldest of Iceland's formations must be reckoned. This formation is called the age of mammalia, and is arranged under two divisions; an older one, which is called the tertiary, and a younger, the post-tertiary. Under the first of these the basaltic formations of Iceland must be ranked, on account of the fossil plants found in them, to which we shall presently allude. During the post-tertiary formation the glacier period occurred, when the whole of Northern Europe and America was enveloped in Jökuls and glaciers; and lavas can still be pointed out in Iceland that were contemporaneous with this formation. The Palagonite formation, which on the whole is of later date than the Lava formation,—and which, moreover, is a formation produced under the surface of the sea,—must therefore occupy the intermediate period, and its formation must thus be dated towards the close of the tertiary and the beginning of the post-tertiary period.

It was on Midsummer-eve, and the sun was shining brightly, when I left Kálfafellsstaðr. The road from thence to Bjarnanes was one of the most beautiful I had yet travelled on. At first it lay on rather high ground, so that I had an extensive view over the blue sea. On my left lay a lofty cliff, Hestgerðishnúkr, 1,190 feet above the sea, on whose top a "dike" of basalts was visible. Next came a plain, partly overgrown with herbage, partly devastated by Jökul rivers, lying in a semicircle, surrounded by crested, snowy mountains and Jökuls. I counted four large, magnificent glaciers sloping down towards this plain; and besides the defiles in which they were, there were five other valleys which seemed to lose themselves in among the mountain-range on the north, which is known by the name of Heinabergs-Jökul. Towards the close of the day I had to ride over a river named Hornafjördr, which is rather a shallow lake than a river, about three and a half miles in width. As is customary among the natives, my guide had a dog with him. It had waded or swum over the smaller watercourses we had met; but when we came to this one, it commenced howling piteously. Thereupon its master took it up and put it behind him on the horse's back, to the great delight of the dog. This was the only time I saw a dog riding in Iceland.

Dogs are favourite animals with the Icelanders, and they

An Icelandic dog.

keep a prodigious number of them; for, as far as I could estimate, nearly every grown man keeps a dog. On arriving at a house, one is usually received by four, six, or eight yelping curs, whose behaviour towards the traveller is in striking contrast to the hospitality of the inmates. Dogs are necessary to Iceland, otherwise it would be impossible to collect the flocks and to tend them; but their exaggerated number constitutes a literal plague, not so much on account of the quantity of food they consume, as from weightier causes, as the reader will readily allow. For dogs are the indirect cause of the appearance of a terrible disease that attacks both sheep and human beings, and which, until recently, has gone under the name of liver-complaint, but whose true nature has been brought to light by recent investigations.

The Danish physician, Dr. Krabbe, who visited Iceland in order to study this disease, has given some interesting information concerning it.

The disease appears under the form of vesicles, which attack the interior of the system, especially the liver; and so general is this complaint in Iceland, that nearly every fortieth individual suffers from it. These vesicles, it has been ascertained by Professor Eschricht, of Copenhagen, are a species of animal called "hydatid" which not only appear in human beings, but are also found in cows, sheep, goats, and pigs. This "hydatid" appears under three different forms. The first is often found in the adipose membrane of sheep, and frequently attains the size of a duck's egg. Occasionally, in a single sheep, fifty "hydatids" may be found, though not all of the above size. They have, as stated, the appearance of a bladder filled with a watery liquid. The bladder, or vesicle, consists of an outer membrane, within which the worm lies. On carefully rending the external membrane, or capsule, this bladder falls out. It is soft, and immediately collapses, when it resembles a round, flat mass; like the contents of an egg, for instance, that have been poured out from the shell. It exhibits no signs of life; but as it contains a fluid, it assumes a quivering motion on being touched. If one succeeds in getting a "hydatid" entire out of its capsule, immediately after the sheep has been killed, on placing it in a saucer of luke-warm water, the temperature of which is about the same as the interior of the slaughtered animal, it will show signs of animation; and one can see the membrane contract itself, while the folds in it spread with an undulatory motion, without the animal moving from the spot. On each of these bladders a protrusion may be observed of a whiter and more opaque nature than the other parts, and which one might suppose to be the head, with an orifice in it. This is an elongation of the bladder, which has drawn itself inwards, and thereby forms a little tube or hole. By an even pressure on the bladder, the part that has been drawn in can be pushed out, and one can then see that it terminates in a little head about the size of a pin's-head; but with the aid of a magnifying-glass, it will be found that this little head has a peculiar structure; for it has a fringe of more than thirty small hooks, and outside these, four orifices for suction. The little head with the hooks, which had been hidden in the white elongation of the "hydatid," has exactly the same appearance and structure as the head of the common tape-worm in the Icelandic dogs, and is, in fact, nothing else; for when a dog swallows a "hydatid," or its white elongation, the "hydatid" becomes a tape-worm. When a sheep is killed, the "hydatids" are generally torn out, and are devoured by the dogs, which are generally well represented on such occasions. After the dog has swallowed the "hydatid," it becomes dissolved in the stomach under the process of digestion, with the exception of the little head with its hooks and suckers. It thrives well in its new abode, not only defies the influence of the gastric juices, but becomes a living animal, sets its hooks and suckers in motion, and, with the help of these, attaches itself to a point in the fore part of the entrails. The hindermost part of the worm becomes gradually elongated and jointed, and as the joints increase in number and size, after the lapse of a couple of months it becomes a tape-worm of three feet in length.

From experiments that have been made by making dogs eat "hydatids," and then killing them at different times, when the size of the "hydatids" they have contained has been found to correspond with the period that has elapsed since they were eaten by the dogs, it has been fully proved that the process of transformation takes place as described.

Eggs are never found in the "hydatid;" but they are discovered in prodigious numbers in the tape-worm. As has been already stated, it attaches itself to the entrails by means of the hooks and orifices of suction on its diminutive head. It has no mouth, for the tapeworm absorbs nourishment throughout the whole length of its surface, which is covered on all sides by the food in the stomach in a digested state. This food, of course, properly speaking, ought to be the poor dog's property, but the parasite enjoys a large share of it.

In the course of its development, the tape-worm increases in width in its lower parts, while its articulations become larger, and the lowest one is filled with thousands of minute eggs. When these are ripe, the ova-filled articulations become relaxed, and come away with the excrements of the animal; and this can occur repeatedly, as the worm is very tenacious of life, and can constantly produce new articulations.

These eggs, however, which come away from the dog, do not previously receive their development in the sheep. It has been ascertained by experiments, that when a sheep has swallowed the eggs of the tape-worm in a dog, which the dog has got from eating the "hydatid" in the sheep—for there are several kinds of tape-worm in dogs—the sheep is then affected with this very kind of "hydatid;" and it has, moreover, been discovered how this comes about. When, for instance, the sheep has swallowed the egg of the tape-worm, it is hatched out in its inside, and a tiny worm emerges, armed with six small hooks, by the help of which it bores into the membrane of the gut. When it thus reaches a small vein, it is carried along with the blood till its further progress is arrested from the vein becoming too narrow, or from some obstruction coming in its way. Here it grows, and by degrees becomes a "hydatid," as above described. The blood can of course convey it to other places besides the adipose membrane; but as it only develops itself here, it may be assumed that it only finds favourable conditions for its growth in this spot. That sheep frequently swallow the eggs of the tape-worm in dogs is only natural, for these eggs are distributed over the field after coming away from the dog, and are thus readily swallowed by the sheep while grazing.

This, however, is only one kind of "hydatid." Besides this one, whose *habitat* is the adipose membrane, another variety is found in the brains of sheep, and occasionally in those of oxen —though less frequently—which produces a well-known disease, in Iceland called "staggers." This "hydatid," like the above-named, consists of a membrane, filled with fluid matter, but differs from it in this respect, that it is furnished with several small excrescences, containing heads of "hydatids." These often occur in hundreds, and assemble in clusters on one side of the vesicle. If a dog swallows one of these, the same process takes place as with "hydatids" from the adipose membrane: the vesicle, namely, becomes relaxed, while the heads grow into tape-worms, and the eggs of these coming away from the dogs, and finding their way with the grass into the sheep, ultimately become "hydatids." But they will only thrive and flourish in the brain, especially of young sheep. This has been ascertained by experiment. If, for instance, one gives a sheep a large number of the eggs of this tape-worm, the disease quickly develops itself, and an inflammation of the brain takes place, which speedily causes death, as a quantity of "hydatids" appear at once.

The disease always commences after the lapse of a certain time, namely, a fortnight after the sheep has swallowed the eggs of the tape-worm. This species of "hydatid" in the sheep is of much rarer occurrence than the first-named, as also is the corresponding tape-worm in the dog; but, as it has many heads, the dog that swallows it contracts a large number of tape-worms at one time. In corroboration of this, Krabbe has often found 150 to 180 tape-worms of this kind in a dog.

A third kind of "hydatid" occurs in the liver and lungs of cows and sheep; and this is the species which is found in human beings who suffer from "hydatids." No head is discoverable on this "hydatid" with the naked eye. In human beings, it can attain a large size and thickness; but in sheep and cows (it also occurs in goats and pigs) it dies sooner, and shrinks up into a lithic mass. When found in human beings, it generally appears in greater numbers in the abdomen, which becomes puffed up, and, when pressed, causes pain. Swellings frequently occur in the regions of these excrescences, especially after a fall or a blow, when the vesicles come out, of their own accord, through the skin; and as the diseased person can thus be most readily relieved from his pains, the doctors adopt an artificial means of making the vesicles appear to view in this way, either by incision or by blistering. But the swelling can also turn inwards towards the lungs, entrails, or other internal organs; in which case there is great danger, and death often ensues.

The inner side of the coating of these parasites, on being submitted to magnifying power, seems to be occupied by numberless heads of a similar appearance to the first-named, only much smaller. When a dog swallows one of these vesicles, the heads grow and become tape-worms, but do not attain the same dimensions as the first-named, and are, at most, only about a quarter of an inch in length when full grown. On the other hand, they appear in astonishing numbers, in fact, by thousands. In each of these tape-worms, myriads of eggs are formed, so that the number of the eggs of this tape-worm which come away from a dog is often enormously large. Furthermore, these eggs enter into cattle while grazing, and are developed into "hydatids" on reaching the liver or lungs. It has lately been positively ascertained that it is this "hydatid" that occurs in human beings; for puppies, which could not possibly have swallowed the tape-worms of other domestic animals, have been made to swallow the worms from human beings, whereby the corresponding tiny tape-worm has been developed in them.

These three kinds of "hydatids" occur, likewise, in other countries—the last-named, both in animals and human beings—but are far from being so common as in Iceland. Moreover, Icelandic dogs are much more liable to worms than is the case with Danish dogs. From an experiment made by Krabbe, out of a hundred Icelandic dogs, tape-worms of the first kind were found in 75; of the second, in 18; and of the third, in 28; whilst the corresponding proportion in Denmark gave the numbers of 20, 1, and 0·6. Moreover, the number of the individual in each dog is much greater in Iceland than in Denmark. Five other kinds of worms are found in Iceland, in dogs, but they have nothing in common with "hydatids."

It is easy enough to understand how the eggs of the tape-worm enter into animals while grazing; but it is more difficult to ascertain how they enter into human beings. But, still, this can take place in many ways: as, for instance, by letting a dog lick one; or it may occur from a disgusting custom, which is sometimes to be met with in Iceland, of letting the dogs lick the plates and dishes clean, without any further washing; or

MEANS OF CHECKING THE DISEASE.

the dust which is carried along by the wind may contain them. For, if a person rides over a sandy heiði, or mountain-road, when a brisk breeze is blowing, he will naturally get a good deal of sand into his mouth, or, if this be close-shut, into his nose; and, very likely, these fine particles of sand may be mixed with the dust of the dried excrements of dogs. Several other ways may be imagined in which the germs of the disease may enter the human frame, especially when the general uncleanliness of the country is taken into account. And the frequent cases of the disease which occur testify that the germs of the disease are spread far and wide. The means which might be adopted to check this evil (which truly may be called a national evil in Iceland, for not less than 1,500 persons suffer from it), should be sought for in preventing the dogs from eating the infected parts of slaughtered animals, and in considerably diminishing their number. But people do not seem as yet to have entertained this opinion in Iceland, neither will they do so unless a dog-tax be introduced. Sheep-dogs, of course, are indispensable; for, when an epidemic raged a few years ago among the dogs, and consequently greatly diminished their numbers, the peasants had to give a cow in exchange for a sheep-dog. Still, as companions, the number of dogs might well be reduced.

Between Bjarnanes and Stafafell, my next night-quarters, a little bit of mountain-road is met with, a forerunner, as it were, of the large mountain-tracts that form the connecting link between the deep fjords on the east coast. The narrow strip of coast, which, under the form of low-land, occupies the space between the Jökuls and the sea, and which has to thank the Jökellöbs for its existence, is entirely wanting here. Sharp mountain-ridges, which separate the fjords from each other, descend directly into the sea without any marked depression; consequently, when the inhabitants of these parts want to cross from one fjord to another, they have been obliged to seek a track across the mountain-passes; and as these passes, generally speaking, do not offer convenient lines of communication, but, on the contrary, possess most of those qualities which conduce to make a road abominably bad—for instance, they are very steep, and are blocked up with stones and earth, and masses of snow; and, in consequence of their great altitude, the traveller is generally enveloped in clouds or mists —it will be readily perceived that the communication between the fjords is often attended with no little difficulty.

A traveller with a number of loose horses has naturally less difficulty in getting on, especially in the summer time, with the help of a little patience; but for the people of the country who have often to traverse these heights with laden horses, it must be remarkably disagreeable. In winter time, moreover, they are dangerous and impassable. There are small heaps of stone placed here and there to serve as guide-posts for travellers; but when a snow storm comes on very little of them can be seen. In winter time, also, they commonly use "ski" (a kind of snow-shoes) in these parts; and it sometimes occurs that people lose their way and perish from cold, hunger, or fatigue.

A sad occurrence took place a few winters ago on the mountain ridge north of Eskifjördur, which lies further to the north on this coast. Three persons had lost their way in a snow storm. After wandering about a long time, during which, instead of crossing the ridge, which was of no great width, they found their way down to the sea. One of them now sank down from fatigue, declaring that he could go no farther, and that he would lie down and die. The reason of his companions was doubtless affected by the cold and the exertions they had undergone, and as there seemed to be no other means of extricating themselves from their position, they left him to his fate, and continued to roam about. At last they reached the settlement, but were so bewildered, that they were ignorant of the fact, and actually passed by the house, whither they were bound, instead of entering in. They were, however, seen by the inmates, and were taken in. On coming to themselves, they declared that they could not understand how they could possibly have left their comrade to his fate; and when they did so, it never occurred to them that they were doing anything unnatural. Self-preservation was the only instinct their bewildered senses had retained, though death had appeared to them to be a natural consequence. Even in calamities, nature confers a boon on mankind, by diminishing the impressions of fear on the minds of those who are overtaken by them. They were, moreover, respectable men, on the credibility of whose accounts perfect reliance could be placed.

Almannaskarð was, as I have said, a harbinger of the near proximity of the mountain passes, though it was but a short though steep path over the sharp ridge between Klifatinör (2,797 feet) in the south, and another mountain peak in the north-west. The road lay transversely up the slope, and consisted of a narrow beaten path. The midsummer-day sun shone warmly on the grey-coloured mountain side, on whose dry surface some specimens of the *Rhodiola rosea*, and of other plants were growing, whose fleshy leaves compensated them for the dryness of the soil. At Almannaskarð I found a little flower, the *Saxifraga Cotyledon;* it has a rosette of thick stiffish leaves at its base. From this the flower stalk shoots up; but its numerous buds were still so imperfectly developed, that it was impossible to discern what the colour of the petals would be. I put a couple of specimens in a book, which I had brought with me in lieu of a press, and let them remain untouched for a fortnight. But when by chance I saw them again at the lapse of that time, small, white, delicate, and fresh flowers had become developed. The leaves at the base, however, had become dry and shrivelled. It seemed to me a sin to put a flower into a press, that had displayed such tenacity of life. On the other side of Skarðén I descended on to a stony plain, that had been devastated by a Jökul river, and after crossing the river, which as usual was divided into several broad arms, I reached Stafafell in the evening.

Sira Bjarni, in Stafafell, was one of the few native clergy I have seen who reminded me of their brethren in Old Sweden. In the first place he was in possession of a little clerical stomach; and in the second, of an accompanying, if not necessarily so, dignity of person. But pastors in Iceland do not wear their clerical garments every day; and it is possibly the absence of priestly attire that made the difference between an Icelandic and Swedish pastor so striking. Sira Bjarni was rather a notorious character, because he nearly occasioned a breach of the peace between the little state of Denmark and the powerful kingdom of France. For he owned a small eider-duck "holm,"* which had been robbed of its treasures by the French fishing smacks that swarm round the coast of Iceland; and in former days states have declared war for reasons less weighty than this. But now-a-days people have made the discovery that it costs both parties less to accept payment in ready money for such peccadilloes, and to let feelings of honour go to the winds. And, indeed, we ought to be thankful that it is so, for after all it is merely "skin deep" honour. Thus Sira Bjarni may deem himself happy that he came into the world in a more enlightened age, for he has no cause to reproach his conscience with the burden of a war, and

* Holm, a high rocky islet.

with the bloodshed thereby entailed; though he continues to go about uttering complaints against a government that would not see him righted. And it must be allowed to be a vexatious thing when a man sends his boat to fetch fresh eider-duck eggs from his "holm," while he is licking his lips at the thought of their rich yelks, to find it return with only some fragments of English or French newspapers. Moreover, this "holm" was his chief source of income; for it yields him annually 300 to 400 rix dollars in down and eggs, and regarded from this point of view it must be confessed that it was very annoying to be exposed to the incursions of foreign prowlers.

The French fishing-smacks, of which two or three hundred visit the coasts of Iceland annually for a period of at least five months, give rise to a great deal of bitter feeling; the robbing of an eider-duck "holm" or two being among the least of the annoyances they cause. When, for instance, these smacks reach the coast of Iceland in the beginning of April all the cod-fishery is at an end, or, at least, there is but little of it left for the Icelanders, who possess no deck-boats, but only some simple rowing-boats, which are far from sea-worthy, and who, therefore, cannot compete with the well-equipped foreigners. For when thirty to forty French smacks lie along the coast (according to the international law of the sea they have no right to approach land within cannon-shot, or, in other words, within two and a half miles) they appropriate all the fishery to themselves; for they throw the head and entrails of the fish overboard, which, of course, attracts shoals of fish; and as the French smacks can remain lying at the same place, or can drift with the current, they reap the lion's share of the booty. The Icelanders, on the other hand, cannot adopt this method of proceeding, for, with their small boats, they cannot remain out at sea, at the most, for more than twenty-four hours at a time, and, consequently, derive no benefit from the shoals being attracted to the spot from the refuse thrown overboard. And as the Frenchmen, owing to their superior resources, are able to appropriate the fishery to themselves, during the time they lie round the coast, the enormous quantity of fish which they take must necessarily tend to diminish the produce of the fishery, for the number of cod fish which they annually catch in all probability amounts to six or seven millions.

The reason why Iceland cannot herself enjoy the advantage of this source of wealth is deep-rooted. Strange though it may seem, yet it is the case, that the Icelanders, though they are brought up by the sea, and though they derive a great portion of their sustenance from it, are not yet what one may term a nation of sailors. Certainly it seems to require, and it does require, courage to go several miles out to sea in an open boat, and many lose their lives every year, so that it is not from lack of this virtue to meet the danger that the Icelanders dislike the profession of a sailor. The aversion may rather be attributed to a dislike to have to submit to the severe discipline and hard work of a life on board ship; for the Icelander is a very independent fellow, and likes an easy life. Still, whatever the psychological cause may be, it appears remarkable that the descendants of the Norwegian Vikingrs should not like a sailor's life. The explanation of this phenomenon is not to be arrived at till one comes to know the practical reasons that have caused this state of things to exist. These have their root in the oppressive treatment which former governments in Denmark have through centuries shown towards Iceland, which, acting on their rights of possession, have exhausted the energy of the country, and, by means of the revenue it afforded, have promoted the interests of their own mercantile towns, especially of Copenhagen. In the documents relating to the monopoly of

Icelandic commerce by Copenhagen, and in the accompanying enactments against the privilege of Icelanders to export their own products to other lands, or to trade with foreign nations (a state of things which was first established in the reign of Christian IV., and was subsequently in force for two centuries), it was rendered an impossibility for them to be the owners of any decked boats, for the fisheries could not by themselves cover their expense, especially as the value of the fish was depreciated owing to the monopoly. From that period, therefore, may be dated the decline of Iceland as a sea-faring country; and even at the present day the aversion to a sailor's life is so strong in the country, that a merchant who fits out a vessel can with difficulty find a crew of native Icelanders to man it. In order to remedy this defect the Danish Government has of late years offered to take Icelanders on board Danish vessels, an offer which they decline to accept, for they entertain the childish fear that underneath this offer lies the covert intention of subsequently pressing them to serve in the Danish navy.

The praiseworthy endeavours of the government in this direction, however, have come too late, for the attempts of former governments to restrict the commerce to the Danes, that is, to the Copenhagen merchants, a conduct which was neither parental towards Iceland nor of profit to Denmark, have had this consequence, that the Frenchmen, who, together with the Spaniards, are the principal consumers of Icelandic fish, being forbidden to trade directly with Iceland, determined on sending fishing fleets to Iceland, under the very nose of the Danish merchants. The French fishery companies, moreover, are well supported by their own Government, which takes an interest in these voyages to the northern seas, as they form an excellent school for turning out good sailors. Moreover it gives a bounty to every person who takes part in these expeditions, while, at the same time, a high duty is levied upon all fish imported into France by foreign vessels. Hence another difficulty lies in the way of the Icelandic-Danish fish trade, whereby the more enterprising of the Icelanders are hindered from investing capital in the purchase of decked fishing vessels. The injury, however, which the French fishing fleet inflicts on the Icelandic fisheries is a well-known subject for complaint, and Denmark must bear the blame of it. In an ancient Icelandic law it is enacted that foreigners may not fish within nineteen miles of land, and as Denmark naturally can make no other arrangement with the French, or with any other government, which would be more to the interest of Iceland, in the face of the existing law of nations, which fixes the distance from land at which foreign vessels may fish at that which a cannon-ball, when fired from shore, would traverse, it is the universal opinion in Iceland that the Government lacks the ability and the good-will to do so; an opinion which is strengthened by the fact that Denmark has not sought to refute these false impressions by explaining to the Icelanders what changes in the old legislature the modern maritime law of nations demands. Of late the Icelanders have begun to see the impossibility of effecting any alteration in the existing state of affairs by diplomatic means; and eloquent voices have been raised among them promoting the equipment of a fleet of decked boats, in order to cope with the Frenchmen. Means, however, for carrying out this suggestion are wanting; and the unsettled state of affairs renders it difficult to enlist public sympathy in its favour. And though the question is one of vital importance to the country, no steps have yet been taken to carry it into effect, while the prospect of bringing it to a successful issue looks very remote indeed. To such a pitch have the unwise and self-willed actions of former governments brought the country. The recollection of these things helps, meanwhile, to keep alive a feeling of bitterness against Denmark in the country; but this, only in a few exceptional cases, can be ascribed to ill-will; while the occasional annoyances they have to submit to from foreign vessels lying too close to shore, and from the plundering of their eider-duck holms, and from taking other liberties, which neither they themselves nor the Danish Government could possibly prevent, are like burning coals, and only add fuel to the fire.

For the present we will dismiss this subject, while we bid farewell to the worthy Sira Bjarni, in Stafafell, wishing from our heart that in future he may eat his excellent eider-duck eggs in peace, and reap the income derived from his soft down. But as we are speaking of eider down, I will take the opportunity of making a few further remarks thereon.

Owing to the abundance of eider ducks round the coasts of Iceland (one may see flocks of hundreds on the sea-shore at low water, looking out for mussels and perrywinkles among the seaweed), an eider-down coverlet is generally to be met with in Icelandic houses, or else a coverlet of swan down, or of the feathers of other sea-birds, which also make excellent beds; so that there is no cause to find fault with the nature of the bed itself. Still, on taking other circumstances into consideration, a tent will be found a very useful accompaniment in a tour through Iceland. I did not think it worth while to take one as I was alone, but I had cause afterwards to regret that I had not done so; and I therefore advise every one who purposes spending a summer in Iceland, to furnish himself with a small tent. Besides this, it is almost necessary to take some provisions. It often happens that on a journey of ten or twelve hours one does not meet with any house where one's idea of cleanliness would permit of the purchase of food. As I was not aware of this, I had to put up with a great deal at first; for it is no pleasant thing after a not over-abundant breakfast of smoked mutton, bread, and butter not particularly well made, to have to travel for the rest of the day on a cup of coffee, which may be had nearly everywhere. Moreover, on arriving at a "bær" in the evening, there is no table ready laid for the traveller. And if it should be a basin of rice milk that one is expecting, it takes about three hours to make it, according to my experience at least. Sometimes, too, the lamb has first to be killed, especially in the autumn, when this meat is common. Anyhow it is well to have a little bread and butter with one, as I found out on my fortnight's journey from Reykjavik to Berufjörðr. I make these remarks for the special benefit of future tourists in Iceland; to the general reader they will not be peculiarly interesting.

But still another word about the eider ducks. They are strictly preserved over the whole country; and as soon as they build their nest on a "holm" by the sea-coast, which they generally do, for only an occasional pair make their way up into the country, the eggs which they lay become the property of the owner of the soil, as well as the down which the duck plucks off her breast, and lays over the eggs. An eider duck lays from four to six eggs in the first sitting, and when these, together with the down, are taken away, she lays three or four more, and plucks fresh down off her breast. If these are also taken away she will commence laying again, but this time the drake has to contribute his quota of down to the nest. Owing to their being so jealously preserved, the duck becomes very tame during the period of incubation, so tame indeed that she will allow herself to be stroked with the hand while on the nest. Viðey, near Reykjavik, is the largest eider-duck holm in Iceland; and it yields a handsome income in eggs and down. A pound of cleansed down costs six or seven rix dollars in Iceland. The annual export is 5,000 to 6,000 pounds. It is said that the eider duck teaches her young ones to swim by taking them on her back out to sea, and diving—whereby the ducklings remain floating on the water, and naturally begin to splash about.

In Stafafell a wooden house was built in addition to the "bœr," and was used as a summer dwelling. It contained a small keeping room, and a room for the reception of guests. With the exception of a few churches, this was the first wooden building I had seen after leaving Eyrarbakki. But as regards its architecture, too lofty ideas must not be formed, for it was not constructed of timber. The only timber in it was to be found in the framework, while the walls consisted of boards or thin planks, and over the whole a boarded roof, tarred all over outside, and unpainted within. In Iceland they do not seem to know the use of birch bark in roofing. They therefore lay turf on the boarded roof; occasionally a little straw or some rushes are laid underneath; and the consequence is, therefore, that the rain, when it falls continuously for any time—and it can rain in Iceland!—finds its way in in all parts, and makes the damp intolerable and unavoidable even in the best furnished "bœr." The furniture is attacked by the fearful damp in a few years; and what I have already spoken of may thus be conceived, that if, in one respect, the existing style of architecture is cheap, in another, it is dear, unreasonably dear; for the timber work of a house has to be renewed every twentieth year. In the Færoe isles they use birch bark for their roofs, and consequently the houses last much longer there. On going to bed in an Icelandic "bœr" the damp strikes the body to such an extent that it is exactly as if one were lying in water. Rheumatic complaints, therefore, are among the commonest ailments in the country.

The church at Stafafell is an insignificant earthen building, surrounded by a small wall or bank of turf and stones. I happened to be there one Sunday, and as I stood on a little green hill in the churchyard I listened to the singing of the congregation, who, though few in number, seemed to testify by their devout voices that they felt the meaning of the words, " Where two or three are gathered together in My name, there am I in the midst of them." The sun shone brightly and cheerily that day, and all nature around was hushed in repose; only the twittering of a few birds in the meadow below was to be heard. At some distance off lay the bright, blue sea, while in front the sharply peaked mountain ridges reared their crests aloft. A prospect such as this, and on such a day, belongs to the hours that call forth feelings of love towards a land that can produce them; and many such hours have I experienced in Iceland.

Between Stafafell and Hof, in Altafjörðr, I had again to cross a piece of mountain road over Lónsheiði, which though rather steep at the outset, was a mere trifle in comparison with what I had afterwards to encounter. As far as I could see through the fog, which began to gather round me as soon as I had got a short distance up the mountain, the scenery was very picturesque. Along the side of these mountain roads, which usually go in a zig-zag direction up towards the ridge, there is nearly always a rapid cataract to be found, which has cut itself a deep bed between the steep mountain walls, and whose foaming waters may be seen at the bendings of the road. These fosses are nourished from the melting snow "fonds" on the mountains, and the body of water in them, therefore, varies according to the season of the year; but even though there be but little water in them, the din and roar of the foaming mass is heard at a considerable distance, and accompanies the traveller as he rides over a heiði or clambers up a mountain slope; so that it may with reason be said, that the sighing of the forests in Iceland is compensated for by the murmuring of her fosses; for this is the only sound that breaks the deep silence of these barren mountain heights.

Iceland, as above remarked, is almost a treeless country. In some few places, indeed, a low kind of brushwood appears, the branches of which perhaps rise a little higher than the horseman who is riding through them, and every now and then a wooded plot containing trees, with an apology for stems. Usually, the wood one meets with consists of low brushwood, and when the guide volunteers the information, " We call that a wood!" his remark requires a little explanation. But even this so-called wood is a rarity. I had scarcely seen any of it up to the present time. But though the expression a " treeless country" conveys rather a depressing impression to the mind, still this is far from being the case with Iceland. Uno von Troil correctly remarks in his description of Iceland, " that there is not a tree to be found, beneath which friendship and innocence can meet." But woods are not really missed here. And this is, of course, owing to the physical appearance of Icelandic nature. When, for instance, one stands on some eminence, and looks towards a mountain some nine miles distant, which is clad in its dark blue summer dress, or whose summit is enveloped in a cap of snow; or else if one sees it all a-glow from the rays of the setting sun, the absence of forest tracts does not strike the mind. Or if one gazes over a grassy plain, where no disfiguring fences obstruct the view, but where either a river winds along in its sinuous course, or a lake reveals its shining surface to the eye, the senses do not feel the want of forest land, for a plain such as this is not the forest's proper home. Neither is their absence noticed when gazing over the barren sandy wastes, which one knows to be periodically deluged by the destructive waters of the Jökul, or when wondering at some rigid lava stream. And again, if one directs the eye up towards the mountain slopes, which properly should be the forest's home, it finds them covered with such a brilliant carpet of mingled grass and flowers, that no wood is needed; or else they are so steep and inaccessible, that it would be childish to wish a forest to grow there. Wherever one turns the eye one finds an ample compensation, and the impression which the mind receives is, "I do not miss the forests!" No! the feelings would be rather outraged were the prospect to be shut out by the appearance of forest tracts. Wherever trees do grow, on the sloping side of a fjeld or a heiði, owing to their stunted form they resemble more a mossy carpet than a wood; they do not obstruct the view, and therewith the mind is content. Thus the thought of the non-appearance of woods or forests is pushed into the background by the magnificent style on which Nature has revealed herself there; and that is the whole matter! Truly a little wooded land would be acceptable on the bare, bleak heights round Reykjavik; but the sea-blasts rage there with such violence, as to render it an impossibility for trees to thrive.

I will now conduct the reader down from the cloud-capped Lónsheiði. First, then, we emerge into a valley, which opens on to the plain in the interior of Altafjörðr. Lofty mountain walls seem to tower above it. Among these is one of a roundish form, which, owing to the arrangement of the basaltic strata (the intervals of which are filled up with the *débris* of mountain slips), each of which jutted out farther than the one above it, reminded me of an enormous crinoline, whose gigantic wearer, from the crown to the middle, was enveloped in a mystic and impenetrable cloud. The view over the island-studded Altafjörðr is very beautiful. After a short ride from the "heiði," I reached Hof Parsonage, and as experience had taught me not to raise too great expectations from a parsonage house, I, of course, was thankful for what it could afford me. Still I trust I shall not be accused of a want of gallantry towards the fair sex, if I ascribe the want of cleanliness that reigns in most of the Icelandic "bœr" to the ladies; for certainly they do not fulfil their house-wifely duties in this respect.

My landlord at Hof, the worthy Sira Þorarinn, whose acquaintance I subsequently made, was absent from home. I did not await his return, but continued my journey on the following day, in company with a guide, whom I engaged for a lengthened period, as I had reached a place where I purposed staying some time, and thus could derive more benefit from a constant companion than if I had engaged a fresh guide every day. I obtained him at the moderate rate of a rix-dollar a day; for which he was to provide himself with a horse, and find himself in victuals; which, as a guide always lives gratis with his master, is a very trifling item. The pay of a guide differs very much in different parts of the country; for there are no fixed stations for the entertainment of travellers, where a guide can be supplied at a regular tariff. Generally speaking, a guide costs from one to two rix-dollars a day, for which he has to provide himself with a horse; but, of course, he has to be paid for his journey home, which naturally occupies the same time as the journey out. But in dealing directly with the peasants one is often exposed to great imposition. Thus on one occasion I had to pay seven rix-dollars for one day, though my guide only needed the following day to reach home. Still I must allow that such cases were exceptional, at least with me; for I was furnished with letters of introduction to persons of influence, who did all in their power to facilitate my progress, and relieve me of the disagreeableness of bargaining with my guide.

This day I reached Berufjörðr. On riding along the shores of Altafjörðr I saw a large flock of swans (Altafjörðr signifies "swan fjord"). I then ascended a low ridge which separates this fjord from Hamersfjörðr on the north. It is best to reach this place at low water; but as the tide was flowing when I got there I had to ride for some distance into the water along the coast before crossing. Icelandic horses are generally small, and do not reach higher than the breast of a full-grown man. They are, moreover, rather short, but for all that they can go a good pace, and are very comfortable to ride either at a canter or a gallop. It is not, however, every horse that can canter, and some can never be taught to do so. A good canterer in Iceland is prized at a much higher value than a trotter. The first will cost from forty to fifty rix-dollars, while the latter may be bought for twenty or twenty-five rix-dollars. Occasionally a hundred rix-dollars have been given for a horse, but this is something so unheard of, that it is alluded to as if it were a political event of the last importance. In consequence of the low prices of horses, they do not receive much attention at the hands of their owners. On the coast they are allowed to run loose during the winter, when they keep themselves on sea-weed; and by some of the fjords where the herbage is luxuriant on the mountains, they are allowed to search for the grass underneath the snow, that has not been mown in the summer; or else pick up heather, &c., in the fissures and clefts of the rocks. Thus in most parts of the country they have to provide themselves with food. Sometimes they get a little hay in very severe winters. They live, in fact, like the sheep, with the exception of the milch ewes, and have to find their own food all the year round. In the autumn they are assembled on the mountains, and driven home to their parish, where as far as possible, a look-out is kept that they do not starve or freeze to death in the winter. Thus, though there is no trouble in feeding them, all their manure is lost, which in Iceland is a great loss indeed. Horse-breeding, too, as well as many other things, is much neglected in the country. Stallions are allowed to run loose all the year round, so that there can be no choice in the breeding of a foal; and it is well-known, of course, what great influence a careful selection has in this matter. Another result, too, is, that there are an enormous number of foals born every year, whence the owner of a mare is put to the inconvenience of being unable to use her for some time. Mares, therefore, do not fetch nearly such high prices as horses. To obviate the above inconvenience they generally put the foal to a mare that has lost her own progeny. If at first she is not inclined to receive her step-child kindly, resort is had to a clever stratagem. The mare and foal are shut up in a dark place together, and after a little while she gets to be fond of her adopted one. There is no doubt that much might be done in improving the breed of horses in Iceland. Their numbers are rather large. In 1863 there were in round numbers 37,000 horses in the country, or rather more than half a horse for each person. A good many of them are exported. In the above year 828 were exported, principally to Scotland, and a few to Belgium. Owing to their diminutive height they would be very serviceable in coal mines; indeed it is for this purpose they are chiefly bought. The Icelandic horses, though larger than Shetlanders, are smaller than the Norwegian, and are as strong and as stoutly built. In a part of the south coast of Iceland the people eat horseflesh, and thrive on it. It is said to possess the quality of imparting a good complexion. When it is generally known that it possesses this virtue, horse-flesh will probably be sought after in all countries, especially by the fair sex. Possibly it may have been this fare which gave our ancestors those beautiful complexions for which they are renowned in the Sagas; for they were regular gluttons when horse-flesh came in their way. The three commandments of the Catholic priests to their proselytes were—"Not to have more than one wife;" "not to expose their children;" and "not to eat horse-flesh."

At this season of the year, that is, in the middle or towards the end of June, accordingly as the spring has been an early or late one, it is one of the occupations of the Icelanders to wean the lambs, whose mothers they purpose to keep as milch ewes. Very often a well-to-do farmer will have more than a hundred milch ewes. I often rode by flocks of those weaned lambs, which were roaming about and bleating in every conceivable key for their mothers. On the first day of being weaned the poor little things will eat nothing; on the second they eat as little; but on the third day they begin to get hungry, and after the sixth day will graze readily. The older sheep are now driven on to the mountains, where they roam about at pleasure, and require no other bounds to their wanderings than an impassable stream, or an impracticable mountain of ice. The lambs, however, are kept at home, as well as the milch ewes, and are driven to the farm morning and evening. A rich farmer in Iceland will own from 600 to 900 sheep, but this last number is the greatest that any single man owns in the country. On the other hand, the number of cows in the island is unimportant. Generally speaking, a farmer will keep one or two, and if he be very wealthy, from three to eight. Large stocks of cattle are very rare.

In 1863 the number of sheep in Iceland was about 350,000, and of cattle 22,000.

As sheep breeding is rather extensively carried on in Iceland, it is only natural that these animals have a variety of names in the language of the country. One of these is "kindr," and rather an amusing tale is related with reference to this word. It happened once that an Icelandic bishop paid a visit to Denmark, when he was presented to the queen, who, of course, was a German princess. The queen asked him in her own tongue, "Wie viele Kinder haben Sie?" Whereupon the worthy bishop, whose thoughts were doubtless directed to his well-stocked sheep-yard, replied, "Nine hundred, your majesty." The queen, who probably thought this number rather a large one, remarked that it must cost a good deal to feed so many mouths, whereupon the bishop replied, that such was not the case, for in the summer they found themselves in food, and when autumn came a third of them were killed and eaten. At this piece of information, her majesty, who was a Roman Catholic, made the sign of the cross before the barbarous bishop. The worthy prelate, whose name was Jón, had moreover the mishap, on being presented to her majesty, to slip down on the polished floor, whereby he assumed a position that was not quite in conformity with the rules of court etiquette, and was ever afterwards nicknamed "drottningarhlunkr." By way of explanation, it should be added that "drottning" signifies queen, and according to Jonsson's "Old Norsk" dictionary, "hlunkr" signifies a sound from a hollow place.

On my short journey from Hamarsfjörðr to Berufjörðr I had rainy and disagreeable weather, which caused the grey-looking plain to appear still greyer. In rainy weather one naturally does not stay to make many observations; accordingly I could only admire the numerous flat mountain walls, which rose up from the earth like walls of masonry, and intersected my road parallel with each other.

Whilst passing by Hamarsfjörðr I saw a beautiful eagle,

which quietly alighted on a rock about twenty paces off from my little caravan. Bird life in Iceland presents its peculiarities, one or two of which have already been touched upon. Our common birds, our crows and magpies, are wanting there; but their place is occupied by the raven, which is a very common bird, and which commits great depredations on the young lambs and eider-duck eggs, but still is unmolested by the people. It seems almost as if they entertained a sort of respect for black; for it would be easy enough to diminish the numbers of these birds, as in winter time they resort to the "bær" in the country, where they live off refuse, and could therefore easily be killed. However, they are allowed to remain in peace though great complaints are made about their bare-faced depredations.* Crows, therefore, and magpies are not found, but, on the other hand, it is wonderful to see how the wagtail can find its way over the sea. Of small birds, there are the stonechat, a small lark, and two other species, besides a number of song thrushes. The most common bird that I saw was, without question, the curlew. Golden plovers and snipes are also common. There are, moreover, several kinds of wading birds. A little bird, called "Odinshane," which frequents the banks of running or still water, was my special friend. It is about as large as a swallow, but has prettier colours and webbed feet, and might generally be seen drifting over the rippling wavelets of a brook wheresoever the current carried it.

Several beautiful and delicate kinds of grasses and plants are found in Iceland. The commonest flower, perhaps, is the *Dryas octopetala*, or "Mountain Avens," which may be found everywhere both on the fjelds and in the low-lands. It resembles the wood anemone, but its flower is somewhat larger.

* It is said in Iceland that the ravens meet in the autumn in "thing" (assembly), when they determine how they shall distribute themselves throughout the country in the ensuing winter.

The *Silene acaulis* (Moss Campion) and *Statice armeria* (Thrift) are also very common flowers; they are low in growth. The flowers of the moss campion are red, and resemble the wild pink, both in form and size; but the latter is of a pale pink colour, and bears its flowers in tufts. *Andromeda hypnoides* is a small creeping plant, like heather: it is often met with, and bears small white flowers, like the lily of the valley, but smaller and more solitary. There are several kinds of gentian in Iceland, many of which are remarkable for their pure indigo-blue colour. There is also a red kind of stonecrop, *Saxifraga hirculus* (Yellow Marsh Saxifrage) and the *Saxifraga oppositofolia*, which thrive high up on the bare fjelds, and smile a welcome down to the traveller below. The Icelandic flora is, as I have said, of a small and delicate nature, with pretty flowers of a bright colour. *Azalea procumbens* (Trailing Azalea), with its pretty red flowers, is a great favourite with the sheep.

The luxuriant herbage, on the sloping sides of the fjelds, consists of several different kinds of grass, mingled with the leaves of a stunted kind of willow, of a green or greyish-green colour, which is also greedily devoured by the sheep, and with mountain-birch of the same dwarfed growth. On the marshy land, several kinds of sedge may be found; and the meadow-grass on the "tun," or pasture-land near the farm, is over-strewn with the yellow ranunculus. Just as often, therefore, as the fjeld sides are covered with the *débris* from a mountain slip, and present a hideously waste appearance, are the valley slopes clothed with a luxuriant carpet of grass and flowers, and look lovely and inviting.

To return once more to Djúpivogur: the general aspect is rather of a dark nature, although the fjord presents many lovely views.

CHAPTER V.

The Mineralogy of Iceland—Zeolites—The Darwinian Theory again—Búlandstindr—Mountain Guides—Fissures and Mountain Slips—Mountain Formations—Denudation Valleys—Glacial Age—Phenomenon of Friction—Lava from the Glacial Age—The Glacial Age and the Fjords—Expedition to Greenland—Drift Ice—Discovery of Greenland—Discovery of America due to Iceland—Traits of Character—Glorious Sunsets—Reyðarfjörðe—Icelandic Spar—" Lausna" Stone—Mountain Passes—Legend of Hrútafjarðarhúls—Whale Fisheries—Novel Harpoon—A whole Nation fed by a Whale—Fishery of the Færoe Islands—Háskerðingr—A New Prophet in the Whale's Belly—Delicacies of the Sea—Mode of Preserving Fish—Fresh-water Fish.

IN a mineralogical point of view, Iceland cannot be said to be a rich country. Neither gold nor silver, copper, lead, zinc, nor any other ore, except a kind of ochreous iron ore, are to be found there. According to Stephensen, some slaggy fragments were hurled out from the crater of the Skaptár volcano, which contained some copper; and a mineral, also containing copper, was found in the sulphur springs near Krisuvík. But these are too unimportant to speak of. All the metal, therefore, that Iceland requires has to be imported; and perhaps it is as well that her consumption in this respect is not very large.

Hardly any agricultural implements exist in the country, as the ground is neither ploughed nor worked; while iron is not used in the building of small houses. It is principally employed for horse-shoes and nails; for spades, to cut the turf with, or to dig the small plot of "kaal rabi," or the potato land, belonging to the farm; for door-locks, pots and pans, and similar articles.

But though, when compared with its physical geography and its mountain formations, the mineralogy of Iceland falls into the shade, still, the minerals of the country, though few in number, from their beautiful and perfect forms, their white and transparent colours, and from the general beauty of their appearance, form one of the most prominent ornaments of our mineralogical museum.

During the fortnight I spent at Djúpivogur with the hospitable family, the Weywadts, I had abundant opportunities for admiring these beautiful objects of nature; and I found many splendid specimens in the rocks near Teigarhorn by Berufjörðr, at the foot of the gigantic Búlands peaks. These minerals belong to a class known under the common head of zeolites, because, under the blow-pipe, they froth up and phosphoresce. They consist of formations which came into existence subsequently to the appearance of the rocky mass in which they are found, and are therefore the product of the dismemberment of this. Near Teigarhorn, a little farm on the south side of Berufjörðr, there is a perpendicular wall of rock, extending along the shore for about half a mile, whose base is washed, at high tide, by the waves. It is here that the best specimens of zeolite are to be found. They lie in a stratum of basalts, more or less of a calcined nature, which is called amygdaloidal basalt, because the cavities in which they are found are, in mineralogical parlance, called "almonds," owing to their peculiar formation, which frequently resembles an almond in shape. From the constant action of the waves, and the violence of the storms in winter, these rocks break up little by little, and thus the "almonds" are washed out, so that at ebb-tide several specimens may be picked up on the sea-shore. They are, generally, however, more or less injured by the action of the waves, and from the joint influence of the air and the water upon their surface. To find really good specimens, therefore, one must search after them in the rock; that is to say, one must find the opening of an "almond" in the face of the rock, whence its treasures can be extracted in a perfect form. Sometimes they are as large as a man in circumference, and are widely dispersed; but it well repays the trouble to hunt for them. They are filled with a red, sticky kind of clay, which must be carefully washed off, to see the mineral in all its beauty.

There is something extremely captivating, and at the same time ennobling, in looking at a beautiful and perfectly formed crystal. Creative life here appears in such a simple clothing, that it seems almost to be exposed to the light of day; but in whichever way one turns the garment, it must at last be confessed that one is standing face to face with the same mighty Power which has given to the flower its lovely garb, and has provided the human spirit with wings.

But though simple in one respect, the formation of the crystal is in itself as subservient to law as any other of the forms of life with which the world is thronged. Indeed, the crystal, by its simplicity and by its mathematical exactness, affords the very best proof possible of the individuality or peculiarity of its form. "Natura non datur saltus" is an old and trite saying that has sprung out of a theorising brain which did not pay much regard to reality; for in mineralogy, especially, it is evidently and incontestably refuted. And yet within the last few years it has been used as the basis of a system that is now going the round of the world, as a pattern of sagacity and excellence—I mean the Darwinian system of development.

If there were no springs in nature, why should she not, for instance, be able to make an Iceland spar crystal, the main axis of which—that is, the supposed line between two diametrically opposite points on the crystal—should stand in any proportion to the bi-axis, a line similar to the first, but at right angles to it? Nature can form an Iceland spar crystal only where the major axis is a definite number of times greater or less than the minor axis. Thus it cannot form one in which the major and minor axes are of equal length; or in which the major stands in any assumed proportion to the minor axis. This proportion is on the contrary limited and defined, in other words, "Chance is entirely excluded." And yet it must be allowed that there is often a necessity for an Iceland spar crystal not to be nearly so long as, according to its composition, it should be; for instance, where there is not sufficient space for it in the cavity of the rock where it has begun to crystallise. And according to Darwin, the existence of necessity is a sufficient reason for nature to espouse the cause warmly. But how does nature treat the Iceland spar crystal, when it becomes too long for the space in which it is crystallising? By simply breaking it off! And surely this cannot be called fulfilling the self-developing tendency of an organisation; the exact reverse is in fact the case. Further, the same law to which the Iceland spar is in this case subservient, holds good throughout mineralogy. Everywhere there are springs in crystalline formations; and from this single example, compared with the Darwinian theory of development, it may be seen how opposed theoretical devices may be to positive reality. A scientific man of great eminence once remarked, with reference to this oracular expresssion, "Natura non datur saltus," that it appeared to him that the fact of man's being able to walk was a complete refutation of the truth of the assertion, for every step he takes is actually a spring; and in lifting the foot up and in placing it down again on the ground, there is an intermediate space that has been sprung over, both as regards time and distance; and there is a constant interruption in the uniformity with which a man advances in his gait, and his progressive motion is thus caused by springs or "saltus."

But we are wandering, perhaps, too far from the subject before us; we will therefore return to the point from which we set out, viz., to the wall of rock at Teigarhorn, with all its mineral wealth; and from thence set out once more on another excursion of a very practical description. We will therefore commence by scrambling up the colossal pyramid of the Búlandstindr, which rears itself aloft before us, and whose pointed summit literally reaches to the clouds; ay, often reaches beyond their cold embrace. On this day, however, it is quite free from clouds, the sun is shining brightly in the heavens, and the weather is perfectly calm, so that we may commence our journey without fear of danger. I will not, however, weary my reader by taking him up to the actual summit, for the simple reason that I did not ascend so high myself, but will merely ask him to accompany me a portion of the distance, namely, to a height of 3,388 feet above the sea, or about two-thirds of its altitude. Búlandstindr is the extreme peak of the mountain ridge which runs along the southern coast of Berufjörðr. Further inland it is cut into several alpine peaks, whose clefts are filled with masses of snow. On Búlandstindr itself these are wanting, for it is too steep to afford a resting-place for any large quantities of snow in the winter, so that the little that does collect there melts early in the spring. Viewed from the end of the fjord this mountain looks like a three-sided pyramid, raising itself up layer by layer, and terminating in a point. Never does the sea look so beautiful as when its azure blue bosom, glittering in the rays of the sun, is beheld from an eminence of one to two thousand feet. On the other side of the narrow fjord, the jagged and snow-covered mountain range of Kistufell, which further inland rises to a height of 3,499 feet, can plainly be seen from its neighbour on the south shore. The river in the valley below appears like a broad silvery stripe on a green ground, as rapid streams usually do when seen from a commanding height. The ascent of such a "tindr" (peak) requires, as may be imagined, no little exertion. After partly riding and partly clambering some distance up the slope, one has to ascend through a "gil," or gully, in the mountain side, formed by a watercourse in the spring. This "gil" is both narrow and deep, and is full of stones, over which one ascends as if one were going up-stairs. Presently a jutting ledge is reached, where one can rest after the fatigue one has incurred. Thereupon the ascent continues over successive strata of basalts. This is not very difficult work as long as the path lies over the mountain slips, but every now and then a nearly perpendicular wall comes in the way, which must be surmounted by clambering. It is advisable, after having passed over two or three such walls, to pile up a few heaps of stones here and there to mark the route by which the descent shall be made, for a mountain wall cannot be ascended at any and every point; on the contrary, it is necessary to make a very careful choice in this respect, and thus the ascent assumes a zig-zag direction. For it is, of course, always much more difficult to be able to choose the route by which the descent shall be made, owing to the ledges and declivities, which incline outwards, and thus shut out the mountain slope below from view, than it is to choose the route for the ascent.

After I had ascended some distance up Búlandstindr I met, unexpectedly, with two guides, besides the one I had taken with me. These were a couple of rams, who were airing themselves up there, and who, probably, took our approach as a hint to move on, for they at once started off, certainly with much more dexterity and agility than either I or my companion displayed; and as they always selected the easiest path up the slopes, we found it advisable to follow in their tracks.

As I have already stated, I did not reach the actual top of Búlandstindr, for the sun was already beginning to set, and there was still at least 1,000 feet to clamber up. I should, moreover, have been obliged to make a considerable *détour* in order to complete the ascent, for it was utterly impracticable from the side on which I was. At the altitude which I had reached, I was surprised to find strata evidently of lava formation on the mountain; for Búlandstindr is not a volcano; in fact, there are no volcanoes on the east coast of the country. This discovery, therefore, confirms the opinion that has generally been formed, though of late voices have been raised against it, that the basaltic formation is not foreign to volcanic agency, although the period when the basaltic strata were heaved up in a red-hot state from the interior of the earth is very remote, and though it probably took place beneath the surface of the sea. The strata in Búlandstindr, however, were found in the upper, and consequently the younger divisions of the basaltic formation. But in the older divisions, also, there are such convincing proofs of the molten condition in which they must have formerly existed, that there can hardly be much doubt about the matter.

It is extremely interesting to wander along a mountain slope in Iceland without ascending or descending it, but keeping at about the same level. At a little distance from one the slope will appear to be even and smooth, even though it be of a rather undulating nature, and one would imagine that one could go straight on, when suddenly a gully, or a cleft, along which a rapid stream is tearing along, comes in the way, and renders a long *détour* necessary. I noticed this to be the case at the foot of Búlandstindr, where the Búlands stream runs along between perpendicular walls of a hundred feet in height, as well as on other mountain inclines in the country.

The Icelandic basaltic formation is peculiar for its abrupt and precipitous character, while the mountain inclines and lower rocky slopes are very steep, owing to their having been formed by rock slips, and which, though overgrown with grass, assume a sloping position. But the slips of trachytic rocks, on which no vegetation appears, are most difficult of all to traverse. They have no alternation of slip and stratum, for they are not arranged like basalts, but wherever they appear the whole face of the rock is covered with loose stones, so that in ascending one of them one often, in the literal sense of the expression, takes two steps backwards to one forwards. Slips of this character occur in the neighbourhood of Djúpivogur. As I should have had to ascend this in order to reach the firm rock from which it had issued, I first of all took my way through a gully, in order to avoid the slip; but it was a difficult matter to advance, for sometimes we had to crawl on our hands and feet, and even then we did not feel safe; or else we had to leap from one ledge to the other; but when I began to clamber up the slip itself it was with difficulty I could get a foothold, for the loose stones kept rolling down at every step.

Perhaps these short notices (and I will not weary my reader with them any more) may serve to give some idea of the difficulty of climbing up or along an Iceland mountain. It generally takes the best part of the day to climb a mountain of two thousand feet in height. This is no great altitude, certainly, in comparison with the Alps, or the tops of Kjölen and of the Dovre Field, in Norway; but when it is remembered that these latter rise up from a platform which itself is some thousand feet above the level of the sea, while the Icelandic mountains often emerge directly from the sea level, the relation between the two is considerably changed. If, for instance, in order to reach the foot of a mountain which is 5,000 feet above the sea one has first to traverse a plateau of 2,000 feet, in which both valleys and small heights alternate with each other, of course this mountain, in comparison with the plateau below, is not higher than one of 3,000 feet that rises directly from the sea. The position of the Icelandic mountain tops—the greater number of them and the most remarkable among them are usually to be found close by, or in the neighbourhood of, the sea, for the interior of the land consists for the most part of table-land from which the Jökuls rear themselves up—explains the gigantic appearance of even a comparatively low mountain.

An excursion up to the mountain ridge by the side of Berufjorðr conveys a very good illustration of the denudation or detrition to which these mountains have been exposed through the lapse of ages. The upper surface of its jagged ridge, which consists of fragments of basaltic and other rocks, gives evident proofs of the changes it has undergone since its formation. The ridge itself is now so sharp, and so jagged with protruding peaks, that it is only the exception that one can wander along it Only a few scattered traces of the topmost strata of rock, which originally must have been in parallel, or nearly parallel, layers, remain now; all the superincumbent mass has been carried away. We will devote a little further space to this subject.

Valleys or defiles, as it is known, may exist from two causes, which are essentially different to each other. Either a depression in the earth's crust may take place, whereby a valley is formed in the hollow between the elevated portions of the strata of the soil; or by erosion, when the matter which once filled the valley is crushed and carried away in the shape of stones, *débris*, and mud, by the agency of floods, glaciers, and the like. The first we will denominate "elevation" valleys; the second, "erosion" valleys. To this latter class the valleys of Iceland belong; and this may plainly be seen to be the case in the fjords of the eastern coast, and in the valleys which debouch into them. The rocky walls which enclose these valleys—the fjords themselves are nothing else than the elongation of the valleys continued beneath the water—are, for instance, all cut at an obtuse angle; their strata, therefore, are not curved, but maintain a parallel position throughout the whole of their extent; and those strata whose ends rise up and form the fjeld side on one side of the fjord, are generally continued on its other shore. But this may be seen even more plainly to be the case in the gullies which debouch at different places into the valleys of the fjords. In Seyðisfjörðr especially, I remember to have seen gullies in which the basalts on the one side correspond to those on the other side. And to this erosion the sharp and jagged outline, as well as the more rounded form observable in the Icelandic basaltic formation, may entirely be ascribed.

Without any question, this extensive erosion is due to the vast ranges of snow mountains, and the glaciers that accompanied them in former ages. Nearly every low-lying spot in the country, where the hard rock is visible, bears traces of their agency.

When we speak of former ages, we refer to an age which, as far as we know, was anterior to the appearance of the human race on the northern portion of the globe; or, in other words, to that section of the post-tertiary age which is called the glacial age. From certain circumstances that have been observed in the northern portions of Europe and America, it has been ascertained that such a geological age has existed on the globe; but the evident traces of it that exist in Iceland have not, I believe, been sufficiently brought into notice; and it is for this reason that I have wished to direct attention to them.

These traces may be observed on the low heights round Reykjavik, where they appear as small, and mostly parallel, scratches of but little depth on the surface of the rock. These scratches are formed by the action of the glaciers on the rocks beneath them, or rather by the stones which have become frozen into the mass of ice in passing over the rocks. A glacier, it will be remembered, advances with its whole mass: so that it is not only its lowest end which is in a state of progression. It is especially on the heights or in the defiles at the heads of the fjords that traces of the effects the glaciers have exerted can be most plainly seen. Here the scratches are always apparent on the surface of the firm rock; they moreover have a direction parallel with that of the valley, which was also the direction of the glacier during its descent.

This parallelism is especially conspicuous here, as these defiles lie at some considerable depth, whence their direction is always fixed; so that one can pronounce with certainty beforehand as to the direction the scratches should have. The loose rocks, too, frequently show marks of these abrasions, as well as the firm rocks; and thus a proof is afforded of the wide extent of the Jökuls in ancient times. I have noticed these scratches at many places in the country, especially on Fjarðarheiði, over which the usual road to Seydisfjörðr runs, as well as on Eskifarðarheiði, north-west of a fjord of the same name. But I found the most perfect scratches on the heights on both sides of the river Blandá, along the road from Mœlifell over Storisandur. They were of moderate depth, and looked as if they had been made with a plane, and were parallel with each other and with the direction of the valley. Together with this abrasion, the surface of the rock assumes a rounded, almost a polished, form; and these are comprised under the one name of the phenomenon of friction, from reasons which it is easy to comprehend. If the lower portions of the Icelandic basaltic and Palagonite formation were not covered over with sand and earth and stones as they are, the existence of the phenomenon of friction would be everywhere apparent; but as it is, the surfaces of the rocks are to a great extent hidden from view. The most beautiful instances of the rounded surfaces of rocks, which the Swiss call "roches moutonnées," may be seen along the north shore of the interior of Reyðarfjörðr, in the east of the country, near the road leading to Hólmar. The surfaces of the rocks there are quite rounded from the shore to a good distance up the face of the mountain. No doubt that a huge glacier once dashed over them. On these "roches moutonnées" near Reyðarfjörðr lies, moreover, a bank of pebbles, thus affording an additional proof of the intimate connection that exists between banks of sand and pebbles with glaciers.

In order to be able to form a correct idea about Iceland in its existing form, it is necessary to attribute its rent and uneven surface to the influence of the Jökuls; and inversely it is much easier to imagine this to have been the case in Iceland, where the incessant action of the Jökuls can be so readily referred to, than in other countries, like Sweden, *e.g.*, where the phenomenon of friction also appears on an extensive scale, but where the remote position of the glaciers weakens, as it were, one's belief in their former extent and agency. The Icelandic basaltic rocks, with their remarkable illustrations, such as Búlandstindr,

Esja, &c., have thus mainly retained their form from the Jökuls having carried away the masses which united the now dismembered strata into one. Where a deep valley or a fjord is now found, there was once a continuous stratum of rock, which was subsequently carried away. An excellent instance of this is afforded in the neighbourhood of Reykjavik.

The rocks which form the extensive heights round Reykjavik, to the north, to the foot of Esja, and to the south, to Hafnarfjörðr, to the east, over Mosfellsheiði, and which are met with in the district south of Okjökul, consist of old lava, as may plainly be perceived from their composition. Although during its formation this lava flowed in a broad valley or over a lowland, where, like the lava of modern times, it extended in horizontal strata of uniform thickness, it now forms a hilly and undulating country, where it appears on the tops of hills of from one to two hundred feet in height, and on the coast, and even on some of the islands in the sea. But as lava in a fluid state could not possibly at first have occupied such a bed—for of course it could not flow up hill—provided its course was not obstructed, no other theory can be found to account for the formation which it now assumes than that of erosion. And as the bare surface of this lava, moreover, together with the loose stones and *débris* that cover it, bear traces of abrasion from glaciers, there is no need to set up ingenious theories concerning the erosion, which can be proved to have taken place; and further, one can see from this fact the best proof of the glacial theory in olden time.

A celebrated American author, Dana, has endeavoured to prove that all the fjords that intersect the coasts of the northern countries of Europe and America have been produced by glaciers. If the reason be asked why these countries, whose climates are now temperate, should once have been entirely covered with snow and ice, we reply by asking another question. What is the reason why Greenland, even in our days, is entirely covered with a continuous crust of ice, with the exception of the narrow tract of coast on the west, where the Danish colonies are situate—though the southern portion of this land reaches far below the parallel of latitude under which Iceland lies? Unquestionably it arises from the formation of the surface of the earth on this portion of the globe; from the distribution of land and water; the direction of the currents of the sea; the height of the crust of the earth above the sea; and from other causes. It may be supposed, therefore, that similar causes have occasioned the distribution of masses of ice and snow over the northern parts of these two continents.

Now that we are speaking of Greenland, I will briefly mention what has come to my knowledge of the voyage of discovery made to the eastern coast of that country in 1865.

During my first stay at Reykjavik an English steamer arrived, having on board, in addition to its crew, sixteen emigrants, eight of whom were Danish, and eight were Englishmen, or people from other countries, under the conduct of a Mr. Taylor, who, accompanied by his wife and a child of ten months old, and a physician, who also had his wife on board, was bent on seeking land on the east coast of Greenland and on wintering there. Several conjectures were hazarded as to the object of their journey; amongst which the most probable was, that the expedition had been equipped to seek for the costly minerals which are to be found in Greenland. Mr. Taylor had resided on the west coast several years, and had probably received such information from the Esquimaux as to lead to the present expedition, which had been fitted out at the expense of an English firm, and which cost, I believe, 250,000 rix-dollars. The expedition seemed to be well equipped, and the vessel was extremely well fitted out. Among other things which they took out with them was a house, constructed of timber, for use in the colony, together with the requisite furniture, and a quantity of goods to trade with among the natives they expected to find there. The ladies, too, had a pianoforte with them, in order to render their sojourn in Greenland more agreeable. With many good wishes for success, Mr. Taylor set sail from Reykjavik in the beginning of June, but returned in the course of the summer without having been able to find a place where he could land. The distance between Iceland and Greenland is only about three hundred miles. On arriving at a spot half way between them, which with a good wind only takes a day, the Jökuls in either country are discernible. The vessel had reached Greenland in about latitude 63° or 64°, but met a quantity of closely packed drift-ice at a distance of about twenty-eight miles from land. When the vessel was made fast to it, it was found to drift over forty-two miles in twenty-four hours, thus proving that the ice was not united to the shore. With a telescope from the maintop, nothing but snow and ice could be seen, not even the smallest patch of earth; so that the boundary line between the drift-ice, and the ice which was connected with the shore, could not be ascertained with any degree of certainty. Mr. Taylor accordingly altered the course of the vessel four degrees to the north along the edge of the ice, but could never get nearer to land than from fourteen to twenty miles, owing to the vast packs of ice. He, therefore, returned to Reykjavik, but soon started again to try and discover a landing place more to the south. I did not hear anything more about him before I left Iceland. But in November of the same year news arrived from Copenhagen that this expedition, too, had been a failure. They had, therefore, steered through Davis's Straits, and the crew had gone ashore on Cumberland Island, opposite to the colony of Good Hope, on the western coast of Greenland. The year previously Mr. Taylor had undertaken a similar expedition, which had also turned out unsuccessfully. The cold Polar stream which flows between Iceland and Greenland drives the ice against the east coast of Greenland, and renders a close approach to land impossible. It seems, according to Mr. Taylor's observations, that this coast of Greenland is entirely enveloped in ice and snow; if such be the case it must be uninhabitable even if one could get in to land through the belt of ice. The drift-ice visits the northern coasts of Iceland, but seldom passes Lánganæs, the north-east point of the country, as it is met there by the Gulf Stream. It appears every year along the north coast of the country, though it does not always extend so close in to land as to hinder the coasting traffic. After it has become connected with the land it does not affect the climate much, but during the time of its coming and going it is always bad weather.

Occasionally it happens that the ice extends below Lánganæs, and fills all the fjords on the east coast; sometimes, moreover, it reaches to the south coast. Once during the last ten years this occurred, and put a stop to all traffic in that part of the country till the month of August, when it drifted away again. In Faxafjörðr, or in Breidifjörðr, on the west coast, however, the drift-ice never settles. Once two large whales were driven in with the ice into Skagafjörðr, on the north coast, and were in such a weak state that they were killed without difficulty. The ice was so closely packed that they could not dive down through it. Ice-bears sometimes come to land in this way, but are, of course, soon killed.

To Icelanders the honour of being the discoverers of Greenland and of America is due. Gunnbjörn was the first to sight Greenland, when on one occasion he had been overtaken by a tempest and driven out to sea. This occurred shortly after the first colonization of Iceland; but no further attempts were made to find land before the year 982, when "Eirikr rauði" undertook a voyage of discovery thither. After he had employed nearly three years in exploring the coast, and had taken possession of such places as he considered eligible, he returned to Iceland, where he spoke of the new country, which he called Greenland, in high terms. He managed to instil a great desire into the bosoms of his countrymen to explore the land; and accordingly, in the following year, a fleet, consisting of twenty-five vessels, sailed for Greenland, of which, however, only fourteen reached their destination. Between this new settlement and the mother-country a regular intercourse took place; so that, after the introduction of Christianity, about the year 1000, several churches were built along the coast, and a bishop was set over them. Norway, Denmark, and Sweden continued their intercourse with this settlement for a period of more than 350 years. In the year 1406, the last bishop was sent over to Greenland; but from that date, nothing further was heard of the settlement. An access to the east coast of Greenland, where this settlement has by some been supposed to have been situated, has subsequently been impossible, owing to the drift-ice. The fate, therefore, of the settlers is involved in uncertainty. Many persons have been of opinion that the settlement was situated on the western coast, where the Danish colonies now are, and not on the eastern coast at all. In the Sagas, indeed, an east and a west settlement are alluded to; but there is no reason at all why they may not both have existed on the same coast of the country—namely, on the west. When Greenland was again taken possession of by Europeans, in the beginning of the last century, remains of old dwellings were found there. The whole settlement probably died out, or was exterminated by the Esquimaux.

The first discovery of America, too, is due to Iceland in the year 1001. In that year, Bjarni Herjulfssonur, on a voyage from Iceland to Greenland, was driven by a violent storm out into the Atlantic. After sailing for some days, he discovered a beautiful wooded country, where plains and rising grounds alternated with each other along the coast. But, as he could not prevail on his crew to land, he returned to Greenland with a favourable breeze, where he arrived in six days. His glowing descriptions of the country implanted a desire for further investigation in the bosom of his countryman, Leifr Eirikssonnur, who accordingly set out from Norway with a vessel manned by thirty-five men. To the south-west of Greenland, Leifr discovered land, which, according to the description given, is supposed to have been Labrador; but, further to the south, he found the same wooded land which Bjarni had discovered. Thereupon he determined to explore its coast for some distance; and two days afterwards he came, with a north-westerly wind, to an island that was separated from the mainland by a strait. After sailing through this strait, he came to a beautiful inland sea, on the shores of which he erected a winter dwelling. The sea teemed with splendid salmon, and the grass retained its fresh appearance throughout the winter. The days here were not so short as in Greenland and Iceland; for on the shortest winter-day the sun was nine hours above the horizon. One of the crew, who was a German, having discovered that grapes grew wild there, Leifr named the land "Vinland." Subsequently it was visited by Þorvaldr, Leifr's brother, who, however, was killed by the natives; but a settlement which took root in the country continued to trade with them for two hundred years.

During my sojourn at Djúpivogur, the commercial season commenced in earnest. Farmers came in with their wool, to pay what they owed from the previous year, and took fresh supplies home on credit. At such a time, everything is life and bustle. Every comer, of course, is treated to brandy and coffee—it would not do if the merchant were not to observe this custom—and they congregate, and talk and make merry outside and inside the shops; for by nature the Icelander possesses a happy disposition, and is not given to be morose. He is fond of laughing, is given to talking, and, apparently at least, does not allow himself to be depressed by the cares and vexations of the world. He is contented and happy, and, as far as my experience goes, has no sour looks about him. He is moreover very witty in his conversation, and sometimes displays an astonishing proficiency in his favourite subjects, history and geography.

An Iceland farmer, therefore, may be very excellent company—provided, of course, that one understands the language—for he will make no foolish remarks, or give stupid answers to questions, as their brethren often do in some other lands! On the contrary, they seem to have uncommonly good heads on their shoulders, which the merchants—this by way of parenthesis—rather regret than otherwise. It is the custom, for instance, for the farmers in a district to club together, and to send a man to the trading stations to enquire at which house goods are sold the cheapest. This being ascertained, they all deal there. In consequence of this, the merchants are obliged to observe uniform prices in the most important districts.

Amongst each other the Icelanders as a rule are ready to give assistance when needed, and are very liberal. If a farmer has had the misfortune to lose his sheep, for instance, the other farmers in the neighbourhood will each subscribe a sheep to compensate him for his loss. When acquaintances meet, they laugh and talk, and kiss and hug each other, using all the while the most endearing epithets, such as, "my good," "my blessed," or "my beloved friend!"

Sometimes it is rather difficult to believe that all this is meant seriously. A Sysselmand in the east of the country told me that once two parties were disputing before the court; and after he had succeeded in reconciling them by arbitration, one of them in a fit of exasperation said to the other, "You lie, my beloved friend!" Still although such an exuberance of heartiness may occasionally be put on, I am convinced that it is often genuine.

I left Djúpivogur on the 10th of July; and followed a stony path along the south side of Berufjörðr, having occasionally to ride up actual flights of steps. Presently I came to a still more stony road over a mountain height named Öxi, which separated the narrow valley at the inner end of the fjord from another deep valley, named Skriðdalr, which again debouches into the wide valley of Lagarfljót. Together with these heights and mountain passes, masses of snow now began to belong to the order of the day; for owing to the late spring and the cold summer there was still a great deal of snow on the lower ledges of the mountains. The ascent of Öxi from the valley below is very steep, and can with difficulty be made on horseback; the terrain is stony, and of a sombre hue, while dark walls of basalts shoot out at several places. Yet though, perhaps, of rather a dull colouring, Berufjörðr is not destitute of natural beauty.

The glorious sunsets I saw from Djúpivogur will long live in my memory. Looking towards the fjord from this spot in the evening, the rays of the sun seemed to unite into a dazzling column of a roseate hue, and presented a sight more lovely than the imagination, at least my imagination, can possibly conjure up. Like an airy cushion it rested for a while upon the water, till it faded and finally disappeared. Only on two occasions do I remember to have seen such lovely and magnificent sunsets in Iceland; once near Reykjavik, where all the mountain tops were dyed purple by the reflection from the brilliantly illumined bank of clouds behind which the sun sank down; and a second time on my journey between Mývatn and Husavík, on the north coast. The sun had already gone down behind a sloping mountain wall, which bounded the horizon on the left towards the north; but presently a little portion of its dark red disc peeped forth from behind the blue rocks, and soon the whole of its orb appeared once more in view upon a cloudless sky. Gradually it seemed to slide down the mountain slope, as if its track lay there, and majestically sank to rest in the bosom of the sea.

Skriðdalr derives its name from a large rock-slip, which covers its bottom with small hillocks; but it is old and overgrown with grass. It is related in Landámabók that a man named Hrafnkell had repaired to this valley; but at night he dreamed that some one came to him and warned him not to remain there. He therefore quitted it, whereupon the slip immediately took place.

From Öxi, through Skriðdalr, the traveller will come to the parsonage of Þingmúli, where the hospitable pastor Sira Þorgrímr will give him an excellent reception. From thence the road lies over a mountain to the east, named Þórdalsheiði, whose summits sleep in eternal snow. It is pretty level and good, though it inclines rather steeply down to the magnificent Reyðarfjörðr, the most important of the fjords on this coast, and which is surrounded with peaked mountain ridges. The name of this fjord, which has been changed by the Danes into Röde-fjord, is derived from an Icelandic word "reyðr," signifying a whale; probably because whales, of which there are sundry varieties on the Icelandic coast, have shown a predilection for this particular fjord. In the same way several other Icelandic names have been Danicised. The genuine Icelander does not approve of this treatment, but the Danes do not seem to pay much attention to his feelings in this respect. At the present day, when maps of Iceland are so easy of access, the names of places ought not to be submitted to this treatment; but so long as this is the case in written language, there is no wonder that it is also done in daily conversation. Many persons may look upon it as trivial and unimportant; but for a little nation like Iceland, that would rather die than sacrifice its nationality, such is not the case.

From the north side of Reyðarfjörðr there is a little lateral fjord, named Eskifjorðr, on the shores of which there is a trading station. The mercantile village of Eskifjörðr is a well-known spot, at least, as concerns the mineralogy of Iceland, as the traveller generally makes an excursion from it to the place where the double spar is found. Double spar is a colourless, perfectly transparent, calcareous spar; the double refraction, which is common to calcareous spar and to a host of other minerals, can therefore be plainly observed in it. This double refraction shows itself thus:—An object viewed through two opposite and parallel surfaces of the transparent mineral appears to be double. This can be best observed by laying a piece of double spar over a written line, when two parallel lines will be seen instead of one. An object is rendered visible, as is known, not from rays of light issuing from the eye to the object, but from the rays of light which are thrown on the object from the sun, or from any other luminous body, being reflected from it upon the human eye. The reason, therefore, that one can see writing is, that light is reflected from the writing to the eye;

and yet it is not the black characters themselves that one sees, for black cannot reflect light, but it is the intermediate space of white whose outline is impressed on the eye. When, however, a piece of double spar is laid over writing, the writing, as I have said, appears to be double. This is caused by the rays of light issuing from the paper, or reflected from the mineral, being divided into two, whereby their direction is somewhat changed. Refraction takes place in all substances of homogeneous density; such as glass, water, sulphuric acid, air, &c. When a ray of light passing through glass is met by the surface of water it breaks or changes its direction; but refraction in connection with distribution, or double refraction, as it is termed, is only found to exist in a certain class of minerals, of which double spar is the principal one, because it is found in large pieces of extraordinary clearness and transparency. Perfectly transparent pieces of one to two hundred pounds weight have been found. Such large pieces, however, are very rarely known. The bed on the north side of Reyðarfjörðr, in which double spar is found, lies in basaltic rock, which in some places is calcined or transformed, and it is clear that the spar is the result of this transformation; for it appears in small veins, alternately with a greenish mineral, which is the surplus of the transformed basalts. But as great things are often hidden under a mean and insignificant covering, so it is the case here. The main mass of the calcareous spar consists only of the common white, coarse-grained spar, in which the double spar must be sought by breaking the mineral up in the usual way. It appears only in scattered cavities of the mass, on the walls of which the transparent double spar has become crystallised. In these cavities it is enveloped in a red clay, like the zeolites at Berufjörðr, which has to be removed, as well as a thin crust of yellowish and nearly opaque calcareous spar; so that one may truly say that it has been well set, as may be seen from its preservation in a state of spotless purity for many thousands of years in the rock.

Sometimes drops of water are found enclosed within the double spar, which, among other things, proves that the agency of water has had a share in its formation. It is quite clear that double spar is a secondary formation; that is to say, the basaltic rock which was heaved up in a molten condition became transformed at a later period, as we have already remarked in speaking of the formation of zeolites, and this took place with the co-operation of water that had oozed through the rock. Double spar is of no especial practical importance, as it is only used in the manufacture of some optical instruments. In mineral collections, however, it occupies a prominent position. In Copenhagen there is (or rather was) a perfectly transparent piece of 160 lbs. weight (176 lbs. Eng.) for sale; it was valued at 400 rix-dollars.

The mountains in the neighbourhood of Eskifjörðr, and near Berufjörðr and Seyðisfjörðr, gave me a little insight into the architecture of the basaltic formation in this part of the country. I will only, however, briefly allude to it. I found that strata of compact or amygdaloidal basalt of ten or twenty, or even fifty feet in thickness, alternating partly with strata of vitrified almond stone, partly with strata of a fine argillaceous tufa, partly also with strata of lava breccia, or strata that looked exactly as if they consisted of compressed floating pieces of lava, as was the case in Grákollur, near Reyðarfjörðr, and like the upper strata of Búlandstindr. This plainly shows that the basalts have been projected from the interior of the earth in a red-hot, molten condition, though, of course, as this took place under the surface of the sea it may be difficult, if not impossible, to ascertain the position of the places from whence they were projected. It may often be a matter of difficulty to decide from whence one or other of the older lava streams originated, and yet comparatively they are much younger than the basalts, and have flowed out after the land has been raised above the surface of the sea; and, moreover, generally they have not been submitted to that excessive erosion that took place in the glacial period. This being the case, how much more difficult must it be to point out the sources from which the older basaltic formations issued in remote ages.

As this is a chapter partly treating of stones, I will here mention a substance which is found on the sea-coasts of Iceland, and which the natives call "lausnastein." It is not, indeed, a stone at all, as they surmise in Iceland, but the fruit of a leguminous growth. It is brought by the Gulf Stream from America, and is round, flat, and as hard as stone, and from one to three inches in diameter.*

This "stone," according to the popular belief, possesses the remarkable property, that when the water in which it is boiled is partaken of by women or animals that are pregnant, it is attended with very beneficial and successful results. This stony fruit undergoes no change from being boiled, and can therefore be used several times. It is held in great esteem in Iceland.

From Eskifjörðr I made an excursion to Seydisfjörðr, on the north, one of the narrowest but most beautiful of the many beautiful fjords on the east coast of Iceland. On riding from Eskifjörðr to Seydisfjörðr one meets with two mountain paths: the first is over Eskifjarðarheiði, and leads from the sea to Lagarfljótsdalr, or Fljótsdalr, as it is called on the map; and the other is over a "heiði," called Fjarðarheiði, leading from the above-named valley to the sea. It is necessary to make a

* The fruits of several other plants are found, such as *Dolichos urens*, *Entada gigalobium*.

considerable *détour* if one wishes to pass from the one to the other of these places, for the direct road over the mountain is impassable for any but foot-passengers, on account of the masses of snow on it and its precipitous character. On both "heiði" there is a good deal of snow. In summer-time it is loose and soft, so that it will seldom bear all the four legs of a horse at one time. First one of the animal's fore-legs will break through, next a hind leg; or else it will lie with its stomach on the snow, with all four legs protruding through the crust of snow, in which case the rider will do best to dismount, as the clever beast will speedily regain its legs. Underneath these snow-fonds streams of different sizes trickle along, over which the snow, which melts on its undermost side, lies like an arch. In crossing over these fragile bridges it is as well to make oneself as light in the saddle as possible, otherwise, should the arch of snow break, a cold bath would be the consequence. The clayey *débris* which the Jökuls have left behind them on these heiði in former days is often so soft that the horses sink down into it up to their knees, and the rider, therefore, is not much better off than when his steed was lying on its stomach in the melting snow. Here and there, too, the "heiði" is filled with large and small stones, with pools of water between.

On the descent from Eskifjarðarheiði to Túngudalr, one of the lateral valleys of the broad valley of Lagurfjót, there is a snow-fond which is so steep that the horses have to be led down it. There is a similar one on the ascent of Hellisheiði, between the above-named valley and Vopnafjördr. These steep ledges are called "brekka." Shortly after my arrival in Reykjavik I had received an initiatory introduction to these kinds of roads, when I crossed Esja; but it was spring then, and I did not think I should have to experience many such tiresome journeys in the summer.

The following story about Hrútafjarðarháls, a "heiði" in the north-west, will give a good idea of the inaccessibility of these "heiði" generally, and of the repute in which they are held even in Iceland. Two old women once were engaged in a quarrel, in which, as is often the case, blows and bad language were freely made use of. At last one of the old women expressed a wish that the other were in the power of his Satanic majesty, whereupon the party thus addressed, who thought such a wish would be even too good for her opponent, wished in return that she might be doomed to ride over Hrútafjarðarháls.

When I rode over Fjarðarheiði, on the 15th of June, snow fell, and on the following night there was a good quantity of snow on the mountains near Segyisfjörðr. The next day was very cold, and was rainy and stormy. On the sea-coast the thermometer only rose to 5° C. On these days the weather was generally bad throughout the country; the snow fell in such quantities in a district in the north that they had to house the sheep; but, naturally, it disappeared after a day or two.

I had two objects in view in visiting Seyðisfjörðr. One of these was to see an interesting mineral formation, namely, a layer of surturbrand, a kind of brown coal, which is found at different places of the country, though in small quantities. My other object was to acquaint myself with a contrivance for catching whales, invented by an American named Mr. Roys. I shall therefore have to lay an embargo on my readers' attention while I allude to both of these curiosities in turn. Let us begin with the whales.

Mr. Roys, who is about fifty years of age, is the son of a farmer in the State of New York, North America. When sixteen years of age, being in a weak state of health, his doctor ordered him to go to sea. Accordingly, he went on board a whaler, took a liking to the occupation, and ever afterwards followed it. His eldest brother manages the farm at home, but four of the younger ones accompany him on his whale-fishing expeditions. Mr. Roys has visited several parts of the world after whales, and has chased the Greenland whale, &c.; but as the whale of these seas is fat, lazy, and stupid, and therefore easier to catch, it has become gradually rarer; accordingly, Mr. Roys has begun to look after some other representatives of the valuable whale family, which he has found in numbers round the coasts of Iceland.

These are certainly not so fat, and are more wary and nimble, in so far as one can imagine nimbleness to exist in a whale, and are, therefore, not so easy to get near as the Greenland whales; but this very fact proved only an additional incitement to Mr. Roys to display his Yankee nature, and to invent some means of catching them. Formerly they employed the old plan of harpooning the whale, and of letting it go for one or two days with the harpoon sticking in it till it died, when it floated on the surface. But if this plan is adopted with the thin whales of Iceland, they will simply sink to the bottom and die, and will not come up to the surface till they have begun to get rotten; and further, the current will have carried them away to some distance. In addition to this, the Iceland whales are more lively in their movements, and therefore expose the harpoon-boats to the greatest danger; and this is the cause of their having hitherto been left unmolested. They are by no means despicable objects to capture, for a whale of 72 feet to 80 feet long yields a return of 2,000 rix-dollars, if it be properly managed. Mr. Roys was fully alive to this fact. Accordingly, he had made an explosive grenade, at one end of which was fastened a sharp, three-edged knife, while at the other, a rocket with a harpoon is attached;

the first to explode the grenade, and the latter to hook the boat on to the animal; and with these instruments he now endeavours, not exactly to blow up the whale into the air, but to kill it on the spot, so that it can neither run off with the boats, or sink before it has been towed to land. The plan succeeded, or at all events succeeded sometimes; thus showing that the principle is correct, even though the result has not as yet turned out to be as satisfactory as was hoped. For Mr. Roys had been sanguine enough to think that he would be able to catch an enormous number of the whales which swarm round the coasts and in the fjords of the country. But in this year (1865) he had not taken more than seven or eight whales; and this he did not consider to be enough. He had, however, shot a score of whales, or more; but of course in order to produce the proper effect, it is necessary that the shot must strike the whale in a mortal place, so that death may immediately ensue, when it will float on the surface. If they are hit in the right place, death ensues in five or ten minutes; and if the sea is not too heavy they can generally be towed to land. The day of my arrival at Seyðisfjörðr, they were trying to tow a whale that they had killed into the fjord; but the animal was inconsiderate enough to sink at about a mile's distance from the landing-place where it was to have been cut up. On another occasion they had shot a whale, but had probably only hit it on the tail; for it dived down at such a prodigious rate, that they were only just in time to prevent the boat from sinking by cutting the rope. It is supposed that a whale must possess a certain amount of fat to enable it to float, and that therefore it is the thinnest whales that sink to the bottom; and further, that its floating capabilities depend on whether the gas from the powder remains in the whale or escapes from it, which of course depends further on the spot where the shot takes effect.

A NEW HARPOON.

The accompanying picture may serve to give an idea of the instrument used. The knife and the grenade protrude outside the wide iron tube, which rests on the man's shoulder, and which contains the rocket, with four small harpoons attached to an iron rod behind. The rocket is enclosed in an iron cylinder, which is screwed fast to the grenade and to the iron rod to which the harpoons are attached. The iron cylinder in which the rocket lies is about a foot long; and the grenade and knife together make about another foot in length. The first of these,

A harpooner.

which is about as large as two clenched fists, is filled with a pound of powder, which on exploding in the body of the whale causes no little devastation. A rope is attached to the iron rod, the other end of which passes round a reel in the fore part of the boat. The iron tube which encloses the apparatus is provided with a slit for the escape of the gas when the rocket is lighted, and also with a sight, and a contrivance whereby the face of the person who fires it off is protected from the escape of gas. The person who uses it stands upright in the boat, with the gun, or whatever it be termed, on his shoulder, and ignites the rocket by means of a small pistol attached to the cylinder. When the shot is fired, the knife and grenade, the cylinder in which the rocket is enclosed, together with the rod and harpoons, should all of them enter the body of the whale. Consequently it is seldom fired till the boat is within forty or fifty feet of the whale, which has not time, therefore, to dive at the report before it is struck by the shot.

Some people say that whales are very abundant round the coast, especially in the spring. My excellent host, Sysselmand Smith, in Seyðisfjörðr, told me that he has often heard the whales blowing while sitting in his house at the extremity of the fjord, as they were tumbling about among the shoals of herrings which they pursue into this deep and narrow fjord. I have also been told the same thing at Akureyri, on Eyjafjörðr, on the north coast.

Owing to the immense shoals of herrings, and the movements of the whales, the water on such occasions looks as if it were boiling. But I have subsequently spoken with naturalists on this subject, and they are of opinion that whales are not nearly so numerous as is supposed. They maintain that there are only a very few whales round the coast of Iceland, and that for ten consecutive years the very same whale has been seen to frequent a particular fjord. They think, therefore, that the whale fishery cannot last longer than a few years. Whether this prognostication is correct, time alone will prove.

The flesh of the whale is a very favourite dish among the Icelanders, and my readers must not turn up their noses at the mere idea, for when properly dressed, it is really very eatable food. They do not, however, eat the flesh which lies nearest to the bones, but an intermediate layer, called "rengi," something between flesh and blubber. Mr. Roys shoots many more whales than he succeeds in bringing to land to his oil-boiling establishment in Seyðisfjörðr, so that it often happens that whales that have been shot are thrown up at different places along the coast. Before I left the eastern parts of the country, five whales were driven ashore, or were towed in by fishing boats between Mýrdalssundr and Vopnafjörðr. On such an occasion as this the faces of the Icelanders beam with joy; for not only do they get a portion given to them for helping to cut the whale up; but they are also able to buy the fat, boneless "rengi," at rather less than a penny a pound. I will give my fair readers a recipe for cooking "rengi." It must first be boiled for a considerable time—and a little longer, too—to extract the oil, which makes an excellent lamp oil. Then the boiled "rengi" must be laid in vinegar, sour whey, or some other sour liquid, for a good time, when it is ready. It resembles—indeed it has a look peculiar to itself—something between pork and the muscles of a bullock, and is of a whitish-yellowish colour, and tastes like pickled pork. Can I give a more appetizing description of it?

By boiling the blubber, as everybody doubtless knows, train oil is obtained; and in addition to this a fleshy substance which tastes even better than "rengi," at least to an Icelander's palate, though I should fancy it must have rather an oily flavour.

As may be supposed, there is a good deal that can be eaten on a whale. Sysselmand Smith and I made a calculation that from 355 whales all the 68,000 inhabitants of Iceland could each have a pound of blubber or "rengi" daily, all the year round. If we increase that number to 365, there would be a whale for each day in the year; and indeed whales must be fine animals, when one of them can satisfy a whole nation, at least for one meal a day! Mr. Roys, however, does not make use of his whales in this way. He extracts the oil out of the whole animal, even from its flesh and bones, which he boils in a steam apparatus, whereby the strong pressure of the steam drives out all the fatty substance that is not extracted by common boiling.

P

It is the intention of this gentleman to procure a pressing machine in order to compress the boiled flesh into cakes, and then to sell it in England as food for dogs, poultry, pigs, and goodness only knows for what else.

While speaking of whales we must refer to another kind of whale fishery, which is followed, to a certain extent, in Iceland, but on a much larger scale in the Færoe isles. I am alluding to the bottle-nosed whale. It is twenty to twenty-four feet in length, and is found in large schools, containing several hundred each. When a fishing-boat has discovered a school of these whales off the Færoe coasts, it hoists a signal, whereon a beacon-fire is lighted on the islands around, in order to assemble as many boats as possible. The whales are then driven into a bay or bight by throwing stones at them, where they are killed or are driven on land. If the school is not too large, one or two boats can manage to drive it before them on the open sea; but on nearing land, as many boats as possible are needed. A school of about four hundred whales is considered to be the most convenient size. The reason why they allow themselves to be driven and do not dive under the boats back to sea is, that the stones on striking through the water leave a stripe of light behind them, of which the whale is afraid. In order, therefore, that the undertaking should be crowned with success, the boats have to be provided with a quantity of small stones. Stones with lines attached to them are frequently used, so that they can be pulled up and be used again. After the whales have been driven into the bay it often happens that in their terror at the boats they rush up on the beach, where they are immediately killed. Generally, however, they are killed by stabbing them in the water with knives fastened to the ends of long poles. If the first whale is stabbed in the tail with its head turned towards land, it will sometimes dash on to the beach, and the whole school will follow it. If this cannot be managed, they must continue to stab and stick them till they die. When once the water is dyed with blood, there is no fear of any of the whales escaping. For if one of them were to get out into clear water, it would immediately turn back, as the blood seems to attract them. Sometimes a wounded whale will thrust its head up through the bottom of one of the boats, which of course sinks, but as there are plenty of other boats close at hand the crew is immediately saved.

I was told, on reliable authority, that at a "whale hunt" in Iceland it happened that a whale rose by the side of one of the boats in chase. This made the boat heel over considerably, when one of the men instinctively thrusting his hand over the gunwale, happened to lose one of his mittens. A short time afterwards the whale floated on the surface quite dead; it was dragged to land, and, on cutting it up, the missing mitten was found sticking fast in the windpipe of the whale. When the boat heeled over the man, without knowing it, must have thrust his hand into the whale's windpipe. A similar history, the authenticity of which I will not vouch for, is related to have taken place in the Færoes; only in this case it was a tern innocently engaged in fishing that happened to find its way into the windpipe of the whale.

A whale chase in the Færoes is looked upon as an important event by the islanders; in Iceland it is comparatively of rare occurrence. It happened recently that a school of whales entered a fjord where a vessel ballasted with small stones lay at anchor. As they had, therefore, an ample supply of ammunition in the shape of stones they drove the whole school on to the shore.

While speaking of the wonders that are to be found in the

Icelandic seas, we will allude to another kind of fish, the "hásker-ðingr." It is a shark, and, being a shark, is of course greedy and voracious; but, to adopt Mr. Darwin's mode of expressing himself, in consequence of its tremendous voracity it is provided with a large liver, from which a valuable oil is extracted. At the trading establishments in Iceland there are generally to be found one or more small yachts, belonging to the merchants there, which go in chase of this shark. The fishery is a very lucrative one, although it is not carried on on any great scale, or in proportion to the abundance of these monsters with which the sea abounds; for monsters they may well be termed on account of their tremendous voracity, as anything that appertains to flesh does not come amiss to them. According to the "Development Theory" this fish, of course, had not originally the same voracious nature as now, but swam, like an honest fish, at the bottom of the sea, and was perfectly contented with such food as crabs and snails and an occasional herring. Its liver was then of a proper size; but later, the spirit of evil took possession of it; it began to grow daintier and daintier, and now it is the deadliest foe seals, cod, whales, and many other denizens of the deep possess: and not only so, it does not object to devour a poor shipwrecked mariner floating on his plank on the sea. But, as it became more voracious, it could no longer be satisfied with a small liver that was unable to discharge the functions of digestion quickly enough, and give it a fresh zest to renew its Lucullian banquet. Probably, too, it began to take rather more than it could digest, and of course did not feel altogether comfortable. In order, then, to remedy this defect, or rather to appease this craving, nature kindly made its liver grow, so that it now occupies the whole length of the body from head to tail. And it could not well be larger!

On opening the stomach of a "háskerðingr" (the Greenland shark) the most wonderful things are occasionally found inside it; a regular museum, in fact, of all the gastronomical marvels of the sea. Nilsson, in his "Scandinavian Fauna," mentions a "háskerðingr" that had swallowed a whole reindeer, and speaks of another in whose stomach was found a seal, eight cod-fish, four haddocks, and several pieces of whale blubber! As an instance of their greediness I was told that a whale was once found driven ashore in Seyðisfjöðr, into the side of which a "háskerðingr" had eaten its way, without being able to get out again. The story sounds rather improbable, but may yet admit of this possible explanation—that after having first made a hole in the side of the whale, it continued to eat away till the hole became deeper; till at last, by a powerful effort, it got so far in that it stuck fast, and actually became another prophet in the belly of the whale—a prophet, however, which came in from a lateral direction, consequently an apocryphal one.

The flesh of the "háskerðingr" can be eaten as well as that of the whale, though it must be allowed there is something repugnant in eating an animal which eats human beings. Still, will not pigs do the same thing occasionally? But the flesh of the "háskerðingr" cannot be eaten when fresh, as it is then poisonous. It has first to be buried underground, and left there till it becomes rotten, or to express oneself more tastefully, till it has undergone a process of decomposition, after which it is hung up to dry. After six months have elapsed, provided one is not too dainty, it can be eaten instead of butter with dried fish. But it is best to let it hang for three or four years, or even longer, when it is considered by many to be a delicacy. The unpleasantness of eating it consists in the fact that it —well—stinks just a little, and not so very little, perhaps; but this is a quality it possesses in common with sour herrings, "gammel ost"* (rotten cheese), and other delicacies of northern Europe. After a person has partaken of "háskerðingr" he can be smelt far and wide; but it is said not to taste so badly after all. Naturally, however, it is only the common people who indulge in this food. Whale flesh, on the other hand, may be offered in every house.

Amongst the delicacies which the sea offers, fish naturally occupy the first rank. Icelandic fish may be classed among the best. When the cod fisheries are not so abundant in Iceland, the price of "klip"† fish rises in the Spanish market, where the Iceland merchants send the greatest proportion of their fish. "Klip" fish is cod that is not salted in barrels, but in open heaps, so that the brine runs off; it is afterwards laid on the rocks to be dried. Salted fish is not prepared in Iceland; but what is not made into "klip" fish is dried and eaten with butter without bread.

The accompanying woodcut represents Icelanders of both sexes occupied in preparing fish. The fish that is to be dried, and afterwards placed in barrels and kept for winter consumption, is hung up on scaffoldings. Dried fish has a very pleasant flavour, but it is tough and hard. It is first beaten on a stone in order to separate the meaty fibres a little; for it can then be more easily divided into small pieces, which each person accommodates to the size of his mouth and the state of his teeth; for after the fish has been beaten it is ready for the table. It is then torn in pieces with the fingers, which here usurp the place of knives and forks. Every Icelandic "bær," therefore, has a stone outside it, on which the dried fish is beaten. Haddocks are principally used as dried fish; but in the houses of

---

* I trust Norwegian readers will not be indignant with me for rendering their favourite dish thus.—Tr.

† "Klip" signifies a rock.—Tr.

DRYING FISH.

rich people cod and halibuts are also used. The last-named fish, when cooked fresh, is one of the greatest delicacies of the sea.

The only fresh-water fish in Iceland are salmon and trout. They are of excellent quality, and very numerous in certain rivers and lakes. Englishmen resort to Iceland to boil salmon down. I presume, therefore, that the English people are very partial to this fish as an article of food, for unless I am mistaken, they expend no small sums of money upon catching it!

CHAPTER VI.

Surturbrandr—Its Origin—Snow Fonds—Journey over the Heiði—Alftavíksfjall—Hvítserkr—Sheep-farming and Agriculture—From Hjaltastaðr to Vopnafjörðr—An Adventure—Passage across Jökulsá—Curious way of Crossing a River—Basaltic Columns—Grímsstaðir—Peasant Girls on Horseback—Jökulsú, in Axafirði—Reykjahlíd—Krafla—Sulphur Springs—Mud Springs—Geysirs—Journey to Húsavík—Return to Reykjahlid—Volcanic Crater "Cauldron"—Herðubreið—Solfataras—Excursion on a Lava Stream—Volcanic Craters of Leirhnúkr—Eruptions of 1724-1730—Mývatn or "Mosquito Lake"—Reindeer.

INTERSECTED and laid bare by the two kinds of denudation which we have already spoken of, the mountains of Iceland expose their interior to the light of day. Thus the basaltic formations have been so intersected that their varied contents of compact basalts, amygdaloidal basalt, "wacke" and tufa strata are plainly visible. These latter are neither so thick nor so extensive as the compact basalts, or the amygdaloidal basalts. Still they enclose a formation of great importance, and of pre-eminent interest. The tufa strata, for instance, occasionally lie on a kind of coal which is called "Surturbrandr," in Iceland (surturs-wood). It is a kind of brown coal, which consists partly of carbonised stems of trees, partly of a more coherent layer of coal mixed with schistus. In a practical point of view surturbrandr has no particular importance; certainly in a few cases it may contain enough coal to burn on the little hearth of an Icelandic "bœr," or in the miniature smithy, where they make their horse shoes and nails; but as a source of national wealth it is of no importance, for it is only found high up in the inaccessible parts of the mountains, and the supply would soon be exhausted were it to be much sought after. In Iceland, therefore, Scotch coal is always used as fuel, though it must be confessed there is something alarming in having to carry coals on horseback a journey of several days into the interior.

Surturbrandr generally consists of the stems of trees, which are carbonised in a greater or less degree, and which are pressed flat. They generally retain such a degree of firmness as to cut like wood. Their interior is as black as ebony, and is sometimes worked in the same way as that expensive kind of wood.

In the tufa strata surrounding these stems of trees, numerous impressions of leaves and fruits are often met with. Eggert Olafsen noticed this phenomenon at the close of the last century; but to Professor Steenstrup the honour is due of having first directed the public attention to this interesting fact. It is rather strange that these impressions of fruits and the leaves of plants which do not exist in Iceland, should have escaped the observation of the scientific expedition which was sent out from France under the conduct of Gaimard, in the middle of the year 1830, and which, besides visiting Iceland and other arctic countries, paid a visit to Sweden. Surturbrandr certainly was noticed by this expedition, but they overlooked the impressions in the tufa strata.

The remains of the leaves and fruits which have been found belong to kinds of trees that are altogether wanting in Iceland.

But they bear a great resemblance to those kinds which formerly grew in the tropics of America, for they belong to species which exist no longer. Amongst others, remains of several varieties of beautiful pines, of two varieties of birch, alder, hazel, oak, willow, elm, plane tree, vine, tulip, walnut, and in addition to these, though in smaller quantities, several kinds of plants are found. In all about thirty different species of trees and plants have been found in the surturbrandr strata.

In accordance with the opinion that prevails in geology, that the earth, during its development, has advanced from a warmer to a colder state, and that, in former ages, the heat of the earth was sufficient to maintain a warm climate over the whole globe, the plants, of which remains have been found in the surturbrandr, once grew on the soil of Iceland. Thus, in those remote ages, a forest vegetation must have existed of which scarcely any traces are now to be found; a vegetation, in fact, that comprised totally different growths from those now existing. The period when this was the case must have been millions of years ago, and cannot, therefore, be confounded with the period mentioned in the Sagas, when there was forest over the whole country from the sea to the mountains.

In support of this opinion that the above-named vegetable productions have grown in Iceland, it is maintained that the delicate nature of the vegetable remains, impressions of which have been found, could not have been conveyed any long distance without being destroyed, and that they must, therefore, necessarily have grown on the spot.

According to another opinion, the trunks of trees, of which surturbrandr is composed, have been conveyed as drift timber by the Gulf Stream, in the same way as trees are conveyed at the present day by it from America to the coasts of Iceland.

The upholders of the former opinion, however, in objection

to this theory, maintain that the stems of the trees which are found in the strata of surturbrandr frequently retain their covering of bark, which is always wanting in the drift timber that is washed up on the coast; and they, moreover, point significantly to the impression of the remains of tender plants.

With reference to these two adverse opinions, the following remarks may be made. It is undoubtedly true that the drift wood found on the coast is devoid of bark; it is also undoubtedly true that no remains of delicate leaves and fruits are found on the coast, for, as might naturally be supposed, the action of the surf would soon destroy them; still, specimens of large kinds of fruit are found, as the " lausnastein," *vide* p. 202. Yet, if these leaves, fruits, and stems have drifted with the Stream, and have been tossed about by it at the bottom of the sea, they have certainly never reached the coast, and, therefore, could not have been stript off, or have crumbled to pieces in the surf. In the Gulf Stream, however, in the open sea, they could drift without being knocked about, especially as they would not necessarily drift on the surface, but during the process of decomposition would float in mid-water before sinking to the bottom. In this case, especially as they would not be exposed to the fury of the waves, it seems reasonable to suppose that the most tender specimens might be carried hundreds of miles without perishing. From this point of view, surturbrandr does not testify to the existence of a forest vegetation in Iceland in former ages, but only affords another proof that the Icelandic basalts were formed under the surface of the sea.

During my stay at Seyðisfjörðr, I paid a visit to a stratum of surturbrandr that had been found high up on Brimnesfjall, on the north shore of the fjord. It is situate in a steep slope facing the sea, perhaps at 1,200 or 1,500 feet above its surface.

The surturbrandr consists merely of barkless stems of trees, which are carbonized and pressed flat, lying in the middle of a loose mass of tufa of at least fifty feet in thickness. Above this lies a stratum of basalts, with signs of columnar arrangement. On the top of the mountain ridge the basalts are full of bubbles, and are of a lava nature.

There is a magnificent view from Brimnesfjall over two of the deep fjords on the east of the country—Seyðisfjörðr, which lies below it, and which is of a dark-blue colour, and the narrow Loðmandarfjörðr to the north. These are bounded by ranges of mountains whose snow-clad summits shoot up into the clear sky, and whose mossy slopes and grass-grown inclines will ever leave an ineffaceable impression on my memory. The road up Brimnesfjall was one of the steepest I had hitherto encountered. Often and often we were obliged to dismount and lead the horses up the pricipices, though in my eyes the whole road seemed to be a precipice; and this is the road that is commonly used and which unites the two fjords, and which farmers in market-time, officials on their journeys, and stray travellers, have one and all to use. On the very top of the incline lay a steep snow "fond," on arriving at which we dismounted and left our horses to take care of themselves; for the point we wished to visit lay on the other side of the snow "fond," and the path was too steep even for an Icelandic horse. In order to prevent the horses from running away on such occasions, the following plan is had recourse to. They are bound two and two, so that the head of one is towards the other's tail, and contrariwise; and thus their endeavours to get away result in their continuously describing a circle.

These snow "fonds" are sometimes very troublesome. If the snow is soft, as is usually the case on a summer-day, one can manage to get to the top; and then, by a slight motion of the feet, slide down as if one were on skates. But a small boy, by simply seating himself down on the edge of the snow, could slide down at a prodigious pace in this manner.

In winter-time these steeps are quite impassable unless the traveller takes axes with him to hew out steps in the snow, which is then of the consistency of ice.

To convince the reader that they understood how to live in Iceland, I must inform them that we—that is, myself, Herr Smith, Mr. Roys, and others—drank to the health of the monarch of the mountain in bumpers of champagne. Wine, I may state, is a common beverage in Iceland, especially in the trading stations. Owing to exemption from duty, the price is low; and, indeed, many things may be bought as cheaply in Iceland as in Copenhagen.

After my trip to Seyðisfjörðr, I returned to Eskifjörðr to make some excursions in the neighbourhood. If on my first journey over Fjarðarheiði I had occasion to find fault with the fog and the slud, I was amply compensated on my return journey; for the weather was beautiful, and I was able thoroughly to enjoy the imposing spectacle which Fljótsdalr presented, as I approached it after a long journey of three hours over the "heiði." But it would be vain to attempt to give a description of all the lovely scenery one meets with on a trip in Iceland, provided of course that the weather is favourable. It is literally enchanting. When I first got a sight of the valley in the evening, a stratum of atmosphere, which, though rather misty, and of a whitish-blue colour, was perfectly transparent, lay over it, and cast a magic light on mountain and valley. At my feet, Lagarfljót glittered like a silvery stripe; in the background on my left, Snæfell shot up its snowy summit some 6,000 feet into the sky; while a stupendous range on the other side of Fljótsdalr, stood boldly out with its lofty mountains, Smjörfjall and Diafjall, the latter rising 2,272 feet almost directly from the sea. The sea itself was hidden from view by the mountains intervening.

After descending Fjarðarheiði, the road runs south-east to Eskifjörður. Before reaching the "heiði" of the same name, night began to fall; still there was sufficient light to find one's way. The frost had somewhat stiffened the crust of the snow on the snow "fonds," and it was cold on the "heiði." The stillness and solemnity of the scene after leaving the foaming stream in the valley below was very impressive. On reaching the top of the "heiði," I enjoyed another glorious view over the narrow Eskifjörðr, bounded on the left by the majestic and almost pyramidal Hólmatindr, and on the east by a lofty mountain range. A thick, snow-white sheet of fog had spread itself over the tranquil waters of the fjord, which, from the elevated point where I stood, seemed almost as if it rested on its surface; but on descending, it gradually lifted, and enveloped me and my companion in a thick veil. We had now reached a good and even track, and before long arrived at the trading station near the sea-coast, which was almost concealed from view in the fog and darkness. The night was pitchy dark; and while my companion was occupying himself in knocking up the household, I had ample time to listen to the splashing and quacking of the eider-ducks on the coast, which were doubtless employed in teaching their young ones how to find mussels, and initiating them into the mysteries of diving and swimming. In fact, it was an episode of sea-life,—one which doubtless may suit an eider-duck very well!

On leaving Eskifjörðr, my way lay to the north, through Fljótsdalr, to the parsonage of Hjaltastaðr, which is situated at the entrance of the valley. The worthy Pastor, Sira Jakob Benediktsson, gave me a most hearty reception. He was well known in the neighbourhood as a good rider, and a good judge of horseflesh. From this place I made an excursion to Húsavík, and had to pass over a "heiði" covered with snow "fonds," between the lofty mountains of Beinageitarfell (3,517 feet) and Dyrfell (3,606 feet). This last-named fjeld derives its name from a broad cleft in the form of a gate or door (Dyr—door) on its summit, which is plainly visible from the valley below. In Húsavík I took up my quarters at a rich widow's, who owned both silver spoons and other articles of plate, as my talkative guide informed me. Directly to the south of Húsavík is another small bay, called Alftavík, which is separated from the first-named one by a sharp point jutting out into the sea called Alftavíksfjall. This fjeld presents many geological curiosities. It consists principally of uneven rocks intersected by basalts. The side of the fjeld which is towards the sea is thickly intersected by precipices, which yawn under one's feet almost at every step. The summit is formed of a sharp edge, along which it is difficult to clamber; and occasionally one has to creep on one's hands and feet. The highest point is on the south side, and is about 1,000 or 1,200 feet in height. But the extreme summit is formed of a narrow ridge of detached basalts, which on one side rises to a perpendicular height of 200 feet. To ascend this, sundry upright boulders must be clambered over; and it is a difficult matter to get a foothold on them. Directly under one's foot lies the dizzy abyss; so that in tempestuous weather it is not safe to venture there. A little to the south of Njarðvík, near Borgarfjörðr, it is necessary to ride over a similar slope that goes perpendicularly down into the sea.

After a short visit in Húsavík and Borgarfjörðr, I returned to Hjaltastaðr.

Between Húsavík and Borgarfjörðr there is a mountain

named Hvítserkr, of a very peculiar appearance. It is of pyramidal form, and consists of a ragged, greyish-white rock, which, owing to its light colour, stands prominently out against the dark background, which is so common in Iceland. The slope is interwoven with numerous basaltic rocks, which shoot up from its base, and cross each other in several directions, and finally disappear in a dark bed of basalts that covers the brow of the mountain like a cap.

As the population of Iceland has remained nearly stationary through a long course of years, sometimes increasing and sometimes diminishing, several persons have formed the opinion that the country is really not capable of sustaining a larger number of people; and further, that as its present population, viz., 68,000 persons, is the greatest number it has attained since the introduction of taking the census into the country, it has reached its maximum.

But leaving out of the question those causes which during the last centuries have stagnated the development of the national industry, there are several reasons close to hand which directly refute such opinions. I have already alluded to the low state of development which the Icelandic fisheries have reached. An impetus in this direction would be of vast importance to the prosperity of the country, for doubtless there are still vast sources of undiscovered wealth in the sea, and would divert some of the annual profit which the French reap into the pockets of the Icelandic fishermen. And further it may be stated that the products of the land have not nearly attained their highest degree of development. This any person may discover for himself on travelling through the country, for he will find extensive grass lands which, even as late as the autumn, have never been fed off by the sheep. The parsonage farm of Hjaltastarð affords an excellent example of the progress that can be made in sheep farming in the country. When the present occupier first went there, he found that only 150 sheep had hitherto been kept on the farm, and that it was the universal opinion that it could not possibly support a greater number. Sira Jakob, however, thought otherwise, and during the nine years that he has resided there he has increased the number of sheep to 600, or to four times the original stock. It is by no means to be inferred, however, that a similar scale of increase could be established throughout the whole country, for the neighbourhood of Fljótsdalr is one of the most fertile districts in the country. Still the number of sheep in the island might certainly be doubled. But, in order to attain this desirable end, it will be necessary first to educate the common people; and the proposal, therefore, which has recently been made, of establishing an agricultural school in the country, is of great importance. Some endeavours have certainly been made to promote the cultivation of corn in the island; and, for this purpose, people have repaired to Denmark at the expense of the Government to learn corn farming. But, as might have been expected, these endeavours have not been attended with any particular results.

The summer that I was in Iceland was an unusually favourable one; but I remember to have seen oats which were growing in a garden near Reykjavik far from being ripe even at the end of September, while in the Færoe islands corn was still standing in the fields at Michaelmas. That year, however, they had ripe currants in Reykjavik.

From Hjaltastaðr I travelled along the coast to the trading station of Vopnafjörðr, on the north-west. There are two routes to this place, either by passing over the bridge, or taking the ferry across Jökulsá, the second of the two large rivers which flow out from Vatna-Jökul towards the sea. In the first case the river is crossed at some distance from the sea, after which the route lies over Smjörvatnsheiði; and in the second the road lies over Hellisheiði, after first crossing Jökulsá at a place much lower down towards the sea. I chose this latter route as being the shortest. In both cases Lagarfljót, the largest of the two rivers alluded to, must be crossed in a ferry. There are several ferries over it, so that it may be crossed at different places. In one part of its course the river widens out into a lake, and it is here that the ferries which are principally used are situated, as the water is smoother there. There are also two ferries below this basin, where the river again narrows, and runs with a very rapid stream. It was by one of these, north of Kirkjubær, that I crossed the river, on which occasion I met with an adventure.

And what would an account of travels in a wild country like Iceland be, if the author were not occasionally to meet with an adventure or two? I am not aware whether there are any stereotyped formularies for writing travelling descriptions,' as there are for inditing courting letters, for conversations, and for mercantile correspondence; but it seems to me that if any such do exist, they would be very deficient indeed if one of the first rules to be observed were not—"The traveller should stand in peril of life every now and then." * With such principles in mind, I can only feel rejoiced that I had an opportunity of observing this rule in a manner of which the reader shall judge for himself.

When I and my guide reached Lagarfljót in order to ferry over, we found that none of the ferrymen were at home. The good woman of the house, however, gave us leave to use the ferry-boat, a dilapidated, worn-out little affair, intended for three

---

* The next paragraph would run somewhat as follows—" But must of course ultimately extricate himself." The reason of this, I think, is obvious.

persons. One oar was missing; accordingly we nailed two bits of wood together, and after taking the saddles off our horses and placing the baggage in the boat, it was our intention to make the horses swim over before us, for the current was too strong to admit of towing them after us, as we did in the Ölfusá and Þjorsá. They were to swim over therefore on their own account, but unfortunately we could not make them do so; and though we shouted at them and threw stones after them, as the usual custom is, they turned back twice. The river was about 800 feet wide, and in the middle of it lay a "holm," which divided the stream into two currents. After the horses had swum a few hundred feet and had begun to get into shallow water off the end of the "holm," the strong current on the further side, which was made more rapid still from the strong wind that blew, seemed to terrify them, for they turned back. We resolved therefore to drive them on to the "holm," and then drive them over the other current. So far our plan succeeded, that we managed to get them on to the "holm;" but we could not follow them ourselves. For after we had got out into the middle of the stream, the only oar we possessed broke in half, and the natural result of this was, that we went spinning down with the current at tremendous speed. It was all in vain that we tried to make for a little reef a short distance from the end of the "holm;" for instead of succeeding we got out into the rapid current on the other side, and went away at express speed, though not exactly in the direction we desired. Frantically I seized a bit of the broken oar, and endeavoured to stay the progress of our bark, while my companion tried to help with the stretcher. Our united efforts succeeded, for we managed at last to reach a little point that jutted out from the shore, and finally gained the opposite bank. And it was high time, for our rotten old boat was half full of water.

Meanwhile our horses were on the "holm," and to return to them was a sheer impossibility, for the current on this side was much stronger than on the other, and the wind was blowing great guns. We sent, therefore, a lad who had accompanied us, to a neighbouring farm for the loan of an oar; and in about half-an-hour's time he returned, followed by a man on horseback with the oar in question. It blew now a perfect hurricane, and the man pronounced it to be madness to attempt crossing to the "holm." There was, therefore, nothing to be done but to submit to our fate; accordingly we left our horses to their devices on the barren "holm," while we repaired to the "bær" close by. Hitherto we had made fun of our adventure. While drifting down stream, my companion thought that anyhow we should have been all right when we reached the next ferrying place, nearer to the sea; but the good people in the house assured us that had we not been so fortunate as to have landed on the point we must inevitably have been carried down a foss lower down the river, of which my guide knew nothing about. They said that no boat had ever lived there. No wonder if our after-thoughts were of a rather serious nature!

It was noon when we set out on our venturesome trip across Lagarfljót, and it was not till evening had set in that the weather permitted us to cross over it again for our horses. But the sagacious animals, finding nothing to eat on the rocky "holm," had returned from whence they had come, allured by the tempting grass that grew there. But we ultimately found them somewhere about ten o'clock at night. It was too late to continue our journey any further, for we were afraid if we reached Jökulsá in the middle of the night, the ferryman on the opposite shore would not notice us, and we should have to spend the rest of the night in the open air. Accordingly we prudently decided upon remaining at the "bær" till the following morning, when

CROSSING A RIVER. Page 229.

we left our good-natured host, and after a short ride and after crossing several arms of the Jökulsá, at length reached the main stream and succeeded in drawing the attention of the ferryman on the opposite shore. He soon came, and our horses this time were not slow to swim over, for they saw green meadows before them, while on the sand-bank where we were standing not a blade of grass was growing. The ferryman was a tall powerful fellow, and carried us easily in his arms to the boat, for he was unable to bring it up close to land, an attention, however, which I thought was superfluous, seeing that I was already wet through and through. This time our boat did not try to resemble Charon's ferry, and after we had happily reached the opposite bank, we continued our route over some low land; after which we crossed Hellishciði, and then rode along the south bank of Vopnafjörðr, and reached the trading station at the end of the fjord some time in the evening.

The accompanying sketch will serve to give some idea of the passage of a river in Iceland. The baggage, &c., is conveyed over in the boats, together with the two-legged members that form the caravan. Some of the horses are in the act of swimming across; a man on the opposite bank is trying to persuade the others to follow their companions. The horses to the left seem as if they do not care to cross, for the men in the boat are returning to shore.

Before leaving the memorable Fjótsdalr, which, with Jökuldalr, through which the Jökulsá flows, is one of the richest pasture-districts in the country, I will mention another way in which this river is crossed. Higher up in the valley, at a place where the river flows between deep but narrow banks, two ropes have been stretched across the stream, to which a chair is attached. The delinquent, as he may not inappropriately be termed, seats himself upon it, and manages to pull himself across. The horses are driven over a little higher up. This method of crossing is termed "at fara i kláf"—to go in a basket. It requires a strong head to do it.

The trading station at Vopnafjörðr resembles all the others in the country, and consists of a few black, tarred wooden houses, with a ditto, ditto planked roof; for in Iceland they are not accustomed to colours. The fjord itself is very broad, and therefore the mountains which surround it seem to recede, and thus their imposing appearance is in a measure unnoticed.

To the west of Vopnafjörðr the mountains rise up from a table-land, and consequently do not appear to be so high as they are in reality; moreover, they were not so much covered with snow as was the case on the east coast,—for I went in a westerly direction from Vopnafjörðr to Mývatn,—and in the interior were altogether free from snow, and were thus, in my opinion, shorn of their best adornment. Indeed, on the whole, the landscape seemed to me to have lost a part of that imposing character to which I had so long been accustomed, and appeared flat and dull. It was the contrast no doubt that produced this impression; for every day since I had first set foot in Iceland, I had been used to gaze up at the snow-covered heights which majestically towered aloft, so that it took some little time before I became accustomed to the monotonous dark blue of the bare mountains before me.

Vopnafjörðr presents a point of great interest in natural history in the appearance of some strata of surturbrandr, which lie on the south side of the fjord, in the neighbourhood of the farm of Vindfell. One of these is to be found close to the seacoast, under a bed of basalts, which rises in a perpendicular wall of more than 200 feet in height, and consists of very beautiful upright columns. At the foot of the wall there are strata of tufa with surturbrandr, covered with a columnar wall of basalts. At the base of this, on the right, are small "Fingal's caves," formed by the surf, which serve to enhance the imposing nature of the landscape.

Whilst I was staying at Vopnafjörðr, an English yacht arrived, towing a whale after it which had been found dead at sea. It was a magnificent specimen, and was about 72 feet in length. All was life and stir in Vopnafjörðr; for, as I have already remarked, feelings of joy are awakened in an Icelander's breast when he hears that a whale has floated in; and the whole popu-

Basaltic columns at Vindfell.

lation of the neighbourhood hasten to offer their assistance in cutting it up—it is only the blubber and the "rengi" that are cut off—and to buy portions of it for their consumption. I rowed round the whale as it lay in the sea before it was cut up; but the gaseous exhalations that emanated from a place where the entrails protruded, gave out a most unpleasant perfume. What else could be expected from a carcass of 72 feet in length?

This is the principal place of export for the Icelandic mutton.

It is sold fresh to the factory, and is salted there. In 1862, 1,042 barrels of salt meat were exported from Iceland; and 326,117 pounds of tallow.

At Vopnafjörðr, I met, according to previous arrangement, Sysselmand Smith, from Seyðisfjörðr. He was going to Húsavík, on the north coast, so we determined to travel in company. After passing a day and a night at that excellent parsonage at Hof, in the interior of Vopnafjörðr—Pastor Halldor Jónnson, of Hof, is one of the most esteemed of Iceland's clergy—we started upon our journey to Mývatn, a large lake in this part of the country. Our route lay over Dymmagil, a defile between two mountain ridges, on the plateau which we had to traverse in order to reach the farmhouse Grímsstaðir, where we purposed passing the night. After crossing the grassy hills round Hof, we presently came to a sandy waste, which continued nearly all the way to Mývatn, being only interspersed here and there with a few patches of vegetation.

Grímsstaðir is one of the most elevated "bœr" in Iceland, being about 1,365 feet above the sea. It was doubtless owing to this cause that the day we passed there the thermometer was only at 4° C.,—a temperature which, it will be allowed, is not very great for the last day of July. Grímsstaðir is a well-built farmhouse; but I was surprised beyond measure to find the walls papered, and edged with gilt mouldings; mahogany furniture, and everything else in accordance; for it is at least a two days' journey for packhorses from the trading station, while, generally speaking, the "bœr" near the sea-coast are devoid even of floors. However, I was lodged in the farmer's own room; for in the room with the gilt mouldings there was only one bed, and Smith and I were not accustomed to lie double!

From what I have stated of the customs and manners of the Icelanders in general, and of the style displayed in the guest-room at Grímsstaðir in particular, I trust that the reader has long ago seen that, although poverty, an absence of forests, and other unhappy conditions, have in some respects exercised a depressing influence on the domestic arrangements of the natives—I am alluding especially to their style of building, their dirty habits, &c.—yet, considered as a nation, the Icelanders have a perfect right to be classed among the other civilized countries of Europe. I have already mentioned that all the Icelanders can read; the greater number, too, can write; and if it be borne in mind that this state of things is brought about without any assistance whatever being rendered on the part of the public authorities, it will be seen how far the national spirit is removed from a barbarous state of ignorance. Their proficiency in history and geography, which are their favourite studies, is frequently astonishing.

The exploits of the first Napoleon seem especially to interest them; while they are perfectly well acquainted with the eventful career of Bernadotte, even in the minutest details. With the geography of the north they are especially conversant, in consequence of the numerous remarks and allusions made concerning it in the ancient Sagas. There is no fear, therefore, of an Icelander, at least one of the better classes, appearing at a loss when the important question of our geographical relations is discussed.

"Svíar" and "Svíþjóð," as they call the Swedes and Sweden, appear to them to be old acquaintances, for whom, if I am not mistaken, they entertain a brotherly affection, which might easily be kindled into a flame. And this is the more worthy of remark, as there is scarcely any communication at the present day between Sweden and Iceland.

But to return to Grímsstaðir. The morning I spent there was a Sunday, and the peasant girls were mounting their horses to go to church. The saddles of the Icelandic women consist of a chair furnished with a high back and a stool, in which they seat themselves, with their backs turned towards the side of the horse. It requires, therefore, a good seat for the horse-woman to keep her saddle from swinging to and fro—especially when the girths get rather loose—and herself from turning a summersault backwards. English saddles, however, would hardly be advisable, for in case the horse stumbles, or any other mishap occurs, it would be more difficult for them to dismount; but with the native saddles, however, they can readily jump off. The Icelandic girls are generally very nimble, and can manage their horses as well as any man. The daughters of wealthy farmers wear a black kind of shepherdess's hat, trimmed with flowers, and look rather peculiar as they canter by on their active steeds. I must confess that this fashion, which bore witness to a certain amount of good taste, attracted my attention a good deal; while, on the other hand, I could not but feel surprised at the entire absence of taste which makes the farmers and the pastors ride with black chimney-pots on their heads. Black hats are quite as common with the Icelanders as they are with us. I remember hearing a man complaining about his hat, that it had not only lost all its gloss, after being exposed for a few hours to the rain, but had actually collapsed. Unquestionably, this is the most useless article of apparel possible in a country where everybody rides on horseback, and where storms of rain and snow are of ordinary occurrence. But who is not Fashion's slave?

On leaving Grímsstaðir the farmer took a bottle of port-wine, and offered us a parting glass, like a perfect gentleman. But his house lies on a public road, so that, doubtless, he has ample opportunities for knowing what the customs of the superior classes are in the country.

About an hour from Grímsstaðir one comes to the large river Jökulsá, in Axarfiði, which runs into Axarfjörðr. It rises on Vatna-Jökul, under the same parallel of latitude with the Lagarfljót, and the "Jökulsá with the Bridge," as it called, and runs, with a northerly course, along a hollow in the plateau on which Grímsstaðir lies. It is one of the most desolate-looking rivers one can possibly imagine. We approached it over a barren, sandy plain; and on the opposite side of its muddy, repulsive water, "Mývatns öræfi," as it is termed, a large sandy "heiði," with but little signs of vegetation growing on it, extended itself before us. Moreover, the wind drove the fog along the ground and the surface of the river, and, as I thought, made the scene look more desolate than it otherwise would have done; but I was assured that such was not the case, and that in clear weather its desolateness was even more apparent still. Here then was a place which could not be called beautiful, though it certainly was imposing; for, from whence came those enormous masses of sand, which we had passed over, and which still lay before us? Doubtless they are partly the remains of the glacial age, when the surfaces of the rocks were crushed to fragments by the glaciers; partly they are formed by the volcanic sand, which the wide volcanic belt between Mývatn and Vatna-Jökul has vomited forth at different times.

Jökulsá had to be crossed by ferry, and the horses had to take care of themselves in this river, as well as in the two preceding ones. They had evidently a hard battle with the stream and the waves. Only once is this river said to have been ridden over. A horse-dealer from the northern or western parts of the country had been practising the tricks of his trade to the east of the river, and had so exasperated the peasants that they set off in pursuit after him, and came up with him on the bank of the river. But as he had no relish for being "over-trumped," and as his conscience probably did not lead him to expect much forbearance at the hands of his persecutors, he played his last trump card, rode into the river, and came out safely on the other bank. His followers, meanwhile, not caring to follow suit, returned on their steps crestfallen. When the snow melts up in the mountains the force of the current is so increased, that sometimes the surface of the middle part of the river is actually raised up. This will give some idea, perhaps, of its impetuosity.

It was late in the evening and there was a dense fog when we reached Reykjahlíð, a well-known farmhouse by Mývatn, so that we were unable to notice the points of interest we had passed by. There were the Krafla volcano, and the so-termed "namar," or sulphurous springs and boiling mud cauldrons, which lie to the south. It was only necessary to open one's eyes to know that one was in a volcanic district. The lava protruded here and there from the sand; but on approaching Namafjall by Mývatn the scoriæ form themselves into a coherent lava stream, that is, they are not covered with sand, but consist of younger, uncovered "hraun," without any vegetation. The same is the case between Namafjall and Mývatn, as well as round the lake. The volcanic craters, however, do not lie exactly by this road, but are found dispersed along a volcanic fissure, which runs north and south on the eastern side of Mývatn. A crater named Hverfjall is, as the name intimates, a little mountain by itself, and is some hundred feet in height. As one side of it is somewhat lower than the other, one can observe the saucer-formed basin on its top at some distance off.

In order to visit Krafla from Reykjahlíð on horseback it is

necessary to retrace one's steps over Namafjall, and thence to proceed to the north along the eastern side of Dalfjall. The eastern slope of this mountain, which is covered with brushwood, has a very inviting appearance, but, by way of contrast, in the bottom of the valley there lies a lava stream, which seems to say "beware." That Dalfjall has contributed to form this stream may be concluded from the fact that at one place the stiffened lava comes to the very foot of the mountain wall. The fissure, however, from which the stream has issued is visible on the ridge above. The mountains to the north-east of the valley form an extended ridge, the summits of which go by various names—Jörundr, Hrafntinnuhrýggr, and Krafla, which is the most northerly and the loftiest. On the flat valley bottom between Dalfjall and this mountainous ridge, the lowest slopes of which are called Sandbotnafjall, there is a little Sæter or Chalet, by which there flows a small stream coming from the hot springs at Krafla, the only water that is to be found on these arid regions, for, owing to its porosity, volcanic sand is a bad retainer of water.

Krafla is very easy of access; one can ride to its very summit; no rocky wall obstructs the way, for it is covered everywhere with a fine-grained sand, which has rounded off the unevenness of the soil. On the summit of the mountain, however, the hard rock shows itself, which is generally, if not universally the case in all the volcanoes in Iceland, Palagonite tufa. At the present time, however, Krafla possesses no volcanic appearance. Its form is a sloping ridge; no lava stream that may have issued from it is exposed to view, everything is covered over with sand. But on the north side of the mountain, at its base, lies a crater. It has a fearful name, for it is called Hell, or in Icelandic Helviti, though it does not now correspond to the title. It is a cavity in the ground in the form of a cauldron, and is about 100 feet in depth, and some hundred feet in diameter, and is surrounded by slanting walls of sand and lava, with a basin of beautiful bluish-green water at its bottom. Not more than fifty years ago this smiling lake was a boiling pool, and is said to have had a most repulsive appearance, which naturally procured the above repellent title for the crater. Henderson, who visited the spot in 1815, in describing this basin, says, that every five minutes a column of black muddy water was thrown up to a height of 30 feet from its centre. If from one point of view it may be said that by going to the nether regions one is visiting a place that one would prefer to avoid, so on the other hand it may be urged that, in this particular instance, the locality in question is by far the most agreeable spot in the whole of that desolate tract. Hell here has lost its sting!

There is said to be an excellent view from Krafla; but it blew so hard when I was up there, that it was all I could do to stand on my legs; besides, the plain below was enveloped in a perfect cloud of sand, so that it was impossible to see any distance.

A short distance from Krafla lies Hrafntinnuhrýggr—a ridge, as the name expresses, consisting of an uneven lava, which in some places is formed of obsidian: a very beautiful mineral, of a dark, shining, glossy appearance. The natives call it "hrafntinna." The obsidian of the Lipari isles is manufactured into brooches, buttons, bracelets, &c., for which this mineral is peculiarly adapted, owing to its hard nature (it will even cut glass) and its showy appearance. But the obsidian of Iceland has never been worked in this way, doubtless from the simple reason that there is no encouragement to cultivate this branch of industry. It would, however, be a patriotic as well as a remunerative undertaking to work in this stone, which is found in abundance. In this case, the cost of transport need not be

SULPHUR SPRINGS.

a deterrent cause, for out of a few hundred-weight of obsidian a large quantity of small articles might be manufactured.

On the return journey from Krafla, I visited the "námar" or sulphur springs, which I have before alluded to. They are called there "hliðarnámar." They are situated along a bare mountain-ridge, covered with a deep, loose sand, of a reddish hue, which, owing to its colour, strikes the eye at a considerable distance off. The sulphur springs are of two kinds, which, however, are intimately connected with one another. The first, the actual sulphur springs or "solfataras," consist of hot gaseous exhalations from the earth, which deposit sulphur. They are thus dry springs, if it be permitted to use the expression. The others are the mud springs, or "makkaluber." They are boiling springs, filled with muddy water, of a dark colour, owing to the presence of sulphate of iron. The first-named lie on the mountain-slope, where the water condensed by the aqueous gases cannot collect. The latter, however, are situate on a flat plain, at the foot of the mountain on its eastern side, between it and the lava plains, which extend to the sandy waste. The "solfataras," which partly lie separately, and partly collected in numbers, are externally characterised by small, flat elevations, a few feet in diameter, from the centre of which the gaseous substances are ejected through one or more small apertures, often not larger than the thickness of a finger in diameter. These gases—which consist of sulphuric acid, hydrogen, sulphureous and aqueous vapour, mixed together, and which usually stream forth very peaceably—are partially condensed in the air, and are carried away by the wind under the form of a white vapour, which seriously affects the respiratory organs. But occasionally the gas issues forth with extreme violence, hissing and roaring as when the valve of a steam engine is opened. In such cases, the aperture in the ground is larger.

On the surface these "solfataras" are covered over with loose sand, which does not, however properly belong to them, but which gives them a dirty grey, or a dirty red, appearance. By thrusting a stick through this outside covering, a crust of bright yellow and nearly pure sulphur is found, composed of an infinite number of sulphur-crystals. This crust, which is two to three inches thick, is not very cohesive; it is porous, and can readily be crumbled into a fine, gritty sand. This sulphur is deposited by the gases, when they come up to the surface of the earth and become cool. It is supposed that it is principally caused by the reciprocal action of sulphuric acid and hydrogen,—which gases have no affinity for each other, but decompose each other by becoming sulphur and water. This decomposition takes place in the depths of the earth, and the sulphur is volatilised, or sublimated, in consequence of the heat, just as flowers of sulphur in a manufactory. As we have stated above that the gaseous exhalations of the "solfataras" contain hydrogen, it must only be understood by this that they contain traces of this fetid gas,—for instance, those small quantities of it which have avoided contact with the sulphuric acid.* The quantity of hydrogen is moreover so small, that it would be difficult to test its presence if one did not possess a very delicate indicator. By thrusting a lighted cigar, or any other burning substance, into the gas, a light cloud of steam issues from it.

* Sulphuric acid, as is known, is the gas which is generated by the ignition of sulphur in the air, and hydrogen is the gas which is developed in rotten eggs, and which imparts to them their repulsive odour. These gases cannot combine. If, therefore, one has the smell of rotten eggs in one's nostrils, it is only necessary to light a brimstone match and inhale the vapour, when the former smell disappears. Care, however, must be taken not to hold the nose too close over the match.

Underneath the crust of sulphur which composes that portion of the "solfataras" which is broken up and carried away for exportation, the products of the decomposition are found, which take place from the action of the above-named gases on the palagonite tufa, in which the "solfataras" lie. By the chemical action of sulphuric acid, palagonite—which is a siliceous mineral composed of oxide of iron, clay, lime, talc, soda, and alkali—is decomposed into gypsum and pure or ferruginous clay.

These two latter products of decomposition form layers over each other, of which the one consists of a white clay quite free from iron, and the other of a coloured, ferruginous clay. Gypsum, however, occurs in strata or layers of greater or less extent between these, especially towards the surface, or else intermixed with them. Such are the results of the action of sulphurous acid on the resinish, or dark brown, hard palagonite. Finally, if it be inquired whence the above-named gases which are instrumental in the formation of the "solfataras" derive their origin, we are only able to answer that they proceed from the depths of the earth. The causes of their formation have not been hitherto ascertained; till that has been done we can only accept it as a fact that these gaseous exhalations take place in the neighbourhood of, or in connection with, volcanic eruptions.

Many signs bear witness to the extension of "solfataras" in former ages over portions of Námafjall, where they exist no longer, even up to its very ridge. For nearly everywhere pieces of gypsum of different sizes may be met with.

We will now speak of the "Makkaluber," or mud springs. The most important of these lie almost in a row with each other on the plain, a short distance from the foot of the mountain. There are seven or eight large ones, which have cauldron-shaped openings in the ground of eight or twelve feet in diameter, and which are filled with the boiling black mud

R

which is thrown up on the edges of the cauldron, and elevates them. The chemical processes that take place in these mud springs and "solfataras" are one and the same, although their products occupy a somewhat different position owing to the different nature of the two phenomena. Naturally there is no deposit of sulphur on the surface. But on the plain between the mud springs the activity of the "solfataras" is apparent; and exhalations of gases, sulphur deposits, &c., take place, though on a smaller scale. In such places the earth is undermined. The crust of the earth may seem firm enough to the eye, but should one attempt to walk on it, one's feet penetrate through it into the black boiling-hot clay; so that it requires some caution in making the attempt. The external appearance of the mud springs is not particularly inviting; on the contrary, they have a most repulsive look, though all feelings of disgust are lost in admiration of the imposing grandeur of the phenomenon. In one of these springs the mud is thrown up, by the slow and regular rising of large gas-bubbles through the muddy mixture, to a height of fifteen feet, when it falls down with a splash and a rumbling noise partly into the bottom of the spring, partly upon the sides. The gas-bubbles come up at two places in this spring, which is larger than the others. At one time one gas-apparatus is in active motion; at another time, the other. Thus they take it in turns. For a few seconds the surface may be perfectly calm, or only a slight tremulous motion may be observable over the above-named points; but presently a bubble rises, and breaks with a splash on the surface, followed by a larger one, which throws up the mud on the edge of the spring, and still by a larger bubble which ejects the mud even yet higher. And this goes on till the eruption gradually grows weaker and less violent. All this while the other point will have been in a quiescent state, as if occupied in watching its sister's performances; but no sooner does the one show signs of becoming tranquil, than the other begins to be disturbed, and presently the same phenomenon is repeated over again. When the muddy ejections of these springs, added to the barren desolateness of the surrounding landscape, are taken into account, no one, I think, who has an eye for what is lovely, and a taste for the beautiful, would care to linger long in this spot.

Far different, however, will be his emotions should he go to see the beautiful and inviting fountains, which I visited on the following day on my journey to Húsavík. They belong to that description of spring which in Iceland are termed "Geysirs," and of which the Great Geysir, on the north-west of Hekla, is the most prominent example. They consist of a clear, bluish-green water, which deposits siliceous crystals, out of which a little, flattened cone is formed, furnished in the middle with an orifice reaching perpendicularly downwards into the ground, and which at the surface usually widens out into a basin in the form of a flat saucer. These springs, of which the principal one is called "Uxahver," lie at the foot of a grassy mountain slope on a plain which is overgrown with a luxuriant vegetation. Their existence may be ascertained, even at some distance off, from the white clouds of vapour which proceed from the surface of the heated or nearly boiling water. But there is no unpleasant smell attached to them; and when the water is cold, it is perfectly drinkable. Three or four of these springs will especially attract attention. The most important of them, the basin of which is about twelve paces in diameter, is filled to the brim with water, which trickles down in small channels over the flattened cone. The water in it remains tranquil, only giving out a thick steam, through which, when the wind drives it to one side, the pipe that descends into the earth in the centre of the basin, can be discerned. This spring has now entirely ceased to be a fountain. But close to it there is another spring of much smaller dimensions, in the pipe of which the water is in a continual state of ferment, which may be better heard than seen, as the amount of steam generated prevents one from getting a clear view. "Uxahver" is a fountain, and casts out boiling water every three or four minutes, throwing glittering drops of water to a height of about twelve feet. Thereupon the water sinks about one foot in the basin, but immediately rises again till it reaches the brink, when it runs over through a little channel, after which the gas-bubbles again keep rising up in the middle of the basin, till another eruption takes place. The fourth spring has similar though weaker eruptions. The basins of these springs are three or four feet in diameter. Around the larger springs there are sometimes smaller hot springs, which put one in mind of a number of younger sisters playing and sporting round their elderly relative. I must mention, merely on account of the contrast, though there is nothing strange in the phenomenon, that by the side of these hot springs there is often a spring of icy-cold water bubbling up. This latter has its source high up in the mountain side, while the former rise from the bowels of the earth. The characteristics of these springs will be treated of at greater length in my description of the great, world-wide Geysir.

From Reykjahlíð I made an excursion to the trading station at Húsavík, on the north coast. The situation of this place is one of the most brilliant in Iceland. It lies at the head of an open bay, called Skjálfandi, on the west shore of which runs the imposing ridge of Víknafjalls, ornamented with its snow "fonds" and sharp, alpine peaks. At the foot of this mountain is Náttfaravík, celebrated for being the place where one of

Iceland's former colonists settled. The trading station, on the opposite shore of the bay, is surrounded with grassy heights, and some low but precipitous fjelds, which slope towards the shore, and in some places present a nearly perpendicular wall of 200 feet in height. On the lowland above there are a good many houses; and the road along the coast to the north is frequently intersected by mountain streams fretting and chafing in their narrow beds. I travelled along this road a few times on scientific excursions, and had frequent opportunities of obtaining a near view of the quantities of seals that lay basking on the rocks on the shore; for they seemed to trouble themselves very little about the presence of a horseman. Seals are caught here, as in other parts of the country, in nets, at certain seasons of the year when they frequent the coast. Sometimes the capture of seals will amount to 150 at one time; but it is bloody work: for as soon as a seal is caught in the net, it is drawn up to land, and is knocked on the head with a club. Very often it is only stunned from the effects of the blow; whereon the club again comes into requisition, and the blood flows out, and thus the poor beast dies by degrees.

The coast to the north of Húsavík consists of a tufa, which contains fossil remains of periwinkles and mussels in large quantities, belonging to the younger division of the tertiary formation. Rather extensive strata of surturbrandr occur in this tufa, and run for some considerable distance along the coast, and penetrate some way inland. Thus at one place the eye can follow them to a distance of 900 feet along the upper edge of the steep coast; while a little brook, named Skeifa, which has cut itself a channel deep down in among them, and which empties itself into the sea in the form of a beautiful fall over a perpendicular rock, shows that they extend inwards some 500 feet. I had great difficulty in clambering up to these strata, which are at a height of about 150 to 200 feet above the sea; and when I reached them, owing to the smoothness of the rocks, I could scarcely keep my footing, so that I was unable to examine them closely. Of these strata there are four which are of some importance, measuring about one foot in thickness, and separated by a sandy tufa. The topmost of them lies near the surface of the earth. At another place, to the south, the rock was easier to clamber up. Strata of surturbrandr and tufa alternated with each other, so that in a perpendicular height of about 23 feet the united thickness of the strata of surturbrandr, five in number, was about eight feet and a half. They were quite bare for a distance of about 500 feet along the coast. A third stratum to the north of the above-named was about 700 feet in length. Nearly all the strata lie in a horizontal position, or are slightly inclined towards the horizon. As may be perceived, therefore, these surturbrandr strata are of some extent; and it is strange that they are altogether neglected in a district where all the coal that is used has to be conveyed on horseback from the trading stations, and where they might prove of great service to the inhabitants.

The beautiful landscape round Húsavík appeared at its best during my stay there—thanks to fine weather and a clear sky. In the forenoons the sun shone with great power, and made one long after the "hafsgola," or the breeze which blows from the sea on the hot days of summer. I noticed here the highest temperature in the shade this summer. It was 16° C., which, though it cannot be compared with the temperature which prevailed at Upsala at the same time, viz., 36°, yet in comparison with what I had experienced a few days before up at Grímsstaðir, was certainly an agreeable contrast.

From Húsavík I ventured to ride by myself to Reykjahlíð,

some seven or eight hours' journey. This road is one of the best in Iceland. The "heiði" south of Húsavík is free from stones, and is level, although only sparsely overgrown with grass. Neither are there any hills or fjelds to be met with along it, and there are only a few small streams to be crossed. The last few miles north of Mývatn certainly consist of a sandy plain; but it is tolerably level, and the road is pretty good, owing, I suppose, to the sulphur traffic from the "solfataras," near Mývatn, to Húsavík, in former days, in which 100 horses are said to have been employed at one time. But, though the road did not present any difficulties or obstructions, yet it is not an easy matter to ride alone in Iceland, as the loose horses which have to be driven on in front are not always willing to go in a direct course, but will often stray to the right or the left after the fragrant patches of grass. In passing a farmhouse, too, they are sometimes rather refractory, for an Icelandic horse, like its master, will "pull-up" wherever it can, and thus cause the traveller all manner of annoyances. In one respect, it is much easier travelling across the sandy wastes, for there is generally not a single blade of grass growing there to entice the hungry animals.

My principal object in returning to Reykjahlíð was to gain a little further information about the "solfataras" in the district of Mývatn. In addition to the so-called Hlídarnámar, mentioned above, near Namafjall, to the east of the lake, there are some springs of a similar character to the south-east of this, by the northern edge of the enormous stream which, under the name of Ódáðahraun, transforms a large portion of the district north of Vatnajökul into a frightful wilderness. These springs are called Fremrinámar; and it is these which have yielded the most sulphur. About twenty-two years ago, however, the people ceased to work them, and from what a farmer in Reykjahlíð told me, no one had ever visited them since that time. After four hours' hard riding from Reykjahlíð, for the most part over a bare plain, covered with streams of lava or stony heaps, the "solfataras" are reached; they are situate on the northern and eastern slope of a volcanic crater, probably the largest in Iceland. This crater, which is at a great altitude, is not, however, connected with any actual fjeld, but, like many other volcanoes in Iceland, rises up from a table-land. I approached the crater from the side where the lava had issued forth, and as the lava-stream had only a small slope or inclination, and no hill or eminence marked the position of the crater from this side, I was all at once astounded at finding myself on the brink of the abyss, which was about 2,000 feet in width and 200 feet in depth. It is appropriately called by the natives by a word signifying "The Cauldron." Lava streams surround one here on every side. Several important mountains rise up from this plateau, some of which are volcanic. Of these Sellandafjall and Bláfjall are distinguished by their beautiful and rounded forms. In Ódáðahraun, two fjelds rear themselves up aloft, called Trölladýngjur, or the "Trold's sleeping rooms," while to the south-west the snow-clad summits of some of the spurs of Vatnajökul may be seen. The most beautiful of all the mountains here, and, indeed, in the whole of Iceland, is Herðubreið (Broad-shoulder), whose outline, viewed from the crater, assumes the form which the accompanying sketch illustrates. It is one of the loftiest mountains in the country, and is 5,290 feet above the sea; its top resembles the boss of a shield, and is covered with snow, while its steep sides are of a dark blue colour.

The sulphur springs at Fremrinámar consist of hot gaseous exhalations from the earth, which by their deposition of sulphur form low, round eminences on the plain. They are situated on the outer, as well as on the upper inside, slope of the crater-wall. The superincumbent mass, which was two or three inches in thickness, consisted mostly of pure, shining sulphur; but the amount of sulphur contained, not only in this instance, but in all other places in Iceland, is insignificant when compared with what is the case in Sicily. The whole quantity of sulphur produced in Iceland during the years the "solfataras" were worked, was only some few hundred weight,

Herðubreið.

whilst that in Sicily amounted to a million. It may be assumed that when the works at Fremrinámar were closed, about twenty-two years ago, they were pretty nearly exhausted, but the process of reproduction had subsequently been going on to such an extent that my companion was of opinion that the contents would almost correspond to the quantity found there when they began to work them the last time. But, even should they be worked again, the profits could not be large, when it is borne in mind that the sulphur has to be carried a two days' journey on horseback to the trading station; that the price is only three marks per hundred-weight, and that a horse cannot carry more than three or three and a half hundred-weights, while, in addition to this, the expenses of digging up the sulphur from the earth are to be taken into account. Of course, the profit would be larger if the raw sulphur could be manufactured in the country, but, from lack of fuel, this is impossible. Thus, though the Icelandic "solfataras" may put a little into the pockets of a private individual or two, they cannot be called sources of national wealth.

By making Reykjahlíð one's head-quarters several interesting excursions may be made to different places in this part of the country. One of these is the volcano Leirhnúkr, which lies a short distance to the north-east of Reykjahlíð.

One beautiful Sunday morning I set out on foot along the lava stream, which the volcano had discharged in its eruptions of 1725 and 1727, of which I will presently speak. This lava stream runs in a narrow valley, between two high mountains named Hlíðarfjall and Dalfjall, and below these spreads out along the upper shore of Myvatn, and also along the bottom of the lake. In making my way up to the volcano I partly followed the lava stream, which in some places was tolerably smooth, but in others consisted of loose masses of pieces of lava; and partly followed its western side along the foot of Hlíðarfjall. But, after I had gone some distance, fully expecting that the volcano, according to my calculations, should appear in sight, which it obstinately refused to do, and as I had taken no guide with me, I was obliged to direct my steps in that quarter where I conceived it to lie. Under ordinary circumstances this would not have been attended with much difficulty; but in this case the road between me and the volcano consisted of a lava plain of such extent that I could see no limits to it. There was, therefore, nothing else to be done than to direct my course over this obstacle, which I accordingly proceeded to do, first, however, ascending a little mountainous ridge that rose up from the lava stream, in the hope of gaining a better view from its summit. Here I gained another opportunity of acquainting myself with all the peculiarities and vagaries of a lava stream, though it must be confessed it was a lesson attended with a great deal of personal inconvenience. I have remarked above that the surface of a lava stream is partially flat, and flows in a level course. The flat arches of which it is formed are nearly always cracked in fissures along the middle, which, though generally only one or two feet in breadth, are of considerable depth. In other places the surface is jagged and uneven, or is covered with loose heaps of stones about the size of a man's head or hand. They crumble and churn under one's feet; but, though lying quite loosely on one another, they seldom give away, owing to their uneven formation. All these varied formations were exemplified on the lava stream which I had to traverse. After having thus proceeded for about an hour, I became aware of a point where the "abomination of desolation" was more than usually apparent, and in another half hour the broken pieces of slag, of which the surface of the lava was formed, gave evident signs of the proximity of the crater. After a good deal of searching, and crossing and recrossing the crackling lava, I reached the first crater, which was merely an opening in the lava stream, and, therefore, could only be found by a mere chance. At the bottom of this aperture, and at a depth of ten or twelve paces from the surface, hot steam was issuing from two fissures, and which from contact with the cold atmosphere formed a thin smoke. To the north of this there was another aperture of larger dimensions. It was about 200 feet in diameter and 40 feet in depth. At the bottom, which was level, was a cone some 16 feet in height by

12 feet in diameter, furnished at its apex with a perpendicularly descending orifice, a *pseudo* volcanic crater, which served as a chimney for any gases that by chance had collected in the lava.

Close by these, and a little further to the north, was a still larger aperture, which had a weird-looking lava rock rising up from its middle. All these lie at the south foot of "Hnukr," which is a ridge running north and south, along the western side of which a fissure, almost filled up with sand, can be followed for some distance. Parallel with this fissure I noticed thirteen

Volcanic Crater at Leirhnúkr.

volcanic craters of different sizes; the most northerly and the largest, of which a sketch is given, being about 100 feet in height. Hot steam issued from a place in the fissure, as well as from one of the crater walls. Lava had flowed out from most of the craters. To the west and north of Leirhnúkr lies an open plain, over which I made my way to the volcano; it is covered with lava streams, and in some places looks like a boundless plain of lava.

In 1724-30 there were several volcanic eruptions in the neighbourhood round Mývatn. Undoubtedly the eruption which formed the lava stream that issued from Leirhnúkr was the most terrible. When the stream burst forth and reached Mývatn in its course, it made the waters of the lake boil to such a degree, that in a few days they were completely dried up, and all the fish, of course, died. The lake was then filled up with lava streams, which may still be seen protruding here and there above the surface of the water, and forming " holms " or rocky islands in its middle. The lava stream also destroyed the houses at Reykjahlíð, with the exception of the church, which lay on a little eminence, thus causing the stream to divide into two branches on either side of it. Of course the inhabitants looked upon this as a miraculous interposition of Providence. The present farmhouse at Reykjahlíð is built on the edge of the lava stream.

From the hot-springs, on the eastern slope of Lierhnúkr, I could plainly discern the circular opening of Helvíti, at the foot of Krafla; and it was a sight which was very inviting, for it was the only water-basin in the district. But as I had been on my legs since the morning, and did not care to lose my way on these barren wastes; and as, moreover, I had some distance to traverse to Reykjahlíð, I did not make a closer inspection of it. In order to avoid returning over the lava stream, I made my way along its eastern side; and, without wearying my reader too much with the progress of a tired traveller, I will only state that I managed to reach Reykjahlíð before nightfall.

It is also possible to reach Leirhnúkr on horseback—and certainly, as far as comfort is concerned, this is by far the most agreeable plan—but by this mode of travelling many points of interest, which are only accessible to a pedestrian, are not seen.

Before finally quitting Reykjahlíð I must say a few words about Mývatn, or Mygsöen, as it is called in Danish. It owes its name to the swarms of mosquitoes (myg is Danish for mosquito) which infest it, concerning which travellers complain bitterly. With the exception of the last day of my stay there, I was not inconvenienced by them, thanks to the season of the year and the state of the weather. Mývatn is one of the largest lakes of Iceland, but it is of no great depth, seldom more than twelve feet, one of of the farmers there told me. There are plenty of trout in it, and numbers of water-fowl swim about on its surface, such as ducks, gulls, sea-swallows, and other species.* The trout naturally feed on the mosquitoes, and the water birds feed on the trout and mosquitoes too, and the demand and supply is kept up to the mutual satisfaction of all parties concerned; and as the fish, as well as the birds (especially the eggs of the latter), are important sources of income to human beings, I suppose the mosquitoes are perfectly at liberty to sting, so long as they devote their attentions to the natives and leave strangers in peace. At the bottom of the lake there are several warm springs, round which the fish are fond of congregating. Owing to these the lake is not frozen over in winter.

The desert plain of Ödáðahraun, to the south of Mývatn, and its barren environs, are the principal resort of the wild reindeer in Iceland. Reindeer were introduced into the country in 1770, when three animals were brought over from Norway. They multiplied quickly, but, as above stated, principally frequent the extensive barren wastes. They are of little or no use to the natives, for it is seldom any of them are killed, and they do a good deal of damage to the grass, besides devouring the Iceland moss, called in the language of the country "fjallagras," which the people are very fond of eating themselves.

I had been led to form rather grand ideas of Reykjahlíð, as

---

* Amongst the wild fowl frequenting Mývatn may be mentioned the Scaup Duck, Long-tail Red-breasted Merganser, Icelandic Golden Eye, Black Scoter, Red-necked Phalarope, Gadwall, Wild-duck, Widgeon, Pintail, Harlequin Duck, &c.—Tr.

I was told that the only "station-house" in the whole country was to be found there. The public room was certainly cleanly, about as clean as in second-rate stations in Sweden, but the first meal I ate there taught me that I must come down in my ideas—which, however, had not soared higher than clean butter, milk, and the like—for the butter was as full of hairs as it was at other places in the country; while the national failing, dirt, made itself apparent in a variety of ways. I provided myself, therefore, with butter, bread, and cheese, on my journey to Húsavík. The Mývatn trout, however, were excellent.

My landlord, Pjetr, was a very good hand at taking people in; so that if it is part of the character of a landlord to cheat, mine host understood the art of doing so perfectly. To the honour of the Icelanders, however, I must add that, as far as I at least was concerned, such inhospitable treatment is very rarely met with. It was only at Reykjahlíð, and at Kalmannstúnga, in the western part of the country, that I was exposed to any great imposition; and only in two other places was advantage taken of the lonely condition in which a traveller in Iceland occasionally finds himself, when he is ignorant of the road, or the fording places, &c., and cannot get on without assistance. Such things occur in all countries. I must, therefore, deny the justice of the complaints that have been made of imposition among the Icelanders.

CHAPTER VII.

From Reykjahlíð to Akureyri—Akureyri—Medical Staff—Homœopathy—Epidemics—Icelanders and Scandinavianism—Emigration to Brazil—Iceland, "The Best Land under the Sun"—Wood-carving—Painting—Icelandic Foxes—Tales about Foxes—Catching Ptarmigan—Hot-springs of Reykir—A Night-Ride over the Heiði—A Night under the Open Sky—Stórisandur—Surtshellir—Its Origin—Legend of Surtshellir—Geitlands-Jökul—Legend of Þorisdalr—Attempts to re-discover it—Cracks in a Lava Stream—Almannagjá—Pre-historic Lava Stream—Return to Reykjavik.

FROM Reykjahlíð a road leads over Sprengisandr to the south, passing over the table-land between Hofs-Jökul and Vatna-Jökul, which is more than 2,000 feet above the sea, and along the Þjórsá river, to the inhabited portions of the country north of Hekla. In the autumn it is requisite to take a tent with one on this route, as otherwise three nights will have to be passed under the open sky; for, at the distance of a day's journey from Reykjahlíð, an uninhabited country is reached, which extends as far as Stórinúpr in the south. In addition to this the supply of grass *en route* is very scanty; for instance, a ride of sixteen hours at one stretch must be taken, as there is no pasture to be found for the horses.

The other road to the south from Reykjahlíð passes by Akureyri, the second town of note in the country, lying at the south end of Eyjafjörðr. From Reykjahlíð to Akureyri is a hard day's journey;

but I managed it very easily, for owing to the continued dry weather, the roads were in good condition, while there was not a large quantity of water in the two rivers, the Laxá and the Skálfandafljót, which we had to ford. The Laxá comes from Mývatn and falls out into Skjálfandi bay. What Mývatn is for trout, so is Laxá for salmon; at its mouth an important salmon fishery is carried on. The district immediately north of Mývatn is more inviting than is the case to the east. For it is covered with grass, though it must be confessed it is but a thin covering, for evident remains of volcanic craters and lava streams stick up here and there from the green sward. The country between Laxá and Skújlfandafljót consists of grass-grown heiði, which form excellent pasture ground. From Skálfandafljót, in whose sandy bed an old lava stream peeps out, the road runs through the lovely pass of Ljósavatnaskarð by the lake Ljósavatn. On both sides one is hemmed in by steep walls of basalts till Púls parsonage is reached. I made a flying visit to this comfortable parsonage, and was entertained by the pastor and his amiable daughter, who brought me coffee and thin pancakes—an excellent accompaniment, by the way, to the former, and one often used instead of biscuits in Iceland. Here I rode through the first real wood I had seen during the whole course of my long journey through the country. It was a low birch slop, and the branches of the trees reached a little higher than the horseman!

Akureyri, which lies close to the shore of Eyafjörðr, is a place of much less importance than Reykjavik. One half of the town consists merely of a single row of houses; in the other half there are certainly two long streets, but one of them which runs close along the shore is flooded when the tide is high. The houses are generally tarred over both on the walls and roofs. But Akureyri has one advantage over her sister-city and the country in general; for there are to be found the only

s

large trees of which Iceland can boast. They consist of a few mountain ashes, and when the largest was measured a few years ago, it was found to be 25 feet high, and had a fine crown. Owing to their solitary appearance these trees may be reckoned among the sights of the country. Although the mean temperature for the whole year is much higher at Reykjavik than at this place, nothing of the sort can be made to grow there.*

Possibly the reason may be that Reykjavik lies on an open coast, and is exposed to every wind that blows; while Akureyri on the other hand lies protected by mountain ridges on either side the fjord (of which the eastern assumes an altitude of 2,118 feet, while the western range rises to a height of 2,898 feet above the sea), and is thus less exposed to the fury of the storm.

In Akureyri I took up my abode with Doctor Jón Finsen, the district physician, where I was treated with the usual hospitality and kindness. The system of medical supervision in Iceland is, as might be supposed, very deficient. The seven district physicians, and the so-called "Land-physicus" in Reykjavik compose the whole medical staff of the country. Consequently their districts are of such wide extent, that even with the best will in the world they cannot possibly fulfil the duties required of them. Iceland is about two-ninths the size of Sweden; from which comparison it may be seen how insufficient the staff of medical men must be for the country. When the doctor, as is frequently the case, takes four or five days in order to reach the extreme boundaries of his district, it

---

* The mean temperature for the year is +4·5° at Reykjavik, while at Akureyri it is only +0·52°. This striking difference is doubtless due to the different directions which the sea-currents assume. The coast near Reykjavik is washed by the Gulf Stream, while the cold Polar stream impinges on a part of the north coast.

will be understood that this fact is synonymous with his never visiting those parts at all, and consequently that sick people residing there are entirely without medical advice. This is a very lamentable state of things, as, of course, a great many persons must perish from lack of medical assistance. Health is a capital which Icelanders in general seem to regard very lightly. A doctor in Iceland both can and ought to effect a great improvement in sanitary matters, and the knowledge of this fact has doubtless given rise to the establishment of an institution, which, however excellent it may be in theory, yet as regards its practical utility grave doubts may legitimately be entertained.

For a small remuneration from the state, the "Land-physicus" at Reykjavik has undertaken to turn out "doctores medicinæ" in the course of two or three years, who have authority from the government to fill the post of district surgeons, on the same footing with those who have been examined by the medical faculty in Copenhagen. But it appears to me that by adopting this plan, government has but given its sanction to quackery on a large scale. For that a person by merely studying medicine for two or three years from the period when he leaves school, should be able—except in some rare instances—ever to practise otherwise than as a quack doctor, seems to me to be an absolute impossibility. In Reykjavik, there are no opportunities for carrying out medical instruction; no hospital or any institution of a similar nature; consequently the preparation of the students can only consist in the learning of some general prescriptions against sickness.* Happy would it be for the patient if the same prescription would meet every case! When once the medical appointments in Iceland are filled

---

* The examination is of a piece with the instruction given. At the first examination that was held the examiners were the apothecary and the assessor of the law court,—a somewhat strange mixture!

with such persons, professional science will at the same time be driven out of the country. Surely it would be well to pause and reflect before it is too late.

It is very likely owing to the deficient state of medical supervision in the country that homœopathy has gained such a firm footing in Iceland. The Amtmand over the northern part of the island, who lives near Akureyri, seems to have been the introducer and patron of this branch of medical science. Besides this individual, there are seven practising homœopathic doctors, mostly peasants, in these parts, who have acquired their information from some German books. They are much sought after by the people, for patients come from long distances to consult them, and consequently are held in no mean repute. Indeed, in all countries people are very credulous in such matters. My landlord, Pjetr, at Reykjahlið, asked me whether there were many homœopathists in Sweden. "No," I answered; "and we look rather suspiciously upon such people!" This appeared to surprise him; for he rejoined—"They are all allopaths there, then!"

No country in Europe has been so visited by epidemics as Iceland. According to the annals of the country no less than 134 epidemics have visited it from the year 1306 to 1846, most of which have affected the rate of mortality in the country in a greater or less degree. It must be remarked, moreover, that the older annals only refer to the most important epidemics; in later years, however, they have been given with greater accuracy. The number of epidemics, therefore, seems to have increased; a fact which, though partly attributable to the above cause, is none the less a painful reality. For unprecedented misfortunes visited the country, especially in the eighteenth century, partly the results of the devastations committed by volcanic eruptions, partly owing to the injurious effects of monopoly in commerce. In the fourteenth century, seven epidemics are known to have occurred; in the fifteenth, six; in the sixteenth, twelve; in the seventeenth century, when the system of monopoly was first introduced in all its severity, there were twenty-eight; and in the eighteenth century, forty-one. In the last century, therefore, the land was visited by an epidemic nearly every other year. The most fearful of these occurred in 1704, when it is computed that Iceland must have lost 18,000 out of a population of 50,000; and in 1783-5, when those terrible devastations, which have already been described, took place. According to Dr. Schleisner, to whose interesting work on Iceland I am greatly indebted for much valuable information, it is stated, as the author's firm conviction, that the number of epidemics that have occurred in Iceland is principally due to the wretched construction of the houses, which are built without any regard to ventilation or the admission of light; and where the inmates are packed together in a fetid atmosphere and in damp rooms. Whoever knows anything of an Icelandic "bær" will heartily endorse this opinion. For it is well known how much more severely epidemics rage in the dirtiest quarters of well-built cities and towns, than in those where the laws of health are observed.

To the north of Eyafjörðr, about 22 miles from its mouth, lies the solitary island of Grimsey. It is intersected by the Polar circle, and contains about fifty inhabitants. In the course of last summer (1864) typhus fever broke out among them, and had already carried off twelve persons before the fishing boat which brought the news to Akureyri had left the island. In a place like this, destitute of all medical aid, the inhabitants could readily become extinct. Offers were made to the islanders to come over to the main land. But they refused to leave; "they would rather die there," they said. These islanders depend for their support on fishing and bird-catching, and lead rather an active life, though they are entirely shut out from intercourse with their fellow-men. Some of them, however, visit Akureyri once a year in the summer.

I have already alluded to the views entertained by the Icelanders of Sweden and the Swedes, and will now only make a few additional remarks on the subject. From what I could ascertain they are very favourably inclined towards us. Owing to their proficiency in history and geography the Icelanders are perfectly at home in our affairs. For their ancient Sagas contain the names of many places in Sweden, which shine, therefore, with a certain degree of poetical brilliancy in the eyes of an Icelander, and the mention of which makes his heart throb. When I happened to mention one day that I came from Uppland, they began to say by rote, "Uppland, Wärmland," &c. Presently one person asked me, "Are you really from old Upsala?"* He evinced great feeling in pronouncing the word "old," and I was sorry to have to say that the "old" had been pushed aside to give place for the "new."

On the second or third day after my arrival in Reykjavik I was visited by an Icelander of high official rank. This gentleman introduced himself by saying that he had heard I was a Swede, and would, therefore, be very glad to assist me with any information or advice I might require with reference to my journey through the country. He entertained a great affection for Sweden, he said; and had read several Swedish works with great pleasure, of which Geijer's and Tegnér's writings occupied the first place in his estimation; and he thought he was only paying a debt of gratitude by rendering a Swede some service. "Frithiof's Saga" is a very general favourite, and

---

* Uppsalir is a very common name in Iceland. It signifies a place that is situated on a hill, so that it is visible at a long distance off.

has been translated into Icelandic. The Icelanders, as a rule, are better acquainted with the Swedish language than the Swedes are with theirs, owing doubtless to their intercourse with Denmark. These and other circumstances combined assured me that provided the object of Scandinavianism were attained, Iceland would not be unwilling to enter into a political alliance, naturally a personal union, and not as a subordinate country, a condition for which her remote situation and peculiar circumstances render unsuited. Iceland is certainly not a country, by the attachment of which a material addition of power would be obtained; but she affords a rich field for intellectual cultivation, which would stand a better chance of being developed in union with those who are near of kin to her, and which would not fail to exercise indirectly a beneficial influence upon them.

At a festival held at Reykjavik, on the occasion of the close of the Icelandic Rigsdag or Diet, the author of these pages availed himself of the opportunity of pointing out the mutual bonds that united Iceland with the rest of the north, and the future that might await them were the union to be effected. His remarks were warmly received; whence he concluded that a feeling in favour of the unity of the north, though still slumbering, might readily awaken to life and vigour in Iceland. For the moment, however, intercourse between Sweden and this country is at a very low ebb. Except on the few occasions when a Swedish vessel of war has extended its visit to Reykjavik, on its annual cruise, for the instruction and exercise of her naval cadets, the flag of Sweden never floats in any Icelandic harbour. The Norwegians, however, send several small vessels thither laden with timber; and Sweden might well follow the example of her neighbour by exporting both timber and iron to the country.

It rests then for Swedish enterprise and Swedish commerce to seek Iceland; for, as I have already remarked, the Icelandic trade is principally in the hands of Danish merchants, who naturally enough do all they can to guard against any competition.

The Icelander, like all Northmen in general and islanders in particular, is extremely attached to his Fatherland. It is only quite recently, therefore, that the desire of emigrating has made itself apparent among them. They have not, however, fixed their aspirations upon North America, which is comparatively near at hand, but on Brazil. Whence this strange contradiction arises I have in vain sought to discover; for a contradiction it most surely is, to flit to tropical regions from the Polar Circle, passing by republican North America for Imperial Brazil.

Two years ago two men, it seems, set out for Brazil; they had read about this good (?) land in a book, I was told; and, in due course of time, reached their destination, when they wrote letters home encouraging their friends to follow them. In consequence of this, certain peasants were induced to sell their little property, and to make preparations for emigrating. In the course of last summer 150 persons, women and children included, were in readiness to leave their Fatherland. One of them, who was the soul of the undertaking, had entered into a sort of agreement with the others that he should procure a Norwegian vessel to take them over; but, whether it was owing to intrigues or untrustworthiness, the vessel never came, and the poor people stood homeless and helpless with winter at the door. Icelanders, however, in general regard the desire to emigrate with very unfavourable feelings; in fact, they look upon those of their countrymen who have emigrated as downright traitors to their land; and, with their despotic disposition, bitterly complain that the laws cannot check this desire for travelling.

While this aversion to travelling unquestionably affords a good proof of the Icelander's attachment to his Fatherland (and a well-known Icelandic proverb says: "Iceland is the best land the sun shines on"), at the same time it bears testimony to a theorising and inwardly-directed train of thought which is a prominent national feature, partly an heirloom descended to them from their forefathers, and is partly due to the peculiar nature of the country. The existence of raw material, which in other countries compels the inhabitants to direct their thoughts to practical pursuits, is almost entirely wanting in Iceland. The farmer performs all simple kinds of necessary workmanship with his own hands, consequently there are but few mechanics in the country. Hence it follows, too, that the fine arts are but little cultivated, and that a taste for the beautiful is but little developed. It might almost, therefore, be looked upon as a chance, as a freak of nature, that the sculptor Thorvaldsen was of Icelandic origin; for his father was an Icelander. Still, the art of carving is not entirely unknown, as household utensils cut out in a variety of ways fully prove. But painting, sculpture, music, those acquirements whose nature must be appreciated through the external senses, are but little thought of in the country. There are no national songs, but merely a kind of recitative, reminding one of the songs of the old bards; while instrumental music is represented by the old-fashioned harp or other stringed instrument. They but rarely indulge in dancing. It is true, in Reykjavik there is a clever young painter, Sigurðr Guðmundsson, but he receives little encouragement. His portraits are, however, very good. The only art which seems to be thought of any worth in Iceland is working in gold. Very beautiful articles may be seen in this branch of industry, but even these are memorials from olden days. The national costume, it will be remembered, requires a good many gold and silver ornaments. It can, of course, scarcely be expected that many should be found in a little nation like this to devote their time exclusively to the study of the fine arts, especially as no encouragement is given them. If things were different, most probably slumbering talents would be awakened here, as has been the case elsewhere. The dilapidated appearance and the general uncleanliness of their houses can only be accounted for from the deficiency of good taste and the love of what is beautiful among them; for no one endowed with any perceptions for external propriety could put up with what the Icelander endures in these respects.

It is also worthy of remark, and a further proof of the Icelander's peculiar habit of thought, that so few of these people devote themselves to the study of the natural sciences, although the book of nature lies open in Iceland, and its pages are covered with beautiful handwriting. The inhabitants of the northern parts of Sweden are in this respect on a similar footing. When they devote themselves to study, they generally become philologians or theologians, or else take up some other purely theoretical science. The practical cause for this probably is, that the clergyman in remote and thinly-peopled districts is, if I may be permitted to use such an expression, "cock of the walk;" his learning is the sun whose rays are caught up by those who wish to shine with equal brightness. Amongst the Swedes, however, this state of affairs is beginning to give way, but in Iceland there are no such symptoms as yet apparent. It would scarcely be credited that at the school in Reykjavik no collection of the natural products of the country is to be found, or at least none of any account. When Prince Napoleon visited the island a few years ago, he was shown the collection at the school; and my informant assured me, that they requested him to "take whatever he had a liking to!" Such was the regard in which they held specimens from the rocks and mountains of their Fatherland.

The imposing heights on both sides of Eyafjörðr were enveloped in an obstinate fog during my stay at Akureyri. Shortly before my departure, however, it lifted a little, but soon sank down again over the long, deep valley of Öxna, to the west of Akureyri, through which my road lay. I wished to travel over-land to Reykjavik as quickly as possible, in order to visit those well-known notabilities, Hekla and the Geysirs. I had been waiting for letters from Reykjavik and abroad; but the post in Iceland is so badly organised, that the mail which reached Reykjavik in the beginning of August was not despatched to the northern districts before the middle of September, though it is only a six-days' journey between that place and Akureyri.

The first place I put up at for the night, on my journey to the south, was a farmhouse in Öxnadalr. I met with nothing of note on my first day's journey, unless I reckon a little party of three foxes, two black ones, and one white one, which had selected the road along which I had to ride as a playground, and would scarcely get out of the way of my horse's feet. The fox is the largest and the most dangerous (!) beast of prey among the wild animals of the country; and here, as elsewhere, it maintains its character for cunning.

I will tell the reader two of the stories which were told me about them. Whether they are deserving of credit, I will leave it for him to decide.

In the autumn, when the young birds have grown, the foxes congregate in small bands on the rocks, on whose slopes the birds'-nests lie, in order to concentrate their endeavours in adopting some plan to procure some nice fresh bird-flesh; for the fox is a great gourmand at times. To reach the young birds on the slopes of the rocks, the foxes form themselves into a chain, after the following manner—the one lays firm hold with his teeth on the brush of another, whereupon the descent commences. The oldest and strongest fox, naturally, is the one to form the rearmost of the troop on the top of the rock;

An Icelandic Fox.

for it is on him all the others depend. Gulls and water-fowl, which build on the bird-rocks facing the sea, are the principal objects of their attack.

The other story has to do with ptarmigan. These birds are widely dispersed over the country, and are very tame, as well as very stupid birds. In winter-time, during a snow-storm, they will not move off the spot where they are sitting, and are therefore very easily caught. The fox, with his keen nose, observes this; and when a high wind blows, unaccompanied with any downfall, he lies flat on his stomach on the snow, and creeps stealthily along towards the ptarmigan, taking care to approach him on the windward side. All this while he stirs up the snow, both with his feet and brush, and the wind carries it into the eyes of the bird. The ptarmigan, thinking in its simplicity that the snow comes from the clouds, keeps quite still, and lets the fox get so close to it, that it only becomes aware of its peril when it finds itself in the enemy's power.

Foxes, moreover, frequently commit great depredations among the sheep flocks; for, as soon as a fox has conceived a taste for mutton, it prefers this kind of food to any other. But, as it is not strong enough to master the sheep in single combat, it gets a firm hold of its fleece; whereon the terrified animal scampers off, till it falls down. Reynard thus has a regular hunt.

In Iceland a distinction is made between the foxes. Some are called tame foxes; others, wild foxes. The latter are those which attack sheep; and by the former are understood those which will not do so. I suppose foxes have this weakness in common with dogs, that when they have once tasted sheep's flesh, they can never be cured from attacking them.

In the neighbourhood of Steinstaðir there is a little wooden bridge over an impetuous brook, named Bægisú. I mention this as a bridge is quite an exceptional thing. On the other side of Steinstaðir, the road passes through a narrow, stony pass over Öxnadalsheiði down into Norðrardalr, whose stream runs into the Hèraðsvötn, a river of some importance, flowing into Skagafjörðr. There was a large body of water in the river, and the horses were almost obliged to swim; indeed, the water came up over the shoulder of the horse I was riding. The guide who had followed me across the ford from a farmhouse on the eastern side of the river, had to swim over it on his return-journey. He had missed, by only a hair's breadth, the exact point at which we had crossed over, and had immediately got into deep water. The horse which he rode was fortunately a strong animal, and, after having been driven down by the current for some distance, he succeeded in regaining the shore, when the proper fording-place was speedily found.

The above-named valleys are hemmed in on both sides by steep walls of basalts, the tops of which occasionally peered forth, through the fog, like gigantic forms.

I had to remain a day at the parsonage of Mælifell, which I made my second night quarters, waiting for a guide to Kalmannstúnga, a two days' journey, to reach which I should have to traverse an extensive waste, in the centre of which Stórisandur lay.

Skagafjarðardalr is one of the most fertile parts of the country. Several hundred horses are sent there every autumn from the east coast, in order to seek their winter provender in the mountains. Possibly the internal warmth of the earth may, in a great measure, be the cause of this fertility. At all events, there are several warm springs in different parts of the valley. The most important of these is at Reykir, due north of Mælifell; white vapour may be seen to issue from it a long distance off. I was told that corpses buried in the churchyard at Reykir, which is close to these springs, mouldered away and entirely disappeared in the course of two or three years. The heat of the earth submits them to a process of dry distillation, which greatly accelerates their decomposition. It would answer to lay out gardens at such places as these. Round the warm springs grass will grow luxuriantly, at least where the siliceous water, which is destructive to vegetation, is not thrown about.

Mælifell is an excellent place to stay at; and the traveller will bid farewell to the venerable pastor and his amiable wife with feelings of regret. From thence the route lies at the foot of Mælifellshnúkr (3,476 feet), which, owing to fog, was invisible, and afterwards across a stony and barren heiði, called Haukagilsheiði. Owing to the dense fog, which entirely shut out the top of the mountain from view, my guide expressed grave doubts at being able to pilot me over the waste that lay before us, as he had only once crossed it in his life two years ago. I, too, was beginning to get tired and disgusted with the fog, which had now for a whole week shut out the landscape. Great, therefore, was our joy when, on coming out of Mælifellsdalr on to the "heiði," we sighted the snowy summits of Hofs-Jökul in the south-east, and the round, snow-crowned top of Láng-Jökul in the south, at a distance of about forty miles. With joyful anticipations of a prosperous journey, we hastened along on our course, crossed the large river Blandá in the afternoon, and proceeded to continue our route across the barren "heiði," until darkness overtook us.

The goal of this day's journey was a small mountain, named Sandfell, where we knew we should be able to find fodder and water for our horses; but we were very nearly not reaching it, for in the evening the clouds again descended and obscured the view; and as the road was only marked out by horses' hoofs, which even in broad daylight might easily be mistaken, it was a matter of great difficulty to keep to the right road in the dark. When we got out of it I adopted the precaution of halting my own horse and the loose ones, and making my guide ride round in a ring till he had taken up the trail again. After proceeding in this way for some time, we came to a little brook where there was some grass. We deemed it prudent to halt here, whether we were close to the foot of Sandfell or not. When the fog dispersed a little, we found that we were going in the right direction. It was now about nine in the evening; and as it was impossible to continue our journey in the dark, for a sandy waste lay before us, in which no halting-place could be found, we determined to pass the night where we were. That night I slept on the ground, covered up in my cloak; and as the night was calm, though the season was rather far advanced—it was the night of the 16th and 17th of August

—I should have slept "as sweetly as on a bed of flowers," had it not been necessary for me to waken up every now and then and stir up my snoring companion, to make him go and see after our horses, as I feared we might lose them, although they were hobbled, in the dense fog. My companion and his dog crept as close to me as they could during the night, but I always managed to keep a space between us; and as this space was very wet and damp, I felt it would be an insuperable trench against the onslaughts of the only nocturnal wanderers I was afraid of. That evening, therefore, I laid me down to rest with a joyful heart, glad at not having to bestrew myself over with insect powder in order to enjoy a good night's rest.

The next morning we were early astir, and after some searching about found our way on to the sand, where, to our great joy, we came on the fresh tracks of a caravan which had gone in a northerly direction, so that we could now steer our course in spite of the fog; but, after we had proceeded on our way for a few hours, a brisk wind began to blow, the clouds lifted, and the sun shone out. Before us lay snowy mountains bathed in a deep purple hue. It was a glorious sight, one of the most lovely I have seen in Iceland; for what more can be desired than a clear sky, a bright sun, and a boundless mountain of snow, the summit of which seems to melt into the distant atmosphere, and—the reader must not smile—an illimitable sandy plain? What is it that makes the sea so imposing? Is it not its vastness? What makes the star-bespangled sky so enchanting? Is it not because it is infinite? Why, then, may not an extensive plain of sand, to which the eye can perceive no limits, present a grand and imposing spectacle, whatever the disagreeables be which the imagination may connect with the mere thought of Nature clothed in such a form?

The crest of Láng-Jökul was even and rounded on this side,

and without peaks; light-blue glaciers sloped down its precipitous walls. Another mountain on the north side, named Eyriks-Jökul, whose top was covered with a crown of snow, and whose sides were adorned with snow fonds and glaciers, was a real feast to my eyes for a great part of the day.

After journeying over the sand for three or four hours, we reached a "heiði," sparsely overgrown with grass. It is called Arnarvatnsheiði, from the number of large and small lakes, which, in number about fifty, occupy the desert terrain north of Eyriks-Jökul, and are called Fiskivötn, under one general name. They are a favourite haunt for swans; and we could see the majestic birds swimming over the blue water, and could hear their melodious tones.

After crossing the "heiði," and a small Jökul river named Norðlingafljót, we came to an old lava stream, which contains one of the wonderful sights of Iceland. This is the cave Surtshellir, or rather a tunnel in the earth, about a mile in length, between 50 and 60 feet in breadth, and about 36 feet in height at its commencement. The descent into this tunnel is through a large opening in a vaulted arch that has given way. It is sufficiently lighted from the entrance and from an opening in the roof, for a person to grope his way in on his hands and feet. The bottom is very uneven, from the large blocks that have fallen down from the roof. The roof, moreover, looks as if it would not last much longer, for every here and there the daylight peeps through small apertures in it, whence it may be inferred that it will follow the example of the portion of the arch that has fallen in. The main tunnel extends behind the second opening; it is only furnished with three small apertures, which are not nearly sufficient to illumine the cave. Indeed, it was nearly pitch dark; and as I had no candles or torches, I could not go far in. From what other travellers, however, have reported, it is uniform in character throughout, only with this difference, that the roof naturally becomes depressed towards the extreme end of the cave. It branches off in several lateral directions. The water drips through the lava on the roof and walls of the grotto; and a damp atmosphere pervades the place.

The origin of Surtshellir has given more than one traveller a "bee in his bonnet." Some have thought it to be nothing more than a huge bubble formed in the lava stream from the collection of gases, in the same way as the arches on the surface of lava streams are produced. But as an objection to this theory, may be alleged its great extent in all directions; and it must be allowed that it seems incredible that gas alone could have caused its existence. Had such been the case, the arch of the cave would be elevated over the surface of the earth; but this is not so. It is more natural therefore to suppose that its formation is due to the natural characteristic of lava streams to congeal on their surface, while the mass underneath continues in a fluent state. On this supposition, then, the surface of the stream became rigid, while the mass underneath continued to flow, thus leaving the cave in its present form.

Surtshellir has not only acquired its notoriety from the fact of its being a natural curiosity, but from its having been a place of refuge for "utilegumenn," or outlawed people, who, in olden days, were said to resort to the mountains, where they subsisted on plunder and robbery, though at the same time it must be stated that the Icelanders of the present day do not seem to have very clear ideas about the fact of their existence or non-existence.

When, for instance, as it sometimes happens, a number of sheep perish on the mountains in stormy weather, the blame is put on the shoulders of the "utilegumenn," instead of being attributed to the carelessness of the owners. It is therefore not uncommon to hear intelligent people ask, in a half-credulous, half-doubting way, "How can these 'utilegumenn' live now?" It may, however, be safely concluded, that they are no longer in existence, for no one has seen anything of them for centuries; and moreover, when the people in the neighbouring districts were being starved to death in numbers, it is scarcely probable that the "utilegumenn" should have escaped. But the strongest reason why they, or rather their descendants, are not existent at the present day, one of my Icelandic friends informed me, is, that there is no reason why they should remain up in the barren wastes; for no one would do them any injury if they did come down into the inhabited districts.

The exploits of those "utilegumenn" have given rise to various tales of greater or less credibility. Amongst these, one that relates to Surtshellir, is one of the best, if not the most probable. It is related, for instance, that the youth who used to frequent a school at Hólar, in Skagafjörðr, where, it may be stated *en passant*, was in former days the one episcopal see in Iceland, conceived the innocent idea of building a snow man; but unhappily in order to carry out their project, they took it into their heads to make use of an unfortunate old woman, who happened to be passing by, as a mould or skeleton for their figure. As might be expected, the consequence was that the old woman perished in the snow. The lads were terribly alarmed, and in order to escape punishment, fled for refuge to Surtshellir, where they subsisted on robbery and plunder, till at last they were exterminated by the peasants, who had banded together for that purpose. The plan they adopted was as follows: they induced a boy to seek out the delinquents, and under the pretext that he had run away from home, to ask permission to become one of them. His request was granted, but in order to secure themselves against treachery, they adopted the precaution of ham-stringing him. But in course of time the wounds healed up, and one day while the band were out on a plundering expedition, the boy hobbled off home, and acquainted the people with what he knew. Thereupon the peasants assembled in a body and set off to Surtshellir, where they found the robbers sleeping in a little valley in the neighbourhood of their retreat. They killed them all with the exception of one who managed to escape to a Jökul, which received the name of Eirikr after the fugitive. In one of the lateral caves of Surtshellir a quantity of bones of sheep and other animals have been found, which, it is said, were carried there by the robbers.

I soon reached my next night-quarters in Kalmannstúnga, and set out on the following morning along the road to Þingvellir, the most classic spot in Iceland. After riding over two Jökul rivers, which are the sources of the large Hvítá river running out into Borgafjörðr, I came on to a road consisting only of sharp-edged blocks of stone, named Skulaskeið. In olden days a man named Skúli, in fleeing away from his pursuers, had made his horse "skeiða," or canter, along this road. At the present day, however, it is only possible to proceed along it at foot-pace. On the other side of Skúlaskeið is the commencement of a narrow valley called Kaldidalr, doubtless so-called because it can sometimes be very cold there, owing to the masses of snow and glaciers on either side. These latter hang over rather than rest on the steep sides of the Jökul, and the blue masses of ice of which they consist afford a most pleasing contrast to the white field of snow further up on the Jökul, and to the black walls of rock, and greyish-brown *débris* in the valley below.

At the south end of Geitlands-Jökul there is a remarkable valley, which has obtained the name of Þorisdalr. The following is related concerning its discovery in the ancient Grettissaga, one of the principal Sagas of Iceland:—

"Grettir went to Geitland in the autumn, where he waited for fine weather; he then went up on Geitlands-Jökul, taking a kettle and matches with him. At last he found a long and narrow valley in the Jökul, hemmed in on all sides by overhanging masses of ice. On descending into it, he found the slopes covered with luxuriant grass and brushwood. There were also warms springs there, whence he concluded that volcanic heat was the reason why the Jökul had not spread over the valley. A little river flowed through it, the banks of which were covered with grass. Owing to the depth of the valley, the sun was only visible for a short time in the twenty-four hours. He could not count all the sheep which he found in the valley; but they were fatter and superior to any he had ever seen before. Grettir established himself there, and built a house out of the wood he found on the spot. He killed one of the sheep, and found that it was as good as two elsewhere. A lamb, for instance, had forty pounds of fat on it, and its flesh was very delicious. But there was something uncanny about it: for its mother used to scramble every night up on Grettir's house and bleat so that he could not sleep. Every evening, too, he heard a shepherd's voice calling the sheep, which always ran to a certain spot. A 'jætte' (giantess), or 'þurs,' named Þórir, ruled over this valley. She had given Grettir permission to remain there, and he called the valley after her. This 'jætte' had daughters, who likely enough were very glad at the presence of a handsome young stranger in their lonely valley. But in winter the time hung very heavily on Grettir's hands, so that he could not endure it any longer; accordingly he left the valley, and went in a southerly direction across the Jökul, till he came to the north side of Skjaldbreið, a volcano lying to the south of the Jökul. There he erected a flat piece of rock, and cut a hole in it, and said that if a person put his eye to the hole he could see right into the cleft of the rocks leading out from Þórisdalr."

After Grettir's time, an uncertainty prevailed whether this valley was really in existence, or whether it only existed in imagination; accordingly two pastors determined to make an expedition to it, in the year 1664, in order to throw a little light upon the matter. They managed to ascend the Jökul, and saw the valley beneath them, but were unable to get down into it.

In the last century two notable travellers, Bjarni Paulsen and Eggert Olafsen, the latter of whom wrote a classical work on Iceland in two thick quarto volumes, renewed the attempt in 1753, but were obliged to turn back for the snow without accomplishing their object. The last attempt was made by Björn Gunnlaugsson, of Reykjavik, and was crowned with success. This gentleman, though but very inadequately assisted by the government, travelled through Iceland for a period of eighteen years, in order to execute that excellent chart of his country, which every traveller in Iceland makes use of at the present day.

Without doubt, Gunnlaugsson is the most be-travelled man in Iceland. His visit to Þórisdalr occurred in 1835. He discovered that the valley lay in the spot as described by the Grettissaga, but that it was filled up with *débris* and ice, without any vestige of vegetation. Nether did he find any warm springs there, so that Grettir's tempting description seems only to have been the offspring of his own imagination, unless one supposes that the volcanic heat and warm springs have disappeared, an occurrence by no means impossible, and, as a natural consequence, every trace of vegetation with them.

At the south end of Kaldidalr, which is a continuation of the stony Skúlaskeið, and is equally barren, there stands a little solitary beacon, probaby erected in order to mark the entrance to the valley between the mountains. The Icelanders call it the "Kerling" (old woman). The dark-brown cliffs, which stand like sentinels on either side the entrance into the valley, give evidence that we have again reached the domains of Palagonite tufa. The barren, rugged bottom round Skúlaskeið, however, is due to a lava stream, which is of older date than the modern streams; that is to say, it falls within the limits of the glacial period. Here and there the hard rock sticks out under the loose stones; its surface is generally furrowed and scored, but in some places retains its original appearance. This lava doubtless issued from Okfjall, on whose slopes the same kind of rock may be seen, and is perhaps contemporaneous with the lava rock forming the upper stratum on the low lands round Reykjavik. Its mineralogical similarity is exact, and the latter kind has likewise furrows on it from the glacial period.

When greater attention than has hitherto been bestowed, comes to be devoted to the peculiar and marked denudation which has furrowed the surface of the rocks in Iceland, they will doubtless discover and be able to follow up the ancient lava stream of the glacial age in other places besides the one above named. These lava streams form the natural transition between the modern lava and the basaltic formation, and a more intimate acquaintance with them is of the last importance with regard to the relations existing between the older and younger formations in Iceland. This lava is frequently covered over with more recent lava streams, and with deposits of alluvial mud, and with stones and earth from the Jökuls. It is always scored and furrowed from the glaciers, whence its superficial conditions have undergone a transformation, so that its original level appearance has been furrowed out into deep valleys and precipices. But it still retains certain signs which characterise it as a lava stream, as well as certain peculiarities which were called into existence by the conditions of the face of the country at the time when these lavas were erupted. Thus one may expect to find them occupying the ridge of the lower table-land, from the sea up to the foot of those mountains which belong to extinct volcanoes; further, the construction of these lava streams must be clearly and distinctly marked, because they are lava streams, that is to say, because they did not originate under the surface of the sea. In all essential points, therefore, they must correspond to a modern lava stream, but as their upper stratum is often more or less destroyed, it is not to be expected that the same fluidity will be observed on the surface, as in the case of recent lava, but the very reverse. We cannot, however, enter into further details in this place. By investigation and research sundry of the ancient lava streams of extinct volcanoes during the glacial period may be discovered; and it is the importance of this fact that we have sought to render evident. Okfjall and the neighbourhood of Reykjavik are, as far as I am aware, the sole instances; but then these parts of the country are far better known than the rest.'

After having left the "Kerling" behind me, I proceeded along the barren and gently sloping table-land to the south of Kaldidalr and Ok, and, after riding for about seven hours, again reached a grassy plain, where a short halt was decided upon. Þingvellir was about three hours distant. A fog now again enveloped our little caravan. We passed over Skaldbreið's lava streams, over small sandy heights, between narrow defiles, and at last reached the famous lava stream which on one side extends up to its source, in the snow-covered Skaldbreið (skjöldr, shield, and breiðr, broad); and, on the other, runs into Þingvallavatn, the largest lake in the country. In this lava stream the famous fissures, Almannagjá and Hrafnagjá, are to be found (gjá, fissure, crack). Almannagjá is a crack of about one geographical mile in length. It is bounded on its left by a perpendicular wall; the highest point is 140 feet above the bottom of the crack. The bottom is level, and about

Cracks in a lava stream.

as broad as the height of the wall. This wall, I should state, is of nearly equal height throughout; the other wall, however, has fallen down in two places, and is lower and more uneven than the first. Almannagjá on the western, and Hrafnagjá on the eastern side of the lava-stream from Skaldbreið, have been formed by the depression of the intervening stream, which is a geographical mile in breadth. The west wall, therefore, of Almannagjá, and the east wall of Hrafnagjá, form, as it were, two lateral walls, from which the corresponding walls became separated, when the mass of rock collapsed from the depression of the intervening lava strata.

A good deal of grass grows on the above-named lava stream, and gives it, therefore, an inviting appearance; the fissures in it also have grass growing at the bottom, forming a striking contrast to the dark walls. A river, named Oxará—so called because in olden days a man is said to have lost his axe in it, while cutting a hole in the ice—dashes over the western wall in Almannagjá in a lovely waterfall, after which it flows along the bottom of the fissure for some distance, and over the other wall into the plain between Þingvalla Church and Almannagjá, and thence into the sea. Up to the year 1800 the plain on both sides the river used to be the place of meeting for people who were going to the Althing, the ancient popular assembly of Iceland. Some stone heaps, called boðar, still mark the points where the chieftains used to assemble; and the ancient Sagas are full of histories connected with this spot. Near to the spot where the Althing was held—viz., a "holm" in the Öxará, which is now no longer in existence, owing to the alteration that has taken place in the course of the river through the lapse of ages—on the east bank of the river, is the Lögberg, or "law rock," whence sentences were pronounced. It is not, properly speaking, a rock, but a detached wall of lava, only a few paces in breadth, though 300 or 400 feet in length, bounded on either side by gigantic fissures with perpendicular walls. The bottom is filled with bright clear water, of a bluish hue. These two fissures unite at the northern end of the Lögberg. The spot, which was thus naturally protected against intruders, was excellently adapted for the purposes for which the assembly met, for the ancestors of the present race were not such a peaceable people as their descendants.

Almannagjú and Lögberg, the green-clad lava stream, the extensive surface of Þingvalla lake, and the precipitous mountains round it, form a picture which, without regard to his-

ALMANNAGJÁ. Page 283.

torical reminiscences, is one of the most lovely and most remarkable in Iceland. The deep, mystical fissure of Almannagjá is especially striking on approaching it from Reykjavik. One goes over a portion of the same lava stream without suspecting the existence of the fissure, till suddenly, at a turn in the road, one finds oneself on its upper edge, while a romantic path leads down by a flight of stair-shaped ledges into the bottom of the fissure. It is a glorious sight.

The lava stream containing all these points of interest that belong both to the world of nature and of man, is pre-historic. The ancient Sagas speak positively on this point. When the question of the introduction of Christianity was laid before the Althing, in 1000, a volcanic eruption took place at the same time in Ölfus, south of Þingvallavatn. As soon as the heathens, who were opposed to the introduction of the new religion, heard of it, they cried out—"What wonder if the gods are angry!" Whereupon Snorri Goði rose up and said—"With whom were the gods angry then, when the 'hraun' on which we now stand was flowing?" For the country was uninhabited then. This question was considered to be decisive; the meeting adjourned for one day, and when they met again the introduction of Christianity was determined upon.

Before the Öxará leaves the fissure, it forms a narrow but deep basin in it, bounded by sharp peaks and crags. In former days, women who had murdered their children, and were condemned to death, were thrown into it. It was also used as a swimming bath, an exercise in which the old Northmen were adepts. Icelanders of the present day seem in general to have forgotten the art.

Some distance from Lögberg is a spot where witches in former days used to be burnt for witchcraft. Men were not condemned to death, as is probably known, in the old times but were declared to be outlawed, which meant that anybody might kill them with impunity. In the middle ages, however, a gallows was erected in a secluded part of Almannagjá.*

From Þingvellir to Reykjavik I travelled alone; it is a six or seven hours' ride. After quitting the lava stream which bounds the lake of Þingvalla on the left, one comes up on a "heiði," about 400 feet above the sea. Its name is Mosfellsheiði; in some parts it is very stony and difficult for travelling, though generally speaking the road was well trodden and easily discernible. I was already acquainted with a portion of this road, from Reykjavik to Seljadalr, and therefore felt myself quite at home. At last I reached Reykjavik in safety, and beheld with feelings of joy its well-known houses, its harbour, with the ships riding at anchor, and other familiar points of interest in the neighbourhood. Once more I took up my abode at my old quarters in the hotel, and rested for some days after the fatigues I had undergone.

* At the present day, when a criminal is condemned to death in Iceland, he has to be conveyed to Denmark to undergo his punishment, as no Icelander can be found who will undertake the duties of a public executioner!

CHAPTER VIII.

Discovery of Iceland—Colonisation of the Country—Political Divisions—Ancient Laws—Lost Independence—Iceland and Denmark—Iceland under the Norwegian Kings—Calmar Union—What country is Iceland ?—Financial Matters—Iceland's Decadence—Monopoly: Its Effects—Free Trade: Its Happy Results—Brandy Imports—A Banquet—The Dessert.

THE following detailed account is given of the discovery of Iceland, and its colonization, in the "Landámabók."

A celebrated Norwegian Viking, Naddoddr, who had been obliged to settle down in the Færoe islands, as the only spot he could find where he could dwell in safety from the attacks of the persons he had robbed, was, on the occasion of his return from a journey to Norway, overtaken by a storm, and driven to the coast of Iceland, about the year 860. After sailing into one of the fjords on the east coast, he ascended a lofty rock, from whence he had an extensive view, but could discover no traces of the country being inhabited. In the autumn he again put to sea, and, owing to the quantity of snow which fell on the mountains, called the island "Snow-land." In 864, it was again discovered by a man of Swedish origin, named Garðar Svafarsson, who was bound for the islands off the western coast of Scotland, where he was going to take possession of some property that had been bequeathed him, and who was also driven to the coast of Iceland by tempestuous weather. He sailed round it, and thus ascertained that it was an island. He called it Garðaskólmr. He sailed into the fjord which now goes by the name of Skjálfandi, and landed on the east shore, where Húsavík now lies, where he built himself a house, and spent the winter, returning to Norway in the following spring.

The tempting description he gave of the country aroused the adventurous spirit of the Northmen; and Flóki, another renowned Viking, determined to seek out the new-discovered country and take possession of it. The compass, at that time, was of course unknown; but Flóki took with him three ravens, to act as guides, which he had first consecrated to the gods at a sacrificial banquet. After reaching Hjaltland and the Færoe islands, he let go one of the ravens, but it immediately returned to the Færoe isles; the second one mounted high into the air, but soon returned to the vessel, but the third directed its course towards Iceland, where Flóki landed a short time after. Not being particularly pleased with the appearance of the east coast, where he first touched, he sailed round the south coast to the western part of the island, till he came to Vatnsfjörðr (in Barðastranðarsyssel, on the southern shore of the north-western peninsula), where he took a portion of land into possession. But, during the summer, he occupied himself with fishing, and entirely neglected the hay harvest; the consequence of which was, that all the cattle he had brought with him died in the winter. Vexed at his loss, and being quite dispirited at the cold of the ensuing spring, and having moreover discovered that one of the fjords, which he saw from the top of a mountain, was entirely filled with ice, he resolved to return to a warmer part, after having given the name of

Iceland to the country—a name which it ever afterwards retained.

Flóki passed another winter in the country, somewhere near Hafnarfjörðr, and returned to Norway in the following summer, quite resolved on giving up all thoughts of settling in Iceland.

Flóki, however, seems to have been a misanthrope, or else to have been fond of looking at everything in a dark light, for his two companions, Herjólfr and Þórólfr, give quite a different description of it. The first describes it as a very pleasant country; and the other, unable to draw a better picture of its fertility and wealth, describes it as a land "where butter was dripping from every plant."

In 870 Iceland was again visited by two Northmen, Hjorleifr and Ingólfr, of whom we have already spoken. So captivated were they with its general appearance, that after they had wintered there they returned to Norway, in order to take the necessary steps for settling down permanently in the island. This they did in 874; and from this date, therefore, may be reckoned the colonization of the country. In accordance with the custom observed by several of his countrymen, who subsequently established themselves in the country, Ingólfr left it for chance to decide where he should settle, naturally under the superstitious idea of the co-operation of the gods. On nearing land he threw out the props or supports of the "high seat," which he had brought with him from home, into the sea, with an oath that he would build wheresoever they came on shore. They came ashore near Reykjavik, where Ingólfr, true to his oath, established himself, though his serfs whom he had sent out to search after the props, ridiculed him for choosing such a barren and sandy place, instead of one of the fertile districts they had passed through on their journey from the eastern part of the island.

Nothing, however, promoted the colonization of Iceland so much as the oppressive rule of Harald the Fair Haired, king of Norway, who united the kingdoms of the petty sovereigns under his own sceptre.

By this achievement Harald succeeded in making Norway a kingdom. But the subjugated "Odels"-men,* chafing under the new rule, preferred to flee the country rather than remain. Accordingly they emigrated in great numbers with their families and slaves, and settled in the Hebrides, the Orkneys, Shetlands, and the Færoe isles. But they principally settled in Iceland, where they were partly allured by the description of that "land of promise," partly from the hope of being able to escape the yoke of the oppressor there. These Norwegian colonists were a good deal mixed up with emigrants from Ireland, concerning whom history has not much to say.

During the lapse of little more than half a century the coasts of Iceland were taken possession of by the colonists; and in order to put a check on the spirit of emigration, Harald was obliged to impose a heavy tax on all persons who emigrated from Norway to Iceland. In order that the emigrants should not appropriate to themselves more land than they absolutely required, it was enacted that no person might possess a larger quantity of land than he could walk round in one day with fire in his hand.

In this way every person who arrived in the country got a piece of land; for the old settlers received the new-comers with great good will, and assisted them in establishing themselves. It is supposed that a patriarchal government originally prevailed in Iceland; but towards the year 928 the colonists established a free republic, which remained in existence for more than three hundred years. The land was divided into

* "Odels" men were the owners of allodial estates.—Tr.

four districts or Fjorðúngur, called the north, south, east, and west quarters. Each of these quarters was again divided into three "Thing," with the exception of the northern quarter, which was divided into four "Thing;" and finally in each of these thirteen "Thing" were three districts or "Goðorð," making therefore in all nine-and-thirty. The magistrate in each "Goðorð" was called "Goði," and it was his duty to hold meetings concerning general affairs, to preside at these meetings and pronounce sentences; and also to see that the sentences were carried into effect, and to fill the priestly office. These "Goðar" appointed the twelve judges, who had to judge all cases brought before them, at the meeting which was held in the spring of each year, in each of the quarters of the country. And lastly, these lesser districts were divided into "Hreppar" or Communes, a subdivision which exists at the present day. The chief officials of these communes were called "Hreppstjórar," as they are still termed. Their principal duty was to provide for the maintenance of the poor.

The highest authority over the country was vested in the Althing, or General Assembly, which was convened every year for a fortnight in the summer. This assembly made the laws of the republic; and all differences between people which could not otherwise be settled were adjudicated by it. The president of the Althing was called "Lögsögumaðr," or the interpreter of laws. He was chosen by the whole people, and usually retained his office during life. His sentences were final, and could not be set aside. Though he possessed but little or no power, except in "Thing," he was, however, regarded by the people as the principal individual in that assembly, and, as it were, its chief. It was his duty to preserve the written laws, of which the copy which he retained in his possession was considered to be the original. The famous historian Snorri Sturluson, who lived from 1178 to 1241, was more celebrated and more powerful than any other "Lögsögumaðr."

The first code of laws accepted in Iceland was composed by a man named Ulfljótr, a Northman, by birth, who in his sixtieth year took a journey to Norway, in order to consult with his maternal uncle, Þorleifr the Wise, who was very learned in such matters. On his return to Iceland, he travelled about the country, in order to prepare people's minds for his proposed code of laws. At a meeting held in the course of the following year, his proposal was nearly unanimously accepted. The Norwegian code, which is supposed to have been the text-book of Ulfljótr's legislative enactments, was the well-known "Gulathingslov." In 1118 a more complete code was introduced by Berg þór, who was "Lögsögumaðr" at the time. This was the subsequently-famous "Grágás;" and finally, in 1280, the collection of laws, which, under the name of "Jónsbók," is still considered to be the most important code for Iceland, and which in a great measure is still valid, was introduced.

The principles of liberty which the noble families that emigrated from Norway established in Iceland was not retained for long by their descendants. The peace of the country began to be disturbed by intestine quarrels and bloody disputes, which gave occasion for fresh interference on the part of the kings of Norway; for they had steadily kept their eyes directed towards this country, and used all means to bring it under their sway. At last they succeeded in doing so in 1262—64, when Hakon was King of Norway. In 1262, the greater portion of the country took the oath of homage to Hakon, though with the express reservation that Iceland should retain its independence, and should be governed only by its own laws. A special act was made, with reference to the engagements which Iceland on the one side was to undertake to fulfil towards King Hakon, and which he, on his part, was to observe towards Iceland; and, as this act has not yet been repealed with the consent of the Icelanders, it is looked upon by them as the basis of union with another country under the same crown, first with Norway, and afterwards with Denmark.

The conditions under which the country first entered into union with Norway, have, however, owing to the lapse of centuries, and from the absence of that ardent longing for independence which once burned so brightly in the bosom of the people, undergone many changes. For when the country, in consequence of internal discord, could no longer maintain its independence, but fell under regal sway, the colonists gradually lost their influence in the management of the affairs of the island, which accordingly, in due course of time, passed over into the king's hands. The country, however, was never completely incorporated with Norway or Denmark, but in a great measure retained its laws and constitution. The colonists, therefore, did not cease to exist as an independent people, and it is naturally to this cause that the preservation of the ancient language in all its purity is to be attributed.

Iceland and Denmark do not at the present time regard one another with particularly friendly feelings; indeed one might almost be led to surmise that there was something of a tendency towards national hatred between the two people. And yet this expression hardly meets the case; for from what I have noticed in Denmark there is too much indifference shown towards Iceland to amount to hatred. But certainly the feeling between the countries is not of a very friendly character. Meanwhile they seem to have arrived at a kind of mutual understanding; the Danes look upon all the claims of the Icelanders as unreasonable and exaggerated; while the latter insist strongly upon them, though they possibly deserve the use of the above epithets. The fault of the Icelanders is that in many respects they insist on things from an antiquated and obsolete point of view; while at the same time they hold Denmark of the present day responsible for all the acts of injustice which its former governments have committed, and which have only been the results of the misrule of former centuries, in which the present age has had no participation. On the other hand, I am inclined to think that Denmark's fault consists in looking on the claims of the Icelanders as being unwarrantable; in other words, that she is rather prejudiced against them and indifferent about them. With regard to these various claims, however, it may be remarked, that the opinion in Iceland is far from being similar to the opinion of Icelanders residing in Copenhagen. I have at least met with several influential persons in the country, even amongst the native Icelanders, who are far from willing to endorse the sentiments of their countrymen in Copenhagen.

But as the Danes come most in contact with these latter, they may not unnaturally conceive the idea that an exclusively national tendency is the generally prevailing spirit in Iceland, which, though it is not the case, to judge at least by the votes in the Althing, is decidedly embraced by the majority.

Further, the Icelanders are guilty of a great mistake when they confound the Danish people with the Danish government, while the Danes are equally reprehensible with regard to Iceland when they confound themselves with their government. In Denmark the people frequently attack their own government pretty severely; but directly the Icelanders raise any complaint against it, they are thought to be unreasonable. Probably the remote position of the country may be the cause of creating a misapprehension as regards the correct meaning of the terms, people and government.

It may possibly interest some of my readers to have the

main features of the fundamental laws on which the political existence of the country from the year 1264 depends, considered from an Icelandic point of view, presented to them.

We must, therefore, go back to the Act of Union with Norway, in the year 1262, when Iceland first entered into political union with one of the northern states. Before this date the feeling of liberty was very strongly marked in Iceland; and the Act of Union alluded to bears testimony to the fact that, even though the people exchanged a republican for a monarchical form of government, they were exceedingly careful that this union should not bear upon its face the appearance of their subjection to another nation. The union with Norway was, therefore, only a personal union under the same king. The people reserved their rights and privileges in the terms of their ancient laws, and, moreover, framed conditions with regard to future events. The Act of Union concludes with the following words:—" We and our heirs will observe fidelity towards you so long as you and your heirs keep your promises to us, and adhere to the above-named resolutions; but we declare ourselves to be released from our engagements if, in the opinion of the most honourable men, you break faith with us." The compact, therefore, bears all the marks of voluntariness about it. King Hakon despatched an ambassador to Iceland, on whose appeal an oath was given to do homage to His Majesty, and to pay him tax for ever, in accordance with the contents of a document which was then composed relating to the matter. In this way writers, both of olden and modern date, have understood the matter. Thus, Professor Munch remarks that Iceland was united to Norway " without becoming an actual province of it; and neither in an administrative respect could it be accounted so." The participation, too, of the Althing in the legislative authority was, moreover, reserved to it. Hence it is evident that Iceland did not occupy any subordinate position with regard to Norway, but only to the Norwegian king. The land was thus free and independent.

And even supposing positive proofs were wanting in this case—and they are not—it would be the most unnatural thing conceivable that a republican community, which had enjoyed its independence for more than three hundred years, should of its own accord place itself in subjection to another people; in other words, should surrender its legislative power into this people's hands. If, on the other hand, it is supposed that the Norwegian kings, after once gaining a footing in the country, should have desired to extend their authority wider and wider, and that, perhaps, the Norwegian councillors of these Norwegian kings should have had it in view to gain complete control over the country, the supposition is not altogether at variance with human nature. It shows, therefore, the obstinate vitality of the love of liberty in Iceland, that these views either suffered shipwreck, or were only able little by little to make themselves visible.

In the interval that elapsed between 1262 and 1360, during which time Iceland remained under the supremacy of the Norwegian kings, the engagements which these latter had bound themselves to observe towards the country were tolerably well observed. The principal of these was that no law should be imposed upon the country without the previous sanction and consent of the Althing. The oath of fealty was, moreover, made to the succeeding monarchs at distinct times by Iceland; and that this was not merely a matter of form, may be gathered from the reservations which the people at a later period attached to it. In the letter of allegiance of Erik of Pomerania, it is mentioned that the allegiance of the Icelanders was an entirely voluntary expression on their part, in accordance with the laws of the country, and with the reservation that it should enjoy the privileges it had formerly possessed. And that the Icelanders did not on this occasion consider themselves in any way subordinate to Norway, may be concluded from the fact that after Erik's deposition, the Icelanders could not be induced to do homage to his successor, as they continued to regard Erik as their rightful king.

But we have now arrived at that period when Iceland was governed by Danish-Norwegian kings, before the liberty of these people was yet destroyed; for this period was followed, as is known, by an absolute sovereignty. At the commencement of this state of things, we find that the Icelanders began to be treated with less regard by the government. It is supposed that this partly resulted from the increased extension of her sway, which entailed a corresponding indifference for those countries which were the most remote; partly from an ever-increasing indifference towards, and unacquaintance with, the ancient habits, customs, and language of the North, of which Iceland was the last representative; and partly from a proportionately increasing tendency towards everything German. In addition to these causes, the question of a Scandinavian Union attracted a great deal of attention; and, finally, the Icelanders themselves had become more lax and indifferent with respect to their rights; while, at the same time, these rights were more difficult to maintain.

Under the reign of Queen Margaret, an attempt was made to levy taxes in Iceland, which was an encroachment on the privileges of the Althing, with whom alone it rested to grant them. The attempt proved unsuccessful; accordingly, the annals of the year 1392 inform us,—" Then arrived Þjódbjörn in Iceland with Queen Margaret's letter, in which she encourages every man to give her half a mark, old value, with a threat of impeachment for high-treason in case of refusal. To this all gave an unsatisfactory answer at first. Björn Einarsson married his daughter Christína to Jón Guttormsson, and the wedding was held late in the autumn near Vatnsfjördr. Then the 'Statholder,' Vigfúss Ivarsson, took out the queen's letter; whereupon many of the principal persons at once assented to it." The annals for 1393 continue concerning the same subject,—"The 'Statholder' brought forward the queen's demand at the meeting, when all the chief men promised to give sixteen feet of wadmel for Vigfúss' sake—he was very much beloved in Iceland—but on this condition, that it should not be called a tax, and should not be demanded again. But the inhabitants of Eyafjörd refused to give anything."

In the sixteenth, and in the beginning of the seventeenth century, when the Danish kings had homage paid them in Iceland, it was expressly stated by them that they would allow the Icelanders to retain their laws and rights, or rather Iceland's laws and rights, together with their privileges and freedom. And in the present day the Icelanders give plain proofs that they still bear the old Act of Union of 1262 in mind, and are determined to adhere to the old Icelandic laws. It would be impossible to follow out all these proofs in their details in this place; suffice it to say, that on the introduction of an absolute monarchy Iceland was in posession of "a distinct collection of laws; judicial and civil government; distinct institutions, language, and customs;" in a word, she occupied a collateral, but not a subordinate position to Denmark and Norway.

According to the views of the national party in Iceland, the introduction of an absolute monarchy did not entail any legal changes, as the act of sovereignty had only obtained the subscription of the Icelanders by fraudulent means. And this was how it came to pass. After it had been proclaimed in Norway and Denmark, in 1661, the same underhand dealing by which the estates of Norway had been induced to surrender their independence, and to place it in the hands of the king, were adopted in the following year in Iceland. In a letter to the colonists in Iceland and the Vestmanna Islands, dated March 24, 1662, the people were urged to send deputies from the ecclesiastical and secular bodies, together with a certain number of peasants, who should assemble together on the occasion of the meeting of the Althing and take the oath of fealty. Accordingly, at the appointed time, they assembled, but as the king's ambassador, Admiral Henrik Bjelke, did not appear during the time the Althing was sitting, they all repaired to their homes. Shortly afterwards Bjelke arrived, and immediately sent messages round the whole country to assemble the deputies for the purpose of receiving their oath of allegiance. The oath accordingly was taken on July 28, 1662, but not a syllable about absolute monarchism was broached. But after they had given their oath of allegiance Bjelke produced a document, and requested the officials and deputies to subscribe to it. This document was an act of sovereignty for Iceland, similar to that for Norway. It was composed in the Danish language, and it is assumed, therefore, that it was unintelligible to the greater number of the Icelandic deputies. But directly it had been explained to them that the document was worded so that they were to surrender their privileges and liberty into the king's hand they became alarmed, and would not sign it, which, indeed, they were neither authorised to do, as their constituents had not delegated them to act in such a manner. Whereupon Bjelke explained to them that it was by no means the intention to deprive the Icelanders of their rights; that subscription was merely a matter of form, and that no change was contemplated with regard to the position of the country, and that they might safely rely upon the king. At last they gave way, and signed the document, remarking that they confidently expected that the king would fulfil the promises which Bjelke had made in his name. In this way absolute monarchism was introduced into Iceland. It was a political shift, a *coup d'état*, by which the existing order of things was subverted. However, the national party affirm that this caused no change in the position of the country with reference to Norway and Denmark. Like these countries, Iceland has obtained another form of government; but the reciprocal relations between the people has not thereby been altered.

Strangely enough, the kings of the absolute monarchy felt ashamed to act in a despotic way towards Iceland for some time. It seemed as if they bore witness to the promise which Bjelke had given on behalf of Frederick III., and would not forfeit their royal word; though naturally, in lapse of time, such verbal promises are soon forgotten. Iceland, however, had permission to retain her own laws, and the Althing continued in existence long after the introduction of absolute monarchism. It was first abolished in 1800, though its existence as an independent body had ceased almost from the year 1720. Subsequently its functions were limited to hear the laws made by the king read out; for it was always deemed essential to their validity that they should be read out at the Althing. As further regarded the legislature, the government deemed it incumbent on them to maintain the Icelandic laws, to recommend the composition of an Icelandic code, to take the ancient "Jónsbók" as a model, to make use of the language of the country, &c.; all of which circumstances proved that Iceland was not put on the same level with the Danish or Norwegian provinces.

It is remarkable that Iceland, which, in the days of the

Republic, formed a perfectly independent community, did not, when at a later period it paid homage to the kings of Norway, aspire to any title corresponding to its new position; and this fact seems to imply, that although the people had come under the sway of a royal sceptre, they still firmly clung to republican forms and ideas. The principal engagement which Iceland incurred by the Act of Union, was that the country should pay tax to the king; and the only denomination it therefore obtained was a tributary land.

The want of a special title for the country, however, has contributed to increase the confusion of ideas with regard to its legal position. For if the question is asked now-a-days, "What sort of a country is Iceland?" the answer one gets may be, "It is a province of Denmark." But if it were such, it would come directly under the jurisdiction of the Danish "Rigsdag," which it does not. For Iceland is ruled absolutely by the king, while Denmark possesses a constitutional government. Still less is it a colony, as may be immediately perceived from its history; for, even from the earliest days, there never was any mention made of dependence on the mother-country, Norway.

In official language, Iceland's position with regard to Denmark is stated in different terms, which, by the way, seem to imply an indistinct idea of the relationship existing between the countries. At one time it is called a Colony, at another time a Province; and finally, a new word has been coined, and it has been called a Dependency. The Icelanders acknowledge no such title, but simply call it "the Land."

In 1831 an attempt was made to incorporate Iceland with Denmark, and was carried into effect; but as the measure proved to be unpractical, it was repealed by Christian VIII., who re-opened Iceland's Althing in 1843. Thereupon followed the royal proclamation of April 4, 1848, in which the king communicated his determination to introduce a constitutional government into his kingdom; and this proclamation was succeeded by a Patent, of July 7, in the same year, in which the composition of the National Assembly was determined upon, five members being appointed by the king to represent Iceland. When tidings of this intelligence reached Iceland, a petition was despatched to the king, praying him to convoke a distinct Icelandic assembly, which should meet in the country, and have liberty to discuss the projected fundamental law with special regard to Iceland. The petition received a favourable reply, stating that the provisions of the fundamental laws, as far as concerned the position Iceland should hold, should not be decided on till an assembly in the country itself had been heard on the matter. The qualifications of this assembly were decided upon, after a motion by the Althing, in accordance with an elective law of September 28, 1849.

Up to this time the Althing and the Danish government had met each other with alacrity; but now divisions began to appear. The Althing had insisted that the new assembly should be convoked in the course of the ensuing year, 1850; but, owing to some tardiness on the part of the government, this was not done. Moreover, the Althing, which, in pursuance of the law, should have been held in 1851 (the writs for convening it should have been issued in the autumn of 1850), was postponed; and all this gave rise to ill-blood in the country. But matters became more tranquil when the long-promised assembly was convoked, especially as great expectations were raised concerning the new constitution which it was hoped would be procured by the united efforts of the meeting. A measure relating to the constitutional position Iceland was to assume in the kingdom was laid before the meeting, evidently pointing to the subordination of the country to the Danish "Rigsdag." But, as this was not in accordance with the ideas of the Icelanders (for, amongst other things, it was proposed that the indirect taxes should flow into the Danish exchequer, although the Althing had no voice with reference to the making of such taxes; and it was further proposed that the Danish "Rigsdag," in which Iceland was to be represented by four members in the "Folke-thing," and two members in the "Lands-thing," should arrange the Customs' duties of Iceland, which were to flow into the Danish exchequer), an amendment was proposed;—that Iceland should enjoy the same constitutional privileges which other portions of the kingdom possessed. Meanwhile, the assembly had no opportunity for taking the amendment into consideration; for, when the royal "Commissarius" noticed that the assembly would not entertain the government proposals, but took up an independent position, he dismissed it, at the same time pronouncing their conduct to be rebellious,—a line of conduct, indeed, which could only tend to create a bitter feeling, and render an adjustment impossible,—whereupon thirty-six out of the forty members elected by the people repaired to the king with a petition, that the outline of a fundamental law for Iceland, founded on the above-named amendment, should without loss of time be laid before a meeting elected on the same principle as the former assembly. This address, on being sent round the country, received more than 2,200 signatures,—that is to say, it was signed by one person out of every thirty. A royal proclamation followed upon this address, by which the whole matter was shelved. Another proclamation, issued shortly afterwards, on the occasion of an attempt being made to bring the matter forward again, declared that "no change should take place in the constitution of Iceland without first being submitted to the consideration of the Althing." And thus the matter rests; for neither the Althing nor the government are inclined to make concessions of any importance. Iceland, therefore, continues locked in the embrace of absolutism.

The financial relations, moreover, between Denmark and Iceland are the subjects of various interpretations, and thus give rise to as many misunderstandings. Denmark estimates the annual expenses of Iceland at a sum varying from 30,000 to 40,000 rix-dollars, whence the impression has become current in that country that she loses every year that sum by Iceland. But, in this computation, no regard is paid to the very important advantages which commerce with Iceland entails. The yearly imports of the country—and the trade lies principally in the hands of Danish merchants—is estimated at one and a half millions of rix-dollars; no mean amount! And with reference to the current expenses of Iceland, the Danish exchequer has at different times drawn sums of money from Iceland, which sums ought, it appears, to be devoted to this object. First and foremost among these are the sums derived from the sale of crown property in Iceland, with the revenues of which the schools and episcopal see, &c., were formerly supported. This maintenance, formerly derived from property, now amounts to about 20,000 rix-dollars, and ought, therefore, to be deducted from the sum which Denmark sends to Iceland. In addition to this there are other sources of income which by right belong to Iceland; but the subject is one of too extensive a nature to discuss here. Suffice it to say that the present so-called maintenance does not at least exceed the interest of the capital which has been diverted from Iceland into the Danish exchequer; so that it seems Iceland has a legitimate claim to it. Whatever additional sum the Danish Rigsdag may grant the country time alone will show.

The zenith of Iceland's glory was from the beginning of the twelfth to the middle of the fourteenth century. This period produced that remarkable literature which is justly Iceland's pride, and which has been instrumental in preserving up to the present day the knowledge of that language which our forefathers spoke—a language which is of the last importance to the proper understanding of our own tongue; while, at the same time, the historical portions of this literature, the Sagas, are the sources of the ancient history of the countries of the north, whether as regards actual occurrences, customs, or morals. To us Scandinavians, then, it ought to be as important to have a thorough and minute acquaintance with these sources of history as it is to understand Latin and Greek. It is, therefore, to be regretted that while the educational system observed at our schools has in some degree liberated itself from the oppressive chains which a study of the dead languages imposes, it has not at the same time taken a step in the right direction by introducing a more intimate acquaintance with the Icelandic language and literature. Certainly these ought to occupy their proper place; while, on the part of our youth, they would be taken up with interest.

After this brilliant era, which extended over three centuries, a period of enervation succeeded, during which the country gradually retrograded, so that at the end of the last century the nation was hastening with rapid strides to meet its downfall. The introduction of the Reformation is assigned to be the great cause of this retrogressive motion; as the only counterpoise to kingly authority which then existed in the country was thereby done away with; while at the same time, by the suppression of the Roman Catholic priesthood, its wealth was dispersed; and education, which it was the special province of the clergy to disseminate, was driven out of doors. From a political point of view, therefore, the Icelanders do not regard the introduction of the Reformation into the country with any feelings of self-congratulation; on the contrary, they look on it as the greatest misfortune that could have befallen them. A more approximate cause of the country's decadence may certainly be attributed to the misfortunes which those terrible volcanic eruptions, and the sickness and distress they entailed, brought upon the country; but above all, to the oppressive system of commerce, under which the country groaned at the same time. The history of Iceland's commerce is, therefore, one of the most sorrowful, and at the same time most instructive chapters in the history of the country.

When Iceland was united to Norway in 1262—1264, it was provided in the Act of Union which was then drawn up, that the king should guarantee the country an annual supply of six ship-loads of goods, a provision which was naturally considered to be to the advantage of the country, as it originated from the Icelanders themselves; but from this fact, at a later period, the kings of Norway came to look on the Icelandic trade as their own peculiar property. After the union this state of things was altered; for the kings of the union had other things to think about. They accordingly relinquished this privilege, and left the trade with Iceland to the Hanseatic towns and the Copenhagen burghers. At that period, however, the limits of the inland and foreign trade were not so strictly defined as at a later date. In 1602 the Icelandic trade was let by the Danish Government to a company of merchants in Copenhagen for a certain sum of money. This state of things continued up to 1787, whereby the company got the exclusive right of trading in the island, while the Icelanders themselves were by the same means entirely shut out from foreign markets. In order thoroughly to understand the great importance of such an arrangement, it should be borne in mind that Iceland is only a cattle-producing country, which has to import all its corn-stuffs and other produce from foreign countries. Its exports are principally fish and wool. When, partly to enrich the Danish exchequer, partly to benefit the Danish merchants, a system of monopoly was introduced into Iceland by the government, the result was that many of the necessary articles of consumption which the country absolutely stood in need of, unless, indeed, its inhabitants were to perish from starvation or eke out a miserable existence, were considerably raised in value. This method of attracting revenue to the Crown, and of heaping up all the profits in the hands of a few by the establishment of a commercial monopoly, corresponds to an income derived from imposts, and a consequent rise in prices; though the first method of reaching the same goal is more convenient where one has to do with a remote region.

And what was the immediate consequence of that chain with which free trade was fettered by the ordinances of 1602? Naturally this; that the prices on imported goods rose, so much so, that in the three consecutive years they amounted to three or four times their original value, whilst the prices of fish fell. The effect such a state of things must needs exercise upon the development of a poor country is easy enough to comprehend. Its small income became still less; its industries, such as its fisheries and its rearing of cattle, dwindled away; poverty increased, and the population diminished in proportion. In one district of the country alone no less than 800 persons died from starvation in the three years succeeding the introduction of monopoly in trade; while in the whole country it is computed that no less than 9,000 persons perished—in other words, a sixth part of the whole population. These terrible consequences of a trade monopoly might have been foreseen, for when the country previously to this had only been able to produce a sufficiency for the frugal wants of the inhabitants, it is only natural to suppose that it would be a matter of the greatest difficulty, if not actually impossible, for them to exist when the prices of all articles of import were raised to an artificial height; and the consequence was, that the poorest died from starvation, which is, perhaps, the very extremest consequence at which a prohibitory system can possibly arrive.

Meanwhile the Danish Government, without paying attention to such matters, continued to proceed in the line of conduct it had marked out for itself, and drew the chains even tighter still instead of relaxing them. In a proclamation of 1684 it was strictly enacted that the natives should not trade amongst themselves nor with foreigners, but that all traffic should pass through the mercantile company in Copenhagen; that on no conditions should they trade with others, "neither on land, on sea, in the harbours, in the fjords, or in any other place whatsoever;" and that they should not sell the fish from their boats, when out fishing, under pain of the severest punishments.

Of course, by prohibiting a people from conveying the produce of their country to foreign lands, the art of navigation was rendered an impossibility among them; the more so especially as it could not possibly answer their purpose to fit out decked boats in order to participate in the fisheries, when the prices which the mercantile company put on the fish were so very low. Fishing, therefore, was confined to open boats, which naturally could not keep out at sea for any length of time—scarcely over the twenty-four hours—and thereby the danger was considerably increased, while the profits derived were proportionately diminished. Iceland still suffers from the disastrous effects which this system of monopoly left behind it; the natives have still to row from fifteen to thirty miles out to sea in their open boats, and thus lose a great deal of time, while in stormy weather they cannot put out at all, though they know that off the coasts the sea teems with myriads of fish. Neither has the prohibition that all fish caught off the Icelandic coast should first pass through the hands of the Danish company, before entering into the world's markets, been attained. For when the Frenchmen—who are the greatest consumers, as France is a Roman Catholic country, where large quantities of fish are eaten during the fasts—were prevented from buying directly from the Icelanders, who could have supplied them at a much cheaper rate than it would have cost them to catch them themselves, they began, as above stated, to equip vessels and send them out to those far northern waters. Ably and substantially supported by their government, the French companies have made a very good thing of it. In the year 1864, the value of the fish taken by them amounted to no less than sixteen millions of francs, while the entire exports of Iceland in the same year scarcely reached one-and-a-half million of francs.

By the commercial regulations of 1684, the price of all imported goods rose still higher, so that it was doubled over and over again. The commercial companies paid on an average a yearly sum of 45,000 rix-dollars to the Danish Crown.

In the eighteenth century Iceland was a great sufferer from the terrible consequences which those fearful volcanic eruptions entailed; and as her powers of resistance were completely paralysed by the oppressive system of trade, this century proved a most disastrous one to the people. In 1762, a malignant epidemic broke out among the sheep; and about 280,000, or nearly half the whole number of sheep in the country, were slaughtered in this and the years immediately succeeding. In 1783, 11,000 cows died of hunger and pestilence, and 27,000 horses—that is, the greater portion of all the horses in the country and a large proportion of the cows—and 186,000 sheep. In consequence of this the population diminished in a very marked way. Up to that time a diminution rather than an increase of population had taken place. Formerly it had amounted to 50,000 persons, sometimes slightly exceeding this number, at others falling under it; which was an unnatural state of things, as the country was at peace, and ought, therefore, to have been able to reap the fruits which peace entails. In 1783, however, the population of Iceland amounted in round numbers to 48,000 persons; in 1784-5, it sank to 39,000, which number was again diminished by the deaths of 9,000 persons from starvation. In the succeeding year the population was again diminished by 1,200 persons.

In consequence of this unhappy state of things, the Danish Government conceived the idea of removing the inhabitants away from the country, as the means of subsistence there were wanting. As a preliminary step, however, a commission was appointed to inquire into the causes of the retrogressive condition of the country; and it arrived at the conclusion that these causes must not be sought for in the country itself, but that they were rather due to the pernicious course pursued by government, and especially to the heavy pressure under which free traffic and the producing powers of the country in general laboured. In consequence of this, and owing to the great disasters which had overtaken the country, the commercial bonds were relaxed by two succeeding enactments in 1786 and 1787.

But trade was yet far from being free. The harbours were only opened to Danish subjects, and these were not even permitted to take their vessels to Iceland without first touching at some Danish port. Neither might any native Icelander trade except he was in partnership with Danish merchants.

Foreigners, too, were prohibited from putting into an Icelandic port, except in case of distress, and even in such cases they had to leave as soon as possible. But even this limited concession of competition could not but bear good fruits. After the lapse of two years, the products of the country had increased manifold in value; the prices of fish especially rose in a remarkable degree. A "skippund" of fish which, in 1776, cost 7 rdl. 16 sk., in 1792 amounted to 24 to 30 rdl., or to about four times as much as formerly. In the days of the monopoly it had fetched from 30 to 40 rdl. in the markets of the world, while in Iceland it was not worth more than 7 rdl.

The number of cattle, too, increased in a remarkable degree after the commercial fetters had been relaxed; while the population, which had receded rather than multiplied during the whole century, was increased in the years 1788-1800 by 8,500 persons. The number of sailing vessels, which during the days of the monopoly had amounted to about thirty, now rose rapidly. In 1788, there were fifty-five, and in 1790, sixty-eight.

This progress seemed to the Danish Government to be too rapid; or more properly speaking, private interest interfered, and the privileges that had been granted were again to a certain extent withdrawn. The people were permitted to trade only at certain ports. Direct trade from vessels was greatly circumscribed; and the captains of trading vessels were forbidden to remain more than a month ashore, and not to run into more than one of the authorized ports in the course of the summer. The effect of this enactment was that the yearly arrival of vessels diminished in 1793 to forty-nine, and in 1794 to thirty-nine. In the following year a petition was forwarded to the government, praying for an extended liberty of trade, but received in reply the answer that such a concession would act injuriously to the interests of the country. Foreign vessels were thus excluded; and no goods might be conveyed from any foreign place to the country directly without first passing through one of the Danish ports. Consequently at the outbreak of the war, in 1807, between Denmark and England, the Icelanders were put to great straits, as the Danes were afraid to send any vessels to the country on account of the English cruisers. But by the intervention of some persons, the English Government gave permission to Danish vessels to visit Iceland unmolested, subject to certain conditions.

In the following decennium sundry changes certainly took place; for instance, in 1816 foreigners were first permitted to trade on land, though subjected to the heavy duty of 50 rdl. for every ton burden—a duty which no ship could endure.

In 1836 this impost was considerably reduced, and other privileges were granted, until finally, in 1854, a complete system of free trade was introduced. No duties whatsoever are demanded now, and only a trifling tonnage duty. The material and intellectual resources of the country have since then developed in a remarkable degree, in direct proportion to the freedom that has been granted to its commerce. The population, which in the eighteenth century up to the year 1787 had not advanced a step, has now gradually reached up to 68,000 souls. From the year 1800 it rose at the rate of 50 per cent. The exports, too, have increased in like proportion. The average of the exports of tallow for nine years in the seventeenth and eighteenth centuries amounted only to 114,000 lbs. per annum. Of late this article has been steadily rising, while in 1855 the exports of tallow amounted to 933,000 lbs. In 1784 and the preceding years 2,000 lbs. of eider-down were generally exported; in 1855 the exports amounted to 4,000 lbs. In the eighteenth century the export of feathers amounted to 4,500 lbs.

for one year only, and this is the highest sum it reached, namely, in 1753, while in others it sank to some hundreds. Since the beginning of the present century the export of feathers has been steadily on the rise; in 1855 it reached 25,000 lbs. The greatest advance, however, appears in fish and wool. During the last few years of the monopoly about 8,000 "skippund" of fish were annually exported; in 1855 the exports amounted to 24,000, or to three times the former quantity. During the latter half of the last century the exports of wool occasionally sank so low as to some thousand pounds. In 1734 the exports were 107,000 lbs; in 1743, 84,000 lbs.; in 1764, 39,000 lbs.; but in 1806 they rose to 260,000 lbs.; in 1840, to 940,000 lbs.; and in 1855, to 1,600,000 lbs. The export of woollen manufactured goods has, however, diminished, though in a much smaller proportion.

These brilliant results appear to still greater advantage when compared with the prices which obtained in former days and at the present time, both as regards imports and exports. We have already alluded to the article of fish. The price of wool, moreover, steadily rose: in the years from 1840 to 1849 white wool, on an average, fetched 21 sk. the pound; from 1850 to 1859 the average was 30 sk. In the last few years a further improvement has again taken place, owing, no doubt, in a great measure, to the scanty supply of cotton in the great markets of Europe. In 1864 wool fetched 3 marks 6 sk. the pound. The propitious circumstances resulting from free trade have shown themselves in the most advantageous manner; and although Iceland has been visited during the last decennium by years of severity and distress, still she has not only not had to experience those dreadful horrors, famine and starvation, which the disastrous times of the last century produced, but no check of any importance has been given to her advancement. The development of her commerce is best to be seen from a glance at the number of vessels which visit Iceland at the present day in comparison with the number that visited her in former days. From 1856 to 1863 the average number of vessels amounted to 134, with a burden of 6,164 tons; in 1800 to 1807 the tonnage amounted to 2,401, from 57 ships; while from 1848 to 1855 the relative proportions were 120 ships, with a burden of 4,785 tons.

It is natural, therefore, that the people value very highly the advantages which free trade has conferred upon them, while the merchants themselves have not, on the whole, been losers. Of course the few large mercantile houses which in former days usurped the entire trade of Iceland, and which, consequently, amassed a large amount of wealth, have been compelled to give way to competition; but, in their stead, opportunities have been afforded to numbers of small merchants, who were formerly entirely excluded from the markets. The result of free trade, therefore, has been to divide the prize among a larger number of individuals, which, though of course productive of no little grumbling among the few who have made their fortunes in the Icelandic trade, has yet opened up sources of profit to the many who were formerly shut out from it. Moreover, the producing powers of the country, and with these her exports, have considerably increased, as will be seen from the statistics quoted above, and an impulse been given to her commerce in general. The advantages of the new system are, therefore, mutual.

Iceland, then, is in a good way to enhance her material prosperity, so far as a country which has been so scantily endowed by nature, as is the case with her, can expect; and it will, therefore, be a matter of great regret if her progress be retarded by political complications and petty quarrels. It is difficult to comprehend how Denmark could lose anything by granting Iceland a certain degree of political independence; and if such be the case, it can be of no advantage to her to delay this concession any longer. As matters now are, the interests of Iceland stand in urgent need of this concession, for in the meanwhile the most pressing public matters are almost entirely held in abeyance. It is, of course, the right of taxation that Iceland especially craves. We will merely give one instance of the evil results this tardiness and procrastination have produced. Since 1849 the imports of brandy into Iceland have risen 79 per cent.; and with this increase, drunkenness has, as a matter of course, kept pace. The necessity, therefore, of a tax on the sale of brandy is urgent; but the Althing refuses to take the initiative, because it does not possess the right of utilizing the proceeds accruing from it.

If, therefore, Denmark entertains any desire to retain Iceland under the Danish Crown—which may be assumed to be the case, and which, moreover, it is to the interest of Scandinavia should be the case—she ought not to delay to put the constitutional relations of the country on a better footing than they now are. It cannot but cause sorrow to the impartial spectator to see strife and bitter feeling existing between two enlightened races who are so intimately connected with each other; and, should the existing state of things continue for long, it may easily happen that coldness and indifference on the one side, and an exclusively national spirit on the other, will, ere long, be the means of calling forth an "Icelandic question," the solution of which it is easy to foresee, namely, that Iceland will fall, a choice morsel, into the jaws of a foreign power. This appears to us to be a subject worthy of grave consideration; for, although Denmark may not derive very great advantages from her connection with Iceland, it is still a sister country, and, therefore, has a claim upon her friendship; but should ever Iceland be severed from her connection with the north, her national associations will thereby be broken up—a consummation which will never happen with impunity.

This has been rather a serious chapter, and perhaps the reader may require a little dessert after it. With his permission, I will offer him some. I have already mentioned that the Althing, the representative assembly of Iceland, met during the time I was in the country. It usually assembles every other year for a period of six weeks or two months. It consists of twenty-seven members, six of whom are chosen by the king, the others by the people. The year I was there the popular members were composed of ten peasants, five pastors, and six officials. The members elected by the king were all officials. The Althing chooses its own president, who is assisted by a royal commissary* in the discharge of his duties, and who thus forms a connecting link between the government and the people. It holds its meetings in a large chamber in the school in Reykjavik, and the members are seated round a horseshoe-table, covered with green cloth. The debates, of course, are carried on in the vernacular of the country, and are sometimes of rather a lively nature, for Icelanders have great facility of expression and are fond of making speeches. Of this I received proofs, not only from attending at the meetings of the Althing, but, and especially, at the dinner party or banquet which it gave itself and some invited guests, among whom was the author.

The *menu* was as follows:—

1. Soup.
2. Pork.
3. Salmon.
4. Fricassée.
5. Bytingur.
6. Roast.
7. Confectionery.

With the exception of No. 5, the *menu* was quite intelligible; but this dish puzzled me not a little till I ascertained that it meant puddings. If, in addition to this excellent fare, the reader will add several kinds of choice wines, and will wash the whole down with foaming bumpers of champagne, and suppose speeches and toasts to be going on the whole time, he will get a good idea of the whole ceremony. A band of music was the only thing that was wanting to place this dinner on the same level with a banquet in any other land whatsoever. But there were good reasons for this omission, for a brass instrument is scarcely to be found in the country, and still less a whole quartett.

But now the dessert is over, and the author begs permission to turn over to a new chapter.

CHAPTER IX.

Days of the Week—Þingvalla Church—Laugardalr—Subaqueous Bridge—The Geysir System—Great Geysir—Strokkr—Eruptions of Strokkr—Subterranean Noises—Origin of Geysirs—The Geysir not of great Date—A Night by the Geysir—Journey to Hekla—Hekla—Eruption in 1766—Eruption in 1845—Premonitory Symptoms—First Effects—Showers of Ashes—Continuation of Eruption—Lava Stream—Cessation of Eruption—Return to Reykjavik—From Eyrarbakki to Krísuvík—Dangerous Coast—Shipwrecks—Oil on the Waters—Sulphur Springs at Krísuvík—Farewell to Iceland.

I AM quitting Reykjavik for the second time, in order to pay the Geysirs and Hekla a visit. It was Thursday,* August 31, and the autumn had already given signs of its approach by the yellow appearance of the grass, and by the rainy weather. My horses, which had had a good rest after their long journey round the country, were saddled anew, and conveyed me over the old familiar road across Mosfellsheiði to Þingvellir.

On my first visit to this place I had put up for the night

* In Iceland they have not retained the old names for the four days of the week,—Tuesday, Wednesday, Thursday, and Friday. They were altered by one of the Roman Catholic bishops of the country, because he thought them savouring too much of heathenism. They were called instead—Þridjudagr, third day; Miðvikudagr, mid-week day, the same as the German Mittwoche; Fimtudagr,

at the house of a communicative and hospitable peasant in Skógarkot, whose name, if I am not mistaken, was simply "Jón." His "bær" lies about midway on the level lava stream between Almannagjá and Hrafnagjá. Close by the first-named fissure the parsonage of Þíngvellir is situate. The Öxará flows

Þingvalla Church.

by it into Þíngvallavatn, close to which is Lögberg (*vide* p. 282). It is best to make the parsonage one's head-quarters, if it is desired to explore Almannagjá and the places of historical note in the vicinity.

The above sketch represents the little church of Þíngvalla, and Föstudagr, fast day; and these names are still retained. Saturday is Laugardagr, or bathing day, as it is the universal custom to frequent the bath on that day. Neither is time reckoned according to the hour of the day, for in many places a clock is an unknown article, and they consequently have to divide the day according to the position of the sun in the heavens. Thus 9 A.M. is "dagmál," day; noon, "hádegi," high day or noon; 3 P.M., "nón;" 6 P.M., "miðuraptan," mid-evening; 9 P.M., "náttmál," night; midnight, "midnótt;" 3 A.M., "otta," morning vigil; 6 A.M., "miðurmorgun," or "hirðisrismál." "Otta," however, is not the hour at which they usually get up in Iceland; they recently done up and tarred. It stands on a little eminence near the Öxará, which flows between the church and the mountain in the background. This rocky ridge, which can be followed for some distance, is formed, as may be seen, in its most remote parts of a perpendicular wall, which is, in fact, the western wall of Almannagjá, which thus lies enclosed in all its grand magnificence surrounded by the mountain, the eastern portion of which slopes down to the valley of the Öxará. On the left of the church is the parsonage-house, and on the right "Lögberg." On the mountain slope on the right, and on the level ground at its foot, the "búðirnar," or huts, lay, where the old chieftains used to reside during the meeting of the Althing. This spot was often the scene of quarrels and of bloody encounters between the haughty "Odels"-men. The site of these huts is now only indistinctly marked by some masses of rubbish. Here the days that have passed slumber on in their mysterious sleep, and we can merely trace out their half-effaced memorials in silent wonderment.

At Skógarkot, which I also visited, I engaged a guide to the Geysirs. The road over Hrafnagjá, over which we had to pass, is not so picturesque as the one over its twin-fissure on the other side of the valley. It consists of a narrow bridge formed out of stones that have been thrown or have fallen down. On passing over Hrafnagjá the remarkable lava stream from Skjaldbreið is left behind, and the traveller immediately afterwards emerges upon a new lava plain, and a stony, untrodden "heiði," where the road slopes down into a plain lying open towards the south, named Laugardalr, and which is a con-

generally sleep till "midurmorgun," snooze a little before rising, but remain up till late in the evening, a custom which is due to the light nights, for in the summer months the night is nearly as light as the day. In the northern districts the sun remains above the horizon for nearly a whole week about midsummer.

tinuation of the extensive range of lowland with which I have already made my readers acquainted. On descending on to the plain, there are some holes in the tufa mountain to be seen. The northern slope of the valley is set off by a low but luxuriant growth of underwood. Below, the Laugar lake spreads itself out; and further in the distance a lake of larger dimensions, the Apavatn, can be seen. From the meadows in the valley enormous pillars of steam rise up, evident signs of the hot-springs that are found there, of which Reykjahver is the most important. From Laugardalr there is an extensive view to the south and south-east, as far as Eyafjalls-Jökul and Hekla, which happened at the time I was there to be enveloped in a thick fog. This valley or plain forms, therefore, both on a small and on a grand scale, one of the most magnificent landscapes in the country. The road to the Geysirs from this place is good; that is to say, as good as one may expect to find in Iceland. With the exception of a portion of a lava stream, which has flowed out from the mountain slope on the right, and a river named Brúará, so called from a little bridge that crosses it, there is nothing of any particular interest. This bridge is a work of necessity, for the mid-portion of the river-bed is formed out of a broad cleft, which would otherwise be impassable to man or beast. The bridge, however, is only laid over this cleft, and one has to ride through the water to get to it. The water dashes down into the cleft on both sides with great impetuosity, and is dispersed in the form of a greenish-white foam, which is swallowed, as it were, by the yawning abyss below. The bridge consists merely of a few planks nailed together, and is provided with a railing on either side. When the water in the river rises, it flows over the bridge, which thus becomes an "underwater" bridge.

The approach to the world-famed Geysir is over a green

plain, which is bounded on the north by mountains. Close to the springs, for there are several of them, a small detached mountain-ridge, named Laugafell, rears itself up, which from its trachytic composition—for trachyte and obsidian are closely related to each other—reminded me of Hrafntinnuhryggr, near Krafla. This ridge, as may be remembered, consists of an old lava stream; although now of some considerable elevation, it had once, like every other lava stream, flowed down into a valley, which it completely filled up. It is surrounded on both sides by palagonite tufa. The nature of the rock, however, does not resemble the usual lava form, but has probably flowed out of the interior of the earth in a molten mass. It must thus either have taken possession of an old valley or a fissure; and the surrounding mass of rock has then at a later date been carried away by erosion, as at Hrafntinnuhryggr. This will serve as an instance of the way in which certain portions of the surface of the earth in Iceland have originated.

At the eastern base of Laugafell are the celebrated warm springs, of which the Geysir, or more properly, the Great Geysir, is the most important. The word geysir is a common name for all fountains, and is derived from the Icelandic word "geysa," to ascend violently, though it is now almost exclusively applied to the Great Geysir.

The Great Geysir, another spring named Strokkr, together with a number of smaller springs, of which two are called the Little Geysir and Little Strokkr, are the principal objects of attraction. According to Winkler, the number of large and small springs amounts to twenty-two, besides ten or twelve smaller holes, from which steam issues. The distance between the Geysir and Strokkr is about 500 feet. It will further be remarked that the distance between all these springs is trifling, and that the earth is penetrated with holes like a sieve. The nature of the rock in which the springs are situate is palagonite tufa. The greater number of these are boiling-springs. Owing to the siliceous deposit, and to the fact that many of the springs have changed their position in the lapse of ages, vegetable growth is nearly entirely extinct. By the Great Geysir there is, however, a green patch, where travellers generally pitch their tent. In other respects the terrain consists of a reddish-yellow sand, mixed with particles of yellowish-grey siliceous incrustations. In consequence of the petrifying quality which the water possesses, beautiful impressions of leaves, twigs, old newspapers, and the like, which either nature or man have thrown down on the spot, may be found.

After these preliminary remarks, I will proceed to give a more detailed description of the two "lions," the Geysir and Strokkr.

The Geysir consists of a flat, circular arch or hillock, rising about six feet above the ground, and is formed of light grey siliceous incrustations. Its surface is full of small holes, and is uneven, and may not unfittingly be compared to the bark of an old oak-tree, or to the outside of an oyster-shell. At the top of this arch, which is like the section of a sphere, there is a saucer-shaped hollow, between 50 and 60 feet in diameter, and 4 feet in depth; and in its centre the vertical tube, which connects the saucer-like basin with the interior of the earth. This tube is about 9 feet in diameter, and 70 feet in depth.

Imagine a saucer furnished underneath with a tube of suitable length, and you have a miniature representation of the Geysir basin, with its descending canal. When the spring is inactive, the basin is filled to the edge with clear water, which, however, is not at boiling-point—on the surface it only reaches a temperature of between 80° and 90° C.—but runs gently, and emits clouds of steam. From the edge of the basin, the darker colour of the water in the middle, where the descending canal is connected with it, can be plainly noticed. Immediately over this the water is in constant motion, produced by the warm column of water rising up from the canal, and displacing the colder water in the basin, and driving it slowly towards the edges, where it sinks down again, and flows back into the canal along the bottom of the basin, as may be noticed by throwing pieces of paper into it. The motion, in fact, is exactly similar to that which takes place in a saucepan full of water on the fire. The heated portions of water at the bottom of the vessel rise up to the surface, are cooled from contact with the external air, and are forced by the warmer column of water in the middle against the sides of the vessel, when they sink down to the bottom, to commence the same circulation over and over again.

The margin of the Geysir basin is uneven and knotted like the surface of the arch, and on the side which is towards the plain it is provided with a very small channel or waste pipe, through which the superfluous water runs away. The Strokkr, an Icelandic word, signifying a churn, differs from the Geysir in this respect, that it has no basin and no outlet, except one by chance be formed by an eruption. It consists only of a vertically descending tube $7\frac{1}{2}$ feet in diameter at its mouth, which lies level with the surface of the earth, and is surrounded with a little wreath-like bank of siliceous incrustations, of which substance, moreover, the sides of the canal are composed. The surface of the water in this canal is not less than from 9 to 14 feet below the level of the mouth. The water is constantly in a boiling state, and seethes and dashes against the sides of the pipe. The pipe is not cylindrical as in the Geysir, but gradually contracts underneath the surface. At a depth of 26 feet it is only 8 inches in diameter; and the whole depth of the tube, as far as it has been possible to fathom it, is 42 feet.

Before setting out from Reykjavik, I had been informed that the season was too far advanced to admit of any prolonged stay by the Geysirs. Independently of the necessity of pitching a tent near the springs, in order to observe the eruptions, which last only a very short time, the evenings and nights at this season of the year were dark, and thus, of course,

Strokkr.

the difficulty of taking observations is increased, the more so as a clear sky cannot be calculated on.

On leaving Reykjavik, therefore, I was not very sanguine about enjoying the spectacle of an eruption of the Geysir. The eruptions do not take place periodically, so that it is impossible to calculate with any degree of certainty on the time when an eruption will take place. The inhabitants of those parts say that an eruption very often will not take place for weeks together, while at other times several will occur in one day. It is the opinion in Iceland that eruptions occur more frequently in calm than in windy weather; as, in the latter case, the water in the springs is cooled too much to allow of the conditions necessary to an eruption taking place. On arriving at the spot I was informed that an eruption had only taken place on the previous day; and, as no new eruption could be expected with any degree of certainty for several days, I more than half resolved not to waste my time on a possibly fruitless object. The extreme coldness of the night, and a severe storm the following day, decided me on this point. Still my stay by the springs was very interesting and instructive.

As soon as I reached the spot, and had made a hasty acquaintance with its position, I adopted the usual plan of coaxing the Strokkr; for, by throwing stones or turf into it, it will in a few minutes bubble up. It is necessary, however, to be cautious in doing this, otherwise there is great danger of stopping up the spring altogether. This very nearly was the case once.

After having closely examined the Geysir basin, and another beautiful little spring in its neighbourhood, that had water of a bluish-green colour—Winkler compares it to a stalactite grotto, whose light-yellow walls are decorated with the most lovely ornaments—I directed my steps towards the small springs in the southern portion of the terrain. On passing by Strokkr for the second time, I paused for a few moments on its brink and gazed down into its depths, where the water was boiling and seething as before. I had scarcely gone a few paces from its mouth, when behind me I heard a whizzing sound, similar to that which a rocket makes when let off. On turning round, an enormous column of steam issuing from the spring met my eyes. Being on the lee side of the spring the stream drove towards me, so I quickly moved my position and enjoyed the glorious spectacle of seeing it in all its splendour. Swiftly as an arrow, one column of steam after the other shot up to a great height, whilst massive clouds of vapour detached themselves from the pearly drops of water, and were rolled off by the wind. When the eruption had ceased, I found the large stones which I had thrown into the spring lying on its brink. After a little pause, which was only disturbed by the gurgling sound of the water as it flowed back into the pipe, I ventured to look down, but was obliged to beat a speedy retreat, as fresh columns of steam were hurled out. The eruption lasted, on and off, for about two hours. The only remark that can be made against the beauty of this natural phenomenon is that the water is very dirty, owing to the earth and turf which travellers throw down into it. But the white clouds of steam formed by this muddy water looked even whiter than usual from the contrast.

I had hired a little Icelandic tent to pass the night in at the Geysirs. It was just high enough for a person to sit upright, but far from being wide enough to lie down in— that is to say, if he desired to keep his legs under cover during the night. Possibly it was owing to his intimate acquaintance with this circumstance that induced my companion to ask for permission to pass the night in a neighbouring farmhouse; other reasons besides the contracted area of the tent induced me to acquiesce heartily in the proposed arrangement. Accordingly, he left me, as it was growing dusk; and just as I was occupied in arranging myself comfortably in the little tent, which I had pitched on a green plot of ground only a few paces distant from the Geysir, sundry violent underground rumblings close by me made me start up. I hurried out on to the brink of the basin, which trembled under my feet from the continuous subterranean noises. The water in the spring was visibly in motion, and thicker clouds of steam rose from it than before. The water in the basin rose only a very little, so as just to run over its brink; but when the rumbling noises ceased, it sank down about a foot underneath its usual level, which, however, it soon reached again. It was merely one of the minor periodical eruptions of the Geysir, and reminded me of the rising and boiling over and relapse of the hot spring at Uxahvers. They occurred four or five times during the night, and were accompanied by subterranean noises. In a regular eruption, these noises are louder, and the mass of water is hurled out with great impetuosity to a considerable height, as from the Strokkr; but it differs from this latter, partly from the larger volume of water, partly from the form of the ejected columns which assumes a branched appearance, resembling a pine-tree, and which in the Strokkr terminates in a point. After an eruption of the Geysir, the basin and the pipe become empty, so that one can see down into its depth. The height to which they respectively hurl the column of water differs according to the accounts of different travellers; it is, however, clear that only actual measurements ought to be taken into account. Bunsen, the distinguished German physiologist, who is deserving of great credit for the accounts he has given of the peculiarities of the Icelandic springs, estimates the height of the jet thrown out by the Strokkr during an eruption to be 151 feet. The height of a jet of water from the Geysir is generally reckoned at the same height. In 1804, however, it was said to have reached the height of 212 feet, and one of the previous century a height of 360 feet. Von Troil estimates it at 92 feet.

The Geysir system, it should be stated, lies at an elevation of about 360 feet above the sea.

We will not tire the reader's patience with a detailed account of the hot springs in general, and of the Geysirs in particular, but will merely state that, with the exception of some few "ale springs,"* as they are termed in Iceland, or springs impregnated with carbonic acid, in the west of the country, the mineral springs of Iceland may be divided into two groups, according to their general chemical character, namely, into those which deposit gypsum and sulphur, and those which deposit siliceous incrustations.

The night I passed by the Geysir the sky was clear and cloudless, but, though the moon was up for some time above the horizon, it was still dark. I therefore felt convinced that it would be a matter of great difficulty to observe an eruption at this time with any accuracy, because the transparent water-drops would scarcely be visible against the dark-blue background of the sky, and because large volumes of steam are given out at these eruptions. I was not sorry, therefore, to see the night wear away without any eruption taking place. Not the less, however, was the impression that was conveyed to my mind one of extreme solemnity during that short night. For a long time I stood on the brink of the basin gazing down into its dark, mysterious depths, whilst the white steam slowly rolled off the surface of the water, or was carried on one side by the wind. Overhead the northern lights were silently flickering, and the stars revolving in their peaceful courses. But ever and anon dull, subterranean, rumbling noises, like the distant boom-

* In the "Royal Mirror," a curious Norwegian work, supposed to have been written before the close of the 12th century, express mention is made of a celebrated mineral spring in Iceland. The author mentions three things as remarkable about the water. When drunk in a considerable quantity it inebriates; if the well be covered with a roof the water leaves the place and springs up somewhere else in the vicinity; and, lastly, though it possesses the above quality when drunk at the well, on being carried away it loses its efficacy, and becomes like other water. These springs, of which there are several in Iceland, are called by the natives "*öl-kilder*," or "ale springs."

ing of cannon, could be heard, whilst the earth trembled, and the surface of the Geysir was heaved up. Then all became quiet again, and only the plashing murmur of the water served to break the deep silence of the night.

After midnight it began to blow from the north-east. It became cold, and there was every symptom of a storm. Next morning the water in the hollows of the cone of the Geysir was frozen; and as my little tent could not withstand the blast, I had it taken down and packed up.

When my companion had returned, bringing with him a guide to Hekla, I continued my journey southwards. The weather began to be detestable; worse, indeed, than any I had hitherto experienced in the country. The rain drove over the plain across which I had to go, and the storm raged so fiercely that it seemed as if it were trying to lift me off my saddle. Thus it continued till noon. At that time we reached a farmhouse, Bræðratúnga, where I dined and drank coffee in the church. After this, we rode over to Hvitá, the largest arm of the river, which in its lower parts is known under the name of Ölfusá, and with which the reader is already acquainted. Hvitá comes from a large lake, Hvitárvatn, at the foot of Lángjökul. Between the Hvitá and the next river, the Laxá, the plain is interrupted by several mountain ridges running parallel with the course of the river. They belong to the palagonite formation; and the brown tufa appears to advantage against the green spots on the rocky walls and the grass-covered plains. The landscape is certainly picturesque.

I took up my quarters for the night at Stórinúpr, an indifferent parsonage-house in the neighbourhood of Þjorsá, and the following day ferried over the river, and then proceeded across the older lava streams of Mount Hekla, which were partially covered with sand and overgrown with grass, till I reached Stóru Vellir. Here I passed two pleasant days with the pastor of the place, Sira Guðmundr, a venerable and intelligent grey-haired old man. My original plan had been to ascend Hekla from this place, but as the mountain was enveloped in clouds and snow fogs nearly the whole time of my stay, I was obliged to content myself with paying a visit to its foot, where the lava stream of 1845 had flowed down. This point is situated at about one and a half hour's distance from Storú Vellir, at the foot of the mountain slope, for farther than this the lava stream has been unable to flow. The mountain is approached over a plain sparsely overgrown with grass, which is formed out of older and bare lava streams, that serve to remind one of the volcano's proximity. After passing over Rángá one comes to a thick, low copse-wood of birch, the luxuriant verdure of which is greatly owing to the subterranean warmth, and immediately afterwards to the lava stream which has been precipitated down from the heights above, and whose end forms a steep wall on the sandy plain below. It is difficult to clamber up, and, like the surface of the stream, consists of blackened fragments of scoriæ.

Although the summit of Hekla, which is 4,961 feet above the sea, reaches beyond the limit of eternal snow, it is not entirely covered with snow in summer, as the subterranean heat in a great measure causes it to melt. Still, on its western side, a snow "fond" of considerable dimensions slopes down the mountain. According to Sira Guðmundr, who made the ascent of Hekla three or four years ago, the thermometer rose at certain spots in the ground to 90° C. This gentleman also pointed out to me, the same day I arrived at Storú Vellir, a column of steam that was rising from a point on the last lava stream—a phenomenon seldom to be seen at so great a distance, as it is requisite that there should be an entire absence of wind on the mountain. When Kjerulf visited Hekla, in 1850, the thermometer rose, when placed in some holes in the lava whence gaseous exhalations were issuing, to over 100°; but that was only five years after the eruption had taken place.

But we must pause for a few moments in order to consider the position and the history of Hekla.

Hekla, then, lies, as the reader will at once see by glancing at the map, on the eastern side of the large plain just alluded to, which is intersected by the Þjorsá and Hvitá (or Ölfusá, as it is termed lower down in its course). This lowland, which comprises the largest district in Iceland, is one of the most fertile and prosperous parts of the country. On the opposite side of the mountain a complete wilderness commences, which is almost a *terra incognita*, for it is only traversed by peasants in search of their sheep, which have been turned out to graze there during the summer; for, although there are no human habitations to be found there, yet there is some little pasture. Hekla is bounded by the two rivers, East and West Rángá, which are fed by the water that trickles down through the porous masses of slag and lava of which the upper part of the mountain is composed, and through the strata of lava which surround the volcano on all sides. The volcano itself is piled up with slag and ashes, the loose heaps of which are kept together by the streams of lava that have flowed down along the mountain's sides. The foundation of this frail building, as Kjerulf calls it, consists of a ridge of palagonite tufa, running in a direction north-east and south-west, about 2,000 feet in height. This ridge is the middlemost of the five main ridges which conjointly form the mountain system over which Hekla majestically rears its crest aloft. The remaining ridges, which have their respective names, and which are separated from Hekla proper by valley-formed hollows, are also composed of palagonite tufa, the light-brown colour of which stands out conspicuously against the darker hue of the more modern volcanic productions. Tufa itself, as the reader is already aware, consists of ancient volcanic products, which probably arose from submarine eruptions, and which have become transformed into firm masses somewhat resembling sandstone. The large plain, moreover, above alluded to is formed of older tufa and younger lava, and masses of sand, which, however, according to our reckoning of time, may be still of great age.

Hekla thus forms a ridge of long extent, and belongs to the class of those volcanoes which are arranged in linear series, whose crater is not definitely marked, but changes position along the extent of the volcanic fissure. Leirhnúkr, and most of the volcanoes of Iceland, belong to this class. The exterior of Hekla has naturally been subjected to several important changes from the eruptions that have taken place. Before the eruption of 1845, three, or at least two, peaks rose up from this ridge, though not to any great elevation.

Of all the volcanoes of Iceland, Hekla has had the greatest number of eruptions. Subsequently to the colonization of the country, volcanic eruptions have taken place in twenty-seven different places, numbering in all between eighty and ninety. To this number Hekla has contributed twenty-six, Katla thirteen, the volcano in the sea near Reykjanes about twelve, and the other volcanoes a smaller number; but no regularity as regards the time when the eruptions have taken place has been observed in any of these. The shortest time during which Hekla has remained inactive is six years; the longest, seventy-nine years. Neither has the violence of the eruptions been in any proportion to the duration of its inactivity.

We will now speak of the eruptions themselves more in detail.

The first of these occurred in the eighteenth century, a century which proved so disastrous to Iceland. On April 5, 1766, between 3 and 4 A.M., an enormous column of ashes was discharged from Hekla, accompanied with lightning and violent detonations and reports. The night before several shocks of earthquake had been noticed, two of which were of great violence. The column of ashes took a north-westerly direction, and discharged such a quantity of slag and ashes as to cover the surface of the ground in the immediate neighbourhood of Hekla to a depth of two feet. In two hours' time five farmhouses were completely destroyed, large extents of wood were buried, and the pastures suffered enormous injury; scoriæ of two feet in circumference were hurled to a distance of two miles, and thick masses of loose scoriæ covered the surface of the Þjorsá, and dammed up the Rángá river, whereby the low lands were completely inundated. The enormous quantities of scoriæ that these rivers carried down to the sea, actually hindered the progress of the fishing-boats. The coast to the south of Hekla, for an extent of over twenty miles, was covered with them; and in the immediate neighbourhood of the mouths of these rivers the scoriæ lay piled up to a height of two feet. At noon on the day of the eruption a strong southerly wind sprung up, and carried the ashes towards the northern districts, where daylight was turned into pitchy darkness. Deafening reports drove the people away from the neighbourhood of the volcano, and were heard over the whole island. On April 9, a lava stream began to flow towards the south-west, in the direction of the most populous part of the country, and gradually extended to a distance of two-thirds of a mile from the mountain. Two craters were seen to be in activity at one and the same time; the one on the summit of the mountain, and the other lower down, towards the south-west; but at other times

HEKLA. Page 322.

as many as eighteen places could be discerned from whence fire issued.*

On April 21, the column of ashes was found to have attained a height of 17,000 feet, but on several occasions it was considerably higher. Continuous shocks of earthquake accompanied the eruption, whereby several houses were thrown down; shocks, too, were felt both at sea and on land, but more especially on Vestmanna Islands and in the direction of Reykjanes.

Epidemics raged both among human beings and cattle; and this disastrous state of affairs was increased by the quantities of snow that fell, accompanied by storms from the northwest, which lasted in the south of the country from the 12th to the 17th of April, and in the northern districts during a whole week in succession.

We now come to the last eruption, which took place in 1845. This eruption was preceded, just as the eruption of the Skaptarvulcano in 1783, by an unusually mild winter, so that by April everything began to look green. But the expectations of an early and plentiful hay harvest were dashed to the ground, from a drought that lasted the whole summer through, and withered up the grass in the fields. The drought continued up to the 22nd of August, notwithstanding the southerly winds that prevailed, and though the atmosphere was thick with vapour, and the sky overclouded. These winds, it should be stated, always bring rain in Iceland, for they come from the sea, and are laden with moisture, which on reaching the mountains is condensed and falls in the form of rain.

These unusual atmospheric conditions, which on former occa-

---

* Volcanoes, however, do not vomit forth fire; but the column of ashes over the crater is illumined by the molten lava and the red-hot scoriæ underneath. Whence the term "fiery mountain" has improperly arisen.

sions had been the precursors of an eruption, made the people involuntarily dread a volcanic outbreak. It was remarked, moreover, that the snow patches on Hekla's ridge had diminished in a marked way during the course of the summer, a circumstance which, although in a certain degree owing to the little quantity of snow that had fallen during the previous winter, still served to attract people's attention more closely to the volcano.

In addition to these premonitory signs, it was noticed that on the 4th or 5th of August, in the immediate vicinity of Hekla, particularly on the farms to the south of the volcano, there was a sudden and unexpected diminution in the milk given by the cows, and especially by the sheep; so much so that a cow which had before that date given as much as three measures of milk, now gave only one. In the middle of August a similar phenomenon was observed on a farm near Þríhyrningr Fjeld, south-west of Hekla. Schiödte, who mentions this circumstance, attributes it to a general exhalation of acid vapours issuing from the earth previously to the eruption in those districts. Besides these actual or fancied premonitory symptoms, it was observed that the number of hot springs, which are numerous near the foot of Torfajökul, to the south-east of Hekla, had of late years increased in numbers and activity. Hence the comforting conclusion was arrived at that the volcanic heat was seeking to escape by other means; though, in fact, this circumstance only showed that the subterranean heat was approaching nearer to the surface of the earth, and was rather a proof to the contrary.

The earlier eruptions of Hekla had generally been preceded by earthquakes; but in the present instance not a single shock was felt. The dry weather which had prevailed during the spring and summer was succeeded on August 22nd by rain, which continued with but few interruptions to the end of the month. September set in with a hazy atmosphere, a cloudy sky, and occasional rain. As a rule, a depressing stillness prevailed, except when an occasional puff of wind from the south or west produced a disturbance in the atmosphere. This kind of weather still continued, when, on the 2nd of September, the eruption began. Dark, low-lying clouds hid the mountains from sight; but about nine in the morning the attention of the people was arrested by the report of some dull detonations, apparently issuing from the mountains on the east, while a slight vibration on the surface of the earth was simultaneously felt. People, however, who were out of doors either on foot or on horseback, did not pay particular attention to the circumstance; while others supposed the reports to be the rumbling of distant thunder; others, again, were in a state of alarm lest a violent storm from the east should come on, as tempests from that quarter had always been preceded by premonitory symptoms of a similar nature, though never to such an extent as now. But before long the regularity of the rumbling noises made them fear that they really proceeded from Hekla, and that a new eruption of the volcano was imminent. The forenoon, however, passed by without any change occurring; and many an anxious look, therefore, was directed towards Hekla, which was enveloped in darkness, uncertain as to what would happen. Meanwhile, in other parts of the country, more unequivocal signs of the volcanic eruption had begun to spread panic and devastation. Near the coast, to the south-east of Hekla, a dark cloud was seen to rise over the mountains in the west and north-west at about 10 o'clock, while at the same time an unusual crashing and rumbling sound was heard from the same quarter. If any uncertainty had hitherto prevailed as to what it all meant, it was certainly removed when the cloud, which had gradually spread over the whole sky, began to discharge, at about 11 o'clock, a thick rain of greyish-yellow, slaggy pieces, about the size of "fox-shot."

At the same time the darkness continued to increase in intensity; while, at noon, it was as dark as on the darkest winter-night, so that it was almost impossible to see one's hand. Lights had to be burned in the houses, and people who were overtaken by showers of stones out of doors, could scarcely find their way home. After the lapse of an hour, it began to grow lighter, as when the morning is dawning after a dark night, and at 3 o'clock it was as light as it had been before. Large grey-coloured stones and rubbish continued to fall for the space of an hour, whereby the ground was covered to the thickness of half an inch; after which, a dark, shining, volcanic sand began to fall. This sand shower continued to fall, though with decreasing violence, throughout the whole of September 2nd, the following night, and the forenoon of the 3rd instant; so that at noon on that day, the ground was covered with a layer of stones, sand, and ashes, of one and a half inches in thickness.

On the opposite side of Hekla, or in the district on the northwest of the volcano, a similar darkness prevailed on the forenoon of the day of the eruption. But there was no fall of ashes there, which of course was due to the direction of the wind. At first, several of the peasants thought it was an eclipse, and began to hunt about after their almanacs. But the almanac could give them no information, for the eclipse which then prevailed was occasioned by the interposition of a huge column of ashes between them and the sun. Others thought it was a thunder-storm when they heard the repeated sounds of smothered reports, or were of opinion that they were caused by the Geysir in the neighbourhood; which circumstance shows that the reports were not particularly loud. Nevertheless, they were simultaneously observed over nearly the whole country, even in the most remote parts, and various were the explanations given of them.

At Kirkjuvogr, a little to the north of Reykjanes, the people thought that Reykjavík was being cannonaded; at Stapi, south of Snæfellsjökul, they thought a whale must have been washed ashore, and that it was splashing about against the rocks. The sound extended even to Grimsey, and the people there thought the Frenchmen were cannonading some place in Iceland. This widely-extended distribution of comparatively weak rumbling sounds is readily explained by taking into consideration the great depth from which they probably originated; for it is evident that the deeper down under the earth rumbling sounds take place, the more widely will their effects be felt.

At mid-day, on the day of the eruption, the rumbling noises had somewhat abated after two terrific crashes; but towards the afternoon they recurred with unabated vigour, so that it actually seemed as if one cannon was being fired off after the other. About three o'clock the atmosphere became somewhat clearer, when a dark column of ashes, the top of which seemed to melt away in the clouds, was seen to be hurled out from the summit of the mountain, accompanied with flashes of lightning. About half-past seven P.M., when darkness began to set in, a rumbling noise, more violent than any of the former ones, caused the greatest alarm both to human beings and animals. Dogs in the neighbourhood to the west of Hekla were seized with such a panic that they ran howling away from their masters, and did not return home for a whole week. Vaporous exhalations could be seen to issue from the mouth of the crater, brightly illumined by the glare of the glowing mass in the interior of the mountain.

Apparently it seemed as if a sheet of flame, steadily increasing in dimensions, shot out from the summit of the mountain, while huge glowing masses of stone were being hurled up and down in the fearful fiery mass. In the darkness of the night, the lava stream which was flowing from the north-western side of Hekla, and extended downwards along the sloping incline of the mountain, resembled a fiery band.

At the commencement of the eruption, large masses of slag were hurled out on all sides of the mountain; for although the column of ashes appeared to be sharply defined towards the west, and inclined towards the east, the streams on the western side of Hekla carried down a large quantity of mud and earth and stone. The volume of water in Vestri-Rángá diminished about the middle of the day, probably owing to its bed being choked up with ashes and masses of sand; but in the afternoon it again increased, and rose so high that it could not be crossed. Large masses of scoriæ and mud were carried along in its current, making its usually clear water resemble mud soup. The water, too, was so hot that it was impossible keep one's hand in it; and in several places hundreds of half-boiled trout were cast out on to the land. But the rising of the stream, which was due to the rapid melting of the snow on Hekla's sides, did not continue for long; and towards evening it had fallen to such an extent as to admit of being crossed at the usual fording places.

It has already been remarked that the wind on the day of the eruption was rather low in the neighbourhood of Hekla, but in the upper regions of the atmosphere there was a strong breeze from the north-west. Its strength may be inferred from the fact that homeward-bound captains of ships, who on the 2nd and 3rd of September happened to be in the neighbourhood of the Færoes, the Shetlands, and Orkney Islands, were overtaken by a shower of ashes coming from the north-west, which, judging from the time at which the eruption took place, must have travelled at the rate of about 24 miles an hour. On the Færoes and Orkneys ashes also fell shortly after the eruption.

On the 3rd of September, or the day after the eruption, the atmospheric conditions continued unaltered. The column of ashes was inclined towards the same direction as before. Large masses of earth and stone were also hurled over the mountains and the table-land to the east of Hekla; and the Markar river rose rapidly on this and the following days, and carried with it large masses of slag down to the sea, which were cast up by the surf on the shore of the south coast. Þverá, the western arm of the Markar river, was so choked with it that its tributary brooks and streams were dammed up in their course. Eystri-Rángú, whose source lay more to the south than those of the Markar river, was, however, comparatively free; but the rivers which take their rise in Eyafjalla-Jökul and Mýrdals-Jökul were greatly influenced by the effects of the eruption, owing most probably to a continuous downfall of hot pieces of slag on the masses of snow on these mountains. And that this was the cause may further be inferred from the fact that the Jökulsá at Sólheimarsandr, and Múlakvísl, to the east of Höfðabrekka, rose to such a considerable height, that the former of these rivers could not be forded for nearly a fortnight after the beginning of the eruption.

The sheep had not yet been taken in from their summer grazing, for they are usually left out on the sheep-walks till the middle of September. It might, therefore, be supposed that great havoc was committed among them by the hot fragments of falling slag; but this was not the case. Instinct came to their aid, and urged them to seek safety in flight, so that only a comparatively small number was lost. On the first few days of the eruption, they might be seen proceeding along the northern foot of Hekla, between the mountain and the Þjorsá, which river, together with the Túngnaá, had hindered their flight towards the north. They came, bleating piteously, down into the plain; all of them were more or less blackened by the ashes; many had their fleeces singed in places; while others were suffering from severe burns. Those, however, which remained behind, and which did not return home for a week, had fared the worst, for the flesh about their hoofs was cut and bleeding, from the sharp-pointed scoriæ. The lambs naturally suffered the most, and had to be brought home on horseback; they might be seen grazing on their knees for a long time after the eruption. The flocks that had been grazing on the pastures to the south and south-east of Hekla suffered more severely than any, but still the greater proportion of these escaped.

From the 4th to the 9th of September, Hekla was enveloped in rain and fogs; but the rumbling noises showed that the volcano was still in a state of activity, though not to such an extent as before. During this time the wind blew from the sea over the land in a northerly direction, sometimes accompanied with violent storms, and carried the ashes along with it, causing thereby considerable damage to the grass walks in this quarter. Hitherto the settlement or parish itself, thanks to the direction of the wind, had escaped destruction. The violence of the eruption abated in a marked degree up to the 12th; but the lava stream continued to advance, though with what speed it is difficult to pronounce, as, of course, its rate of progress depended on the greater or less inclination of the mountain-slopes. By the 9th of September, that is to say, one week from its commencement, it had scarcely proceeded a distance of half-a-mile from the actual foot of the mountain; its breadth, however, was considerable. Its surface had, in a measure, begun to stiffen according as the supply from above had diminished; but its glowing interior shone brilliantly among the dark masses of slag, and when an iron rod was thrust into it, it became so hot in a few minutes that it could almost be welded. The radiation of heat, moreover, was so great at a distance of two fathoms from the stream, that it was impossible to endure it without covering the face. While thick vapours were generated from the lava, the mass advanced slowly, with a crashing noise, and loose stones kept incessantly rolling down from its edges. On looking down upon the lava stream from an eminence, one could see the glowing mass flowing heavily along under the stiffened crust, and the red-hot matter oozing out of the cracks, like molten metal; but directly it was exposed to the air it became covered with a crust, which by daylight was of a dark blue colour, but by night appeared to be red-hot. Sometimes the lava burst through the crust, and covered the plain below with a mass of red-hot pieces, owing to the sudden stiffening, which made it dangerous to approach too near to the stream. The height of the lava stream at its edge was estimated at 40 to 50 feet,* which, however, gives but an imperfect idea of its dimensions, because it had flowed through a valley, in the middle of which the thickness of the stream may be computed to have been 100 feet. As the lava stream had flowed over nothing but *débris,* or older lava streams, it did not commit any damage.

On September 12 the rumbling noises increased, and in the evening were as violent as on the first day of the eruption;

---

* It may be remarked that a lava stream does not form a plane surface like a river, but runs in a ridge; that is to say, the side walls are elevated above the plain. Neither does it run out at the end, but forms a wall towards the plain.

the lava stream, moreover, rapidly increased. On the morning of the 13th, the column of ashes was as high as it had been at first, and, owing to an easterly wind, inclined towards the west, over the northern part of the inhabited plain, where ashes fell for the first time since the beginning of the eruption. This lasted for two days. The quantity of ashes that fell, however, was not sufficient, even in the immediate neighbourhood of the volcano, to cover the ground completely; but linen, that was put out to dry, became black in a very short time, while white cattle also assumed the same colour. On stamping on the ground, the ashes flew up in clouds of bluish dust. The vegetation was much injured by their influence; cabbages, which were uninjured on the 13th of September, were withered and dried up before noon on the following day; and where the grass had not yet been mown, it was laid flat, and withered away, especially where the ashes fell simultaneously with rain. The cattle, too, suffered; they could not rest, but went backwards and overwards over the pastures, just as in winter, when they are covered with snow. Horses and cows were driven home from sheer hunger, and were glad to crop the grass growing on the walls of the houses, on which the ashes had been unable to find a lodgment.

On the 14th and 15th of September, on which days the shower of ashes continued in the parish, the rumbling noises increased, succeeding each other with such rapidity and regularity as to resemble the continuous roar of a cannonade; they were caused by the sudden development of bubbles of steam rising up from the volcano, and hurling out the molten lava, in fragments of different sizes, and partly in the form of sand. One can form some idea of the enormous force generated by these steam bubbles from a consideration of the height of the column of ashes. According to Gunnlaugsson, it varied in height on the days of the eruption from 7,000 to 14,000 feet.

On the 14th of September, the inhabitants of the parish, or settlement, were alarmed by a fall of ashes, and loud reports from the volcano; neither did the darkness that set in towards evening contribute to quiet their fears. On the following day, that is, on the 15th, the ashes were driven further over the southern settlement, succeeded by an unendurable stench. The noises from the mountain continued with great violence for thirty-six hours; but on the 19th inst., a perceptible abatement in the violence of the eruption was noticed, neither did ashes fall any longer in the parish. Sometimes the volcano was enveloped in a thick fog, so as to be quite hidden from sight; but when clearer weather set in, towards the close of the month, one could observe that it was still in a state of activity. In this way the time passed by till the middle of October without any extraordinary eruption taking place, though shocks of earthquake were frequently felt. But on the 8th of October, a fresh eruption of lava took place, accompanied with loud reports from the mountain, which lasted for a whole week, and a continual shower of ashes. The eruption, however, was diminishing. On the 19th the weather was bright and cold, and snow for the first time was noticed on Hekla, although it had long been lying on the mountains in the neighbourhood; hitherto it had been thawed by contact with the hot ashes.

Towards the end of October, however, on the 26th and 27th instant, the eruption again increased; and on the latter-named day ashes were again hurled out, and committed no little havoc in the parish. After this a period of rest intervened, succeeded by another eruption of ashes and streams of lava between the 4th and 12th of November; and on the 13th, one of the most violent eruptions occurred. On the following days the lava stream made considerable progress, but it did not advance more than 1,325 feet in the 24 hours. Alternate periods of rest and eruptions continued to take place up to the end of the old, or the beginning of the new year. But the eruption did not cease till January the 25th; and even after this, on the following day, fresh eruptions of ashes and lava took place, and continued till the end of the month. In this way matters continued throughout February and March; but after a violent eruption on April 5th, the volcano ceased to rage, and on the following day the last column of ashes was discharged. With this the eruption may be said to have ceased; for on the 10th, patches of snow were lying on the fresh "hraun" below the crater. This eruption, which had thus lasted seven months, is not considered to have been one of the most violent eruptions of Hekla. At all events, it occasioned less destruction than had been the case in the large eruptions of the last century. The lava streams committed no devastation, although the farm Næfurhólt, close by, was abandoned on account of its unpleasant neighbourhood.

On closely examining the summit of Hekla the year after the commencement of the eruption, five craters were discovered,— three large and two smaller ones. The two largest of these were found to be between 200 and 300 feet in depth. The craters, moreover, lay along the ridge of the mountain, where the fissure too was found to be.

We are now homeward bound, and must turn our backs on Hekla, first returning to Reykjavík along the route which we travelled over in the spring. From Stóru Vellir we rode by Oddi, the well-known and excellent parsonage-house in Rángárvallasyssel, and from thence westward towards Eyrarbakki. Thus we again had to cross Ytri-Rángá, ride eighteen times through Raudalœkr, and over the large swamp in front of Sandhólaferja, where the Þjorsá was again crossed in the usual manner. All these streams had been very much dried up during the summer; but the horses (the same which had taken me round the whole island) were just as averse as ever to a bath in the icy-cold Þjorsá. Towards Eyrarbakki the surf was dashing against the flat coast. In winter-time the sea here is tremendously high, and as far as the eye can reach the entire surface is a mass of seething foam. Scoriæ the size of a man's head are cast by the waves high on to the shore: and, occasionally, live fish, which by the reflux of the water are left high and dry on the sand. The mercantile establishment of Eyrarbakki is protected by a breakwater against the sea, which on one occasion was perforated by a monstrous wave, which flooded the whole place. To the north of Eyrarbakki lies the wide plain, which is intersected by the Ölfusá, over which I had to ferry once more. Our company became increased at this place, and from this cause it happened that one of our horses, owing to carelessness, got under water. Fortunately the animal had a halter round its neck, and so we managed to keep its head above water; but the poor beast was so terrified that it refused to move a limb, and lay floating on its side, with its legs stretched out, and in this position was towed across the river, a matter of ten minutes, while a man was holding its head up all the while. But it soon recovered its fright, and swam over the next river as readily as any of its companions.

Not wishing to return to Reykjavík from Ölfusá by the same route which I had used in the spring, I took a circuitous road along the coast to Krísuvík, and from thence northwards to Hafnarfjörðr. Even to one who has seen something of Iceland, this neighbourhood presents many objects of interest. I have already stated at the beginning of this work that the peninsula, at the extremity of which I now was, evinces evident traces of a volcanic nature. By keeping along the coast from east to west, the mountain ridge is of course on the right; this ridge is almost entirely covered with lava streams, from which darkbrown ridges or crests of palagonite tufa stick up with countless volcanic craters. The mountain ridge at first is not very precipitous, and in Selvogsheiði it offers to view a grass-grown tract quite free from lava, extending down to the coast towards the south-west; but further on it assumes the form of a nearly perpendicular wall some 600 or 800 feet high, where the transversely-cut basalts and palagonite are very remarkably prominent.

The coast winds round into bights and bays, and is inhabited by a fishing population. The fisheries of this open coast must be attended with great danger. Eyrarbakki is, as we know, the only harbour on the whole south coast of the country; and this harbour is, moreover, both narrow and difficult of access. It will only hold two vessels, and these can only run in at flood tide, and with a south-westerly wind. Wrecks, therefore, are not uncommon along the coast. The very day we left Iceland a merchant vessel was wrecked in the neighbourhood of Eyrarbakki. The captain, however, who knew the coast well, was able to avoid the surf and breakers, and to beach his ship. In order to diminish the violence of the surf he adopted a plan which, perhaps, may be strange to some of my readers. It consists, namely, in pouring oil over the surface of the sea, which thus prevents the waves from breaking. Directly, therefore, he had come into the surf he knocked the bottoms out of some barrels of oil, and let their contents run out into the sea, and then sailed straight for shore in the belt of calm water which the oil made through the middle of the surf. Small boats are nearly always swamped on this coast. It might be supposed that the action of the waves would throw persons up on to the beach after a boat had been upset, but this rarely happens, for when the surf breaks against the beach it forms an undercurrent, which carries them out to sea instead of casting them on shore. Instances of this kind have often happened where the unfortunate persons have been carried out a long way to sea; in such cases a knowledge of swimming has been of little avail. Owing to the surf the fishermen from Eyrarbakki dare not often put out to sea, though they know it teems with fish; and where the coasts are not sandy and flat, they are generally fringed with perpendicular cliffs, so as to render a landing impossible. The north coast of Faxafjörðr is said to be a very dangerous one when a storm blows from the west; and vessels from Reykjavík are generally wrecked on the point or neck of land on which Snæfells-Jökul lies. True enough there is a harbour named Stapi, but in the darkness of night it is naturally impossible to find it. The last mail-steamer, the predecessor of the *Arcturus*, a sailing vessel, was wrecked off here. A merchant ship had been lying at the same time in Reykjavík harbour, but when the captain of the mail-boat, who was a very good sailor, saw that his companion had run out and was braving the storm, he determined not to be outdone, and followed the example. There were two or three merchants, besides several other passengers, on board. One of the merchants had travelled across land from Akureyri because he considered it safer to go by the mail-ship than by his own yacht, which reached Copenhagen in safety, while the two vessels that ran out from Reykjavík were totally lost. Nothing was ever heard of them; but some goods which were washed ashore, and a quantity of tallow with which the coast off Snæfells-Jökul was covered for a length of time, and of which it was known the mail-ship's cargo consisted, told its tale. Neither were any dead bodies washed up; they were, probably, devoured by the sharks. Another time, when a vessel was wrecked at the same place, it disappeared altogether, and no traces of it were ever heard of; but some time after a hand or a finger with a ring on it was washed up by the waves, plainly telling of its former owner's fate. But we must hurry on.

A visit which I paid on this trip to the parsonage of Vogsósar, in the district of Selvogr, did not convey a very pleasing impression of the prosperity of its inhabitants; for such a state of filth pervaded the place, as I had thought impossible to be found in any clergyman's house. The pastor himself was said to be one of those who did not deny himself indulgence in strong drinks, whence I concluded that matters were left to take care of themselves as best they might. He himself was not at home, but his wife seemed to thrive uncommonly well in dirt; but whether the little child she had in her arms could flourish in such surroundings, I do not feel myself competent to determine. In the evening, I put up at a house named Herdísarvík, about an hour distant from Vogsósar, situate at the foot of the steep mountain wall, in the midst of a barren lava stream, protected in some measure from the south wind and the surf, for an arm of the sea penetrated here.

The good woman of the house, an elderly person of very prepossessing exterior, "thought," she said, "that I should not like to lie in the 'bær;'" and she was decidedly right in her conclusions; for the only habitable "house" contained, or rather consisted of, merely two small rooms, divided off from each other by a boarded partition, the one of which contained five and the other four bedsteads, ranged along the walls, with a passage scarcely a foot in width between them. As each bed will hold two or three, a score of persons can thus be stowed away in these apartments. But there was a little wooden house close by, used as a store-room, and "there I could find room," she said. Certainly there was a perfect museum of different implements and instruments stored away; but a bed was put in for me, and there I made myself as comfortable as circumstances permitted. That night I slept with the image of death overhead in the form of some newly-flayed calves'-skins; but such matters did not interfere with my dreams. After my excellent hostess had brought me my morning cup of coffee—by the way, she knows how to make a most excellent broil of fish —I continued my journey over the lava streams, and reached the sulphur springs of Krísuvík, in which I recognised old acquaintances from the neighbourhood of Mývatn. These offered the same striking characteristics as the former, but the mud springs are not on such a large scale as at Illiðarnámar. A short time ago an attempt was made to turn the sulphur to account at this place—"brennisteinn," as it is termed in Iceland— but after the necessary houses had been built, horses purchased, &c., it was found that the principal ingredient of success was wanting, namely, the sulphur; accordingly, the project was abandoned. These "námar" lie at the foot or on the slope of a steep mountain ridge, called Sveifluháls, over which the traveller must clamber on his road from Krísuvík to the north. There is a beautiful prospect from the top of this ridge. At his foot the spectator has a deep valley, the bottom of which is filled up with a lava stream overgrown with a light-green moss, ending in a crater-formed hollow immediately under his feet. It is called "Ketill," or the Cauldron. The walls of the valley are bounded by steep, dark-brown ridges of tufa, which protrude some distance, but leave the background open, so that the prospect is not shut out. The mountains on the north of Reykjavík—Esja, looking so beautiful, with its blue tints, and Skarðsheiði, which had decked itself during the night with a snow-white mantle along its extensive ridge, hanging far down on either side—here meet the eye. A clear and cloudless sky overhead helped to make the picture complete.

But the reader, perhaps, has long since grown weary of descriptions of scenery, which at best can but give a very imperfect impression of their actual magnificence. We will therefore hurry on as quickly as possible, and not the less quickly as the road between Krísuvík and Hafnarfjörðr is one of the worst in the whole island. It consists, for instance, of lava, and of nothing else but lava, on which a horse can only go at foot's pace; and to ride for four hours right off at a slow walk is calculated to efface the impression of a view even from Sveifluháls. But, to give everything its due, it must be allowed that the neighbourhood presents many objects of interest.

At Hafnarfjörðr, where I made a short halt, I bade farewell to my companion from Eyrarbakki, who took my only horse with him, for I had sold it to a peasant in the neighbourhood, to the far greater regret of the two animals which I engaged to complete the remainder of the journey to Reykjavík than of his master; for he was the laziest beast I have ever had anything to do with. On Sunday, the 10th of September, I again reached Reykjavík, and therewith my long summer tour was at an end. During the interval which elapsed till the mail-boat sailed—that is, for ten days—it rained almost incessantly; so that it was scarcely possible to put one's head out of doors, much less think about making any excursions. The fjelds and the table-land were, during the whole of this time, enveloped in clouds and fogs.

On the 20th the *Arcturus* was ready to sail,—she only had to take a cargo of eighty horses on board,—when a storm from the south-west came, which lasted for five days and nights, during which the barometer sank down to "earthquake." The horses, therefore, were sent ashore again; and of course the passengers followed their example. But on Monday, the 25th, a breeze sprang up from the north, and though the rain and fog continued while we were raising anchor, hopes of a prosperous voyage were entertained, which I am glad to say were happily fulfilled. During the last few days all the mountains had put on their caps of snow, and it was the opinion that they would not doff them again till the following spring.

We steamed out of Faxafjördr towards Reykjanes and Eldey. The well-known mountain-ridge still lay wrapped up in fogs, which, however, lifted somewhat towards evening.

And so I bade farewell to Iceland! A few blue tints on the now scarcely discernible outlines of the distant fjelds was the last impression I received of a country that had become so inexpressibly endeared to me.

APPENDIX.

LIST OF THE ANIMALS, BIRDS, FISHES, MOLLUSCS, ETC., FOUND IN ICELAND;

Extracted from " Un Voyage en Islande, par M. Gaimard."

MAMMALS.

Canis familiaris. Common dog.
C. lagopus. Arctic fox.
C. fuliginosus. Sooty fox; black fox.
Felis catus domesticus. Common cat.
Ursus albus maritimus. Polar bear.
Mus rattus; musculus. Black rat; common mouse.
Cervus tarandus. Reindeer.
Capra hircus. Common goat.
Ovis aries islandicus. Common Icelandic sheep.
Bos taurus domesticus. Common ox.
Equus caballus. Common horse.
Sus scrofa domesticus. Common hog.
Manatus septentrionalis.
Trichecus rosmarus. Arctic walrus.
Monodon monoceros. Narwahl.
Balæna physalus. Fin whale.
B. boops. Pike-headed whale.
B. musculus *vel* rostrata. Round-lipped whale.
B. mysticetus. Greenland whale.
Physeter macrocephalus. Large spermaceti whale.
Delphinus phocæa. Porpoise.
D. bidens.
D. orca. Grampus.
D. delphis. Dolphin, or bottle-nose whale.
D. albicans.
Phoca vitulina. Common seal.
P. leporina. Leporine seal.
P. barbata. Great seal.
P. grænlandica. Harp seal.
P. cristata (leonina). Hooded seal.
P. fœtida.

BIRDS.

Falco albicilla. White-tailed eagle.
F. æsolon. Merlin.
*F. islandicus. Gyr falcon.
F. lanarius. Lanner peregrine falcon.
F. cæsius.
F. ossifragus.
F. leucocephalus. White-headed eagle.
Strix nictea. Snowy owl.
Corvus corax. Raven.
C. cornix. Hooded crow.
C. corona. Carrion crow.
Phasianus gallus. Common cock.
Tetras islandorum. Ptarmigan of Iceland (Yarrel).
T. columba ænas domestica. Stock dove.
Loxia serinas. Grosbeak.
Emberiza calcarata. Lapland bunting.
E. nivalis. Snow bunting.
Fringilla linaria. Lesser redpole.
F. lapponica. Lapland finch.
Sturnus vulgaris. Common starling.
Turdus iliacus. Redwing.
T. pilaris. Fieldfare.
T. merula. Blackbird.
Motacilla alba. Water-wagtail.
Saxicola œnanthe. Wheatear.
Sylvia troglodytes. The wren.
Anthus pratensis. Meadow pipit.
Hirundo rustica. Common swallow.
Hirundo urbica. Martin.

Hæmotapus astrategus. Seapie.
Charadrius hiaticula. Ring plover.
C. pluvialis. Golden plover.
Calidris arenaria. Sanderling.
Ardea cinerea. Common heron.
Numenius arquata. Common curlew.
N. phæopus. Whimbrel.
Limosa melanura. Black-tailed godwit.
Totanus calidus. Red-shank sandpiper.
Vanellus cristatus. Lapwing.
Strepsilas collaris. Turnstone.
Tringa cinerea. Ash-coloured sandpiper.
T. maritima. Purple tringa.
T. alpina. Purre, or dunlin.
T. pugnax. Ruff and Reeve.
T. vanellus. Lapwing.
T. ferruginea.
T. ocrophas. Green sandpiper.
Scolopax gallinago. Common snipe.
Rallus aquaticus. Water rail.
Phalloropus hyperboreus. Red-necked phalloropo.
P. platyrinchus. Broad-billed tringa.
Uria grille. Black guillemot.
U. brünnichii. Thick-billed guillemot.
U. troile. Foolish guillemot.
U. troile leucophtalmos.
U. alle.
Alca torda. Razor-bill.
A. impennis (extinct). Great auk.
A. unisulcata.
*A. arctica. Puffin.
A. deleta.
*Mormon fratercula. Puffin.
Carbo cormoranus. Cormorant.
C. graculus. Shag.
Pelicanus phalacrocorax. Green cormorant.
Pufferinus arcticus. Manx shearwater.
P. major. The greater shearwater.
Colymbus glacialis. Northern diver.
C. rufogularis. Red-throated diver.
Podiceps cornutus. Horned grebe.
P. auritus. Eared grebe.
Fulica atra. Bald coot.
Mergus merganser. Goosander.
M. serrator. Red-breasted goosander.
Anas nigra. Common scoter.
A. spectabilis. The king duck.
A. mollissima. Eider duck.
A. glacialis. Long-tailed eider duck.
A. clangula. Golden eye.
A. marita. Scaup duck.
A. leucophtalmos. Red duck.
A. histrionica. Harlequin duck.
A. strepera. Gadwall.
A. acuta. Pintail duck.
A. boschas. Mallard.
A. penelope. Widgeon.

Anas crecca. Teal.
A. tadorna. Sheldrake.
A. borealis. Garland duck.
A. minata.
Anser segetum. Bean goose.
A. albifrons. Laughing-goose.
A. torquatus. Brent goose.
A. loucopsis. Barnacle goose.
Cygnus musicus. Whistling swan.
Sula alba. Gannet.
Sterna hirundo. Common tern.
Larus tridactylus. Kitty-wake.
L. leucopterus. Iceland gull.
L. glaucus. Burgomaster gull.
L. marinus. Black-backed gull.
L canus. Common gull.
L. varius.
Lestris catarractes. Common skua.
L. pomarinus. Pomarine skua.
L. parasiticus. Arctic gull.
Procellaria glacialis. Fulmar petrel.
P. pelagica. Stormy petrel.

FISHES.

Raia vulgaris maxima.
R. fullonica.
R. clavata.
Squalus acanthius. Picked dog-fish.
S. spinax.
S. glaucus. Blue shark.
S. carcharias. White shark.
S. maximus. Basking shark.
S. pristis.
Chimæra monstrosa. Northern chimæra.
Anarchicas lupus. Wolf-fish.
A. minor. Smaller wolf-fish.
Lophius piscatorius. Sea devil.
Accipenser sturio. Common sturgeon.
Cyclopterus lumpus. Lump sucker.
Muræna anguilla. Common eel.
M. conger. Conger eel.
Trichiurus lepturus. Silvery trichiurus.
Ammodytes tobianus. Sand eel.
Gadus æglefinus. Haddock.
G. morrhua. Common cod.
G. callarius. Doise.
G. barbatus. Whiting pout.
G. virens. Coal fish.
G. molva. Ling.
G. brosme. Torsk, or tusk.
Blennius gunellus. Gunnel.
Echeneis remora. Sucking fish.
Cottus scorpius. Lasher bull-head.
C. cataphractus. Armed bull-head, or pogge.
Pleuronectes hippoglossus. Halibut.
P. platessa. Plaice.
P. flesus. Flounder.
P. linguatula.
P. maximus. Turbot.

APPENDIX.

Gasterosteus aculeatus. Common stickleback.
Salmo salar. Common salmon.
S. carpio.
S. trutta. Salmon trout.
S. levis.
S. alpinus. Charr.
Fario arcticus. Capelen.
Esox belone. Gar pike.
Clupea harengus. Herring.
C. sprattus. Sprat.
Cyprinus pelagicus. Crusian carp.

MOLLUSCS.

Sepia officinalis. Cuttle fish.
Lolligo vulgaris. Common balamary.
L. octopodia.
L. media.
Lernæa branchialis.
L. salmonea.
Clio borealis. Polar clio.
Doris papillosas.
D. arborescens.
D. lavis.
Limax ater. Black slug.
L. agrestis. The field slug.
Patella tessalata.
P. fissurella.
P. testudinalis.
Nerita littoralis.
Helis haliotoidea.
H. grisena.
H. stagnalis.
H. pella.
H. auricularia.
Turbo littoreus.
T. clathrus.
Trochnus cinerarius.
T. divaricatus.
T. striatellus.
Murex clathratus.
M. antiquus.
M. despectus.
M. islandicus.
Buccinum lapillus.
B. undatum. Common welk.
Ostræa edulis.
O. testa pectinata.
O. irregularis rugosa.
Anomia squamula.
A. retusa.
A. arenacea.
Pecten islandicus.
Mytilus edulis.
M. testa ovata oblonga.
M. planniscula.
M. barbatus.
M. discors.
M. pholadis mantessia.
Tellina lacustris.

Cardium edule.
C. grœnlandicum.
Venus islandica.
V. borealis.
Ascidia rustica.
A. mentula.
A. quadridentata.
Mya truncata.
M. arenaria.
M. arctica.
Pholus crispatus.
Teredo nivalis.
Balanus vulgaris.
Lepus balanoides.
L. balænara.
L. tulipa.
L. anatifera.
L. fistulosa.

CRUSTACEÆ.

Chiton ruber.
C. albus.
C. punctatus.
Cancer maja. Crab.
C. araneus.
C. gammarum.
C. pulex.
C. medusarum.
C. homaroides.
Squilla vulgaris. Prawn.
S. lobata.
Bernhardus. Hermit crab.

INSECTS.

Aranea bipunctata. Spider.
A. palustris.
A. crucigera palustris min.
A. scenica.
Oniscuspsora.
O. marinus.
O. asellus.
O. bicaudatus monoculus apus.
O. piscinus.
O. pulex.
Acarus siro. Cheese mite.
A. cadaverum.
A. longicornis.
A. muscarum.
A. aquaticus.
Phalangium opilio. Long-legged spider.
P. pallidum.
P. groesipes.
Lepisma saccharifera.
Podura aquatica.
P. pusilla.
P. ambulans.
P. fimetaria.
P. plumbea.
Pediculus humanus. Louse.

Pulex irritans.   Common flea.
Cimex grilloides.   Bug.
C. littoralis.
Aphis brassicæ.   Plant louse.
Phalæna graminis.
P. betularia.
P. oleracea.
P. lucernea.
P. vaccinii.
P. prunata.
P. undulata.
P. fluctuata.
P. pratella.
P. topezella.
P. pellionella.
P. surcitella.
Phryganea flava.   Caddis.
P. rhombica.
P. bicaudata.
Teuthredo pratensis.   Saw fly.
Ichneumon sarcitorius.
I. manifestator.
I. ovulorum errator.
Apis terrestris.   Humble bee.
Tipula rivosa.   Crane fly.
T. regelationis.
T. pennicornis.
T. monoptera.
T. plumosa.
Musca pyrostris.   Fly.
M. stercoraria.
M. fimetaria.
M. scybolaria pendula.
M. vomitatoria.
M. mortuorum.
M. cæsar.
M. domestica.
M. fenestralis.
M. petronella.
M. ribesii.
M. larvarum.
M. cremitcrorinum.
M. gibba.
Culex pipiens.   Gnat.
C. reptans.
Hippobosca ovina.   Sheep fly.
Cistela stoica.
Scarabæus fimetarius.   Dunghill beetle.
Dermestes lardarius.   Leather eater.
Silpha tabulosa.   Carrion beetle.
S. pedicularis.
Cerambyx testaceus.
C. for.
Dytiscus marginalis.
D. striatus.
D. semistriatus.
D. latissimus.
Carabas vulgaris.   Bullhead.
C. ferrugineus.
C. velox.
C. melanocephalus.

Carabas piceus.
Staphylinus maxillosus.   Rove beetle.
S. fusipes.
S. rufipes.
S. patitus.

ANNELIDES.

Serpula glomerata.
S. spirorbis.
S. lumbricalis.
S. spirillum.
S. triquetra.
S. granulata.
Sabella granulata.
Aphrodita imbricata.
A. squamata.
Nereis noctiluca.
N. pelagica.
N. diversicolor.
N. viridis.
N. maculata.
Mammaria ovata.
Gordius marinus.
G. lacustris.
G. argillaceus.
Ascaris lumbricoides.
A. vermicularis.
Lumbricus terrestris.
L. marinus.
L. littoralis.
L. cirratus.
Fasciola hepatica.
Hirudo complanata.

ZOOPHYTES.

Holothuria priapus.
H. pentactes.
Echinus esculentus.
E. spatagus.
Asterias ophiura.
A. rubens.
A. aurantiaca.
A. papposa.
Medusa aurita.
M. cruciata.
M. capillata.
Actinia senilis.
A. felicia.
A. viduata.
A. grisea.
A. volva.
Hydra pallens.
H. squamata.
Sertularia abietina.
S. antennica.
Millepora polymorpha.
Flustra foliacea.
F. truncata.
Eschora fascialis.
Cellepora crustalenta.
Corallina officinalis.

APPENDIX.

Isis hippuris.
Alcyonum cydonium.
A. manus diaboli.

Alcyonum labatum.
Spongia manus.
S. oculata.

LIST OF PLANTS, ETC., FOUND IN ICELAND.

*Those marked * are supposed to exist there.*

RANUNCULACEÆ.

Thalictrum alp. Alpine meadow ruc.
Ranunculus aquat. Water crowfoot.
R. reptans. Creeping buttercup; spoar wort.
R. glacialis.
*R. nivalis.
R. hyperb.
R. acris. Upright meadow crowfoot.
*R. polyanthemis.
*R. lapponicus.
R. repens. Creeping crowfoot.
Caltha palustris. Marsh marigold.

CRUCIFERÆ.

Nasturtium palustre. Watercress.
Arabis alpina. Alpine rockcress.
A. petræa β. hispida. Hairy wallcress.
A. petræa J. hastulata. Alpine rockcress.
*Cardamine bellidifolia. Cardamine.
*C. hirsuta. Hairy cardamine rockcress.
*C. intermedia.
C. pratensis. Common cardamine rockcress.
*Draba alp. Alpine whitlow grass.
D. muricella. Wall whitlow grass.
D. hirta. Rock whitlow grass.
D. hirta β. oblongata.
D. muralis. Speedwell, leaved whitlow grass.
Erophila vulg. Whitlow grass.
Cochlearia officin. Common scurvy grass.
*C. danica. Danish scurvy grass.
C. anglica. English scurvy grass.
*Thlaspi campestre. Pennycress.
Crucif. marit. Sea rocket.
Capsella bursa pastoris. Shepherd's purse.
*Subularia aquatica. Awlwort.
*Sinapis pratensis. Mustard.

VIOLACEÆ.

Viola palus. Marsh violet.
V. can. Dog violet.
V. tric. Pansy.

DROSERACEÆ.

Drosera rotundifol. Sundew.

*Drosera longifol. Long-leaved sundow.
Parnasia palus. Common grass of Parnassus.

CARYOPHYLLACEÆ.

Silene inflat. β. marit. Sea campion.
*S. rupes.
S. acaul. Moss sea campion.
Lychnis floscuc. Ragged robin.
L. alp. Red alpine lychnis.
Sagina procumb. Pearlwort.
*Spergula arv. Corn spurrey.
S. nodosa. Knotted spurrey.
S. sagin. Pearlwort spurrey.
S. subul. Awl-shaped Pearlwort.
Stellaria med. Chickweed.
S. Edwardsii.
S. humifusa.
S. crassifol. β. sub-alp.
S. biflora.
S. cerastoides. Alpine stitchwort.
Arenaria rubella. Sandwort.
A. rubella bhirta. Hairy sandwort.
A. ciliata β. Fringed sandwort.
A. serpyllifol. Thyme-leaved sandwort.
A. peploides. Sea purslane.
Cerastium vulgat. Mouse-ear chickweed.
C. holosteoides. Jagged chickweed.
C. alp. Hairy Alpine chickweed.

LINCÆ.

Linum catharticum. Cathartic flax.

GERANIACEÆ.

Geranium sylvat. Wood crane's bill.
G. praten. Meadow crane's bill.

LEGUMINOSÆ.

*Lotus corniculatus. Common bird's-foot trefoil.
Anthyllis vulneraria. Common lady's-fingers.
Trifolium repens. White clover.
*T. pratense. Purple clover.
*T. arvense. Hare'sfoot trefoil.
*T. fragiferum. Strawberry-headed trefoil.
Pisum maritimum. Teasel-headed trefoil.

*Lathyrus pratensis. Meadow vetchling.
Vicia cracca. Tufted vetch.

ROSACEÆ.

Spinæa ulmaria. Meadow sweet.
Potentilla anserina. Goosegrass.
P. maculata.
*Tormentilla erecta. Tormentil.
Comarum palustre. Marsh cinquefoil.
Fragaria collina. Strawberry.
Geum rivale. Water avens.
Dryas octopet. Mountain avens.
Alchemilla vulg. Field lady's mantle.
A. β. montana. Common lady's mantle.
A. alp. Alpine lady's mantle.
Sibbaldia procum. Procumbent sibbaldia.
Sanguisorba offic. Common burnet.
Rubus saxat. Stone bramble.
Rosa pimpinella folia v. islandica.
Sorbus aucuparia. Mountain ash.

ÆNOGRARIÆ.

*Epilobium angustifol. Flowering willow.
E. latifol.
E. montan. Broad willow-herb.
*E. tetragonum. Square-stalked willow-herb.
E. palus. Narrow-leaved marsh willow-herb.
E. origanifol.
*E. nutans.
E. alpin. Alpine willow-herb.

HALORAGHEÆ.

*Myriophyllum spicat. Spiked water-milfoil.
*M. verticillat. Whorled water-milfoil.
Hippuris vulg. Mare's-tail.
Callitriche verna. Vernal water starwort.
*C. autumn. Autumnal water starwort.

CERATOPHYLLEÆ.

*Ceratophyllum demersum. Horn-wort.

PARONYCHIEÆ.

*Scleranthus annuus. Annual knawel.

PORTULACEÆ.

Montia fontana. Water-blinks.

CRASSULACEÆ.

*Tillæa aquat. Tillæa.
Sedum acre. Biting stonecrop.

Sedum ann. } English stonecrop.
S. anglic. } English stonecrop.
S. villos. Woolly stonecrop.
S. rhodiola. Rose-root.

SAXIFRAGEÆ.

Saxifraga cotyledon.
S. aizoon. House-leek.
S. stellaris. Starry saxifrage.
S. nival. Clustered alpine saxifrage.
S. oppositofol. Opposite-leaved golden saxifrage.
S. hirculus. Yellow-marsh saxifrage.
Saxifraga aizoides. Yellow mountain saxifrage.
S. rivularis. Alpine brook saxifrage.
S. cernua. Drooping bulbous saxifrage.
S. granulata. White meadow saxifrage.
S. cæspitosa. Tufted alpine saxifrage.
*S. hetræa.
S. hypnoides. Mossy saxifrage.
*S. tricuspidata.
*S. tridactylites. Blue-leaved saxifrage.

UMBELLIFERÆ.

*Hydrocotyles vulg. Marsh penny.
Ligusticum scoticum. Scottish lovage.
*Imperatoria ostruthium. Master wort.
Angelica archang. Wild angelica.
*A. sylves. Wild angelica.
*Œg-opodium podogr aria. Common goat-weed.
Carum carvi. Caraway.

ARALLIACEÆ.

Hodera helix. Common ivy.

CORNEÆ.

Cornus soeciia. Dwarf cornel.

RUBIACEÆ.

*Galium trifidum.
*G. sylves. Slender bed-straw.
G. saxat. Heath bed-straw.
G. palus. White water bed-straw.
G. uliginos. Rough marsh bed-straw.
G. verum. Common yellow bed-straw.
*G. mollugo. Great hedge bed-straw.
G. boreale. Cross-leaved bed-straw.

VALERIANEÆ.

*Valeriana offic. Great wild valerian.

DIPRACEÆ.

*Scabiosa succisa. Premorse scabious.

COMPOSITÆ.

*Leontodon taraxacum. Dandy-lion.

APPENDIX. 359

Leontodon β. tenue.
Apargia taraxaci. Hawkbit.
A. autumn. Autumnal hawkbit.
A. β. asperior.
Hieracium alp. Alpine hawkweed.
*H. pilosella. Mouse-ear hawkweed.
*H. auricula. Auricula hawkweed.
*H. præmorsum.
*H. aurontiacum. Orange hawkweed.
H. murorum. Broad-leaved wall hawkweed.
*H. prenanthoides. Rough-bordered hawkweed.
Gnaphalium alp. Alpine cudweed.
G. rupium. (?) Dwarf alpine cudweed.
G. β. filiforme.
G. uliginosum. Marsh cudweed.
G. fuscatum.
Tussilago farfara. Colt's-foot.
Erigeron alpin. Alpine fleabane.
E. alpin β. uniflor. Alpine fleabane.
Senecio vulg. Common groundsel.
Pyrethrum inod. Scentless feverfew.
P. β. marit. Sea feverfew.
Achillea millefol. Common yarrow.
*Carduus arvensis. Meadow-plume thistle.
C. heterophyllus. Melancholy thistle.
C. acanthoides. Nettled thistle.

CAMPANULACEÆ.

Campanula rotundifol. Common bell-flower.

VACCINEÆ.

Vaccinium myrtill. Bilberry.
V. uliginos. Bog-whortleberry.
V. vitis idæa. Cranberry.

ERICINEÆ.

Erica vulgar. Common heath.
E. tetralix. Cross-leaved heath.
Andromeda hypnoides.
*Arbutus alpin. Black bearberry.
A. uva ursi. Red bearberry.
Rhododendron lappon.
Ledum latifol.
Azalea procum. Trailing azalea.
Pyrola rotundifol. Round-leaved winter green.
P. minor. Lesser winter green.
P. secun. Serrate winter green.
P. unifol. Single-flowered winter green.

EMPETREÆ.

Empetrum nigrum. Common crowberry.

GENTIANEÆ.

Gentiana aurea.
G. nivalis. Small alpine gentian.
G. amarella. Autumnal gentian.

Gentiana campes. Field gentian.
G. tenella.
G. serrata β. detorsa.
G. serrata J. acuta.
Swertia sulcata. Marsh felwort.
Menyanthes trifoliata. Bog-bean.

CONVOLVULACEÆ.

Trientalis europ. European chickweed winter green.
Glaux maritima. Sea milkwort.

DIAPENSIEÆ.

Diapensia lapponica.

BORAGINIEÆ.

Myosotis arvensis. Field scorpion grass.
Pulmonaria maritima. Lungwort.
*Echium vulgare. Common viper's bugloss.

RHINANTACEÆ.

Rhinanthus cris. galli. Cock's-comb.
Euphrasia offic. Eyebright.
*Pedicularis palus. Marsh red-rattle.
*P. sylv. Dwarf red-rattle.
P. flamm.
Bartsia alp. Alpine bartsia.
*Limosella aquat. Mudwort.
Veronica saxat. Rock speedwell.
V. alp. Alpine speedwell.
V. serpyll. Smooth speedwell.
V. beccabung. Short-leaved water speedwell.
*V. anagallis. Single-weed water speedwell.
V. offic. Common speedwell.

LABIATÆ.

Lamium purpureum. Red dead-nettle.
L. amplexicaule. Henbit dead-nettle.
Galeopsis tetrahit. Common hemp dead-nettle.
*G. ladanum. Red hemp dead-nettle.
*Stachys sylv. Hedge woundwort.
Thymus serpyll. Wild thyme.
Prunella vulg. Self-heal.

LENTIBULACEÆ.

Pingnicula vulg. Common butterwort.
*P. alp. Alpine butterwort.

PRIMULACEÆ.

*Primula elatior. Oxlip primrose.
*P. farinosa. Bird's-eye primrose.
*P. stricta.

PLUMBAGINIEÆ.

Armeria marit. Common sea-pink.
Plantago maj. Greater plantain.
P. lanceol. Ribwort plantain.

Plantago marit. Sea plantain.
*P. coronopus. Buck's-horn plantain.

CHENOPODIACEÆ.

*Chenopodium alb. White goose-foot.
Atriplex patula. Spreading halberd-shaped orache.
A. laciniata. Frosted sea orache.

POLIGONEÆ.

Kœnigia island.
*Polygonum amphibium. Knot-grass.
*P. vivip. Viviparous knot-grass.
*P. hydropiper. Biting persicaria.
*P. persicaria. Spotted knot-grass.
*P. aviculare. Common knot-grass.
P. convolo. Bindweed knot-grass.
Rheum digynum. Mountain sorrel.
Rumex domest.
R. acetosa. Common sorrel.
R. acetosella. Sheep's sorrel.

URTICEÆ.

Urtica urens. Small nettle.
*U. dioica. Great nettle.

AMENTACEÆ.

Betula nana. Dwarf birch.
B. alba. Common birch.
B. fruticosa.
Salix pentand. Sweet bay-leaved willow.
S. purp. Bitter purple willow.
S. myrsinitis. Green whortle-leaved willow.
S. myrtilloides. Tea-leaved willow.
S. arbuscula. No English name. *Withering*.
S. arct. Mountain willow.
S. herbac. Least willow.
S. retic. Wrinkle-leaved willow.
S. lanata. Woolly broad-leaved willow.
S. glàuca. Glaucous mountain willow.
S. lapponum. Lapland willow.
*S. repens. Creeping willow.
*S. fusca. Brownish dwarf willow.
*S. versifol.
*S. caprea. Great round-leaved willow.

CONIFERÆ.

Juniperus nana. Dwarf alpine juniper.

MONOCOTYLEDONES.

ALISMACEÆ.

*Triglochin palustre. Marsh arrow-grass.
T. marit. Sea arrow-grass.

Potamogeton natans. Broad-leaved pond-weed.
*P. lucens. Shining pond-weed.
P. perfol. Perfoliate pond-weed.
P. rufescens. Long-leaved floating pond-weed.
*P. crisp. Curled pond-weed.
P. compress. Compressed pond-weed.
*P. pusill. Small pond-weed.
*P pectin. Fennel-leaved pond-weed.
*P. marin.

ORCHIDEÆ.

*Orchis mas. Meadow orchis.
*O. morio. Green-winged orchis.
O. latifol. Broad-leaved orchis.
O. mac. Spotted palmate orchis.
O. hyperb.
O. cruen.
Satyrium viride. Frog orchis.
S. albid. White fragrant-scented orchis.
S. nig.
*Ophrys nidus avis. Bird's-nest orchis.
O. ovata. Common tway-blade.
Corallorhiza innat. Spurless coral-root.

SMILACEÆ.

Paris quadr. Herb Paris.

COLCHICACEÆ.

Tofieldia bor. Northern tofieldia.

JUNCEÆ.

Juncus arct. Arctic rush.
J. squarrosus. Moss rush.
J. lampocarp. Shining-fruited rush.
J. trifid. Three-leaved rush.
J. buffon. Toad rush.
J. biglum. Two-flowered rush.
J. triglum. Three-flowered rush.
*J. bulbos. Round-fruited rush.
Lazula campes. Field woodrush.
L. spicata. Spiked woodrush.
L. pilata. Hairy rush.

TYPHACEÆ.

Sparganium natans. Floating bur-reed.
Zostera marina. Broad-leaved grass-wrack.

CYPERACEÆ.

Carex dioica. Creeping diœcious carex sedge.
C. capit. Small sedge.
*C. pulicaris. Flea carex.
C. microgloch.
C. rupes. Rock carex.
C. incurva. Curved carex.
*C. vulp. Great compound prickly carex.

*Carex norveg. Norwegian carex.
*C. oval. Oval-spiked carex.
C. arenar. Sea carex.
*C. muricata. Greater prickly carex.
C. carta. White carex.
*C. loliacea.
C. lagopina.
*C. elong. Elongated carex.
C. saxat. Russet carex.
C. cæspit. Tufted bog-rush.
*C. acuta. Slender-spiked bog-rush.
C. pulla. Russet sedge.
*C. vahlii. Close-headed sedge.
*C. atro-fusca.
*C. fulig.
*C. pillulifera. Round-headed sedge.
*C. flava. Yellow sedge.
*C. pallescens. Pale sedge.
*C. podata.
*C. ornithopoda.
C. panicea. Pink-leaved sedge.
C. capill. Dwarf capillary sedge.
C. limosa β. rariflora. Mud sedge.
*C. pseudo-Cyperus. Cyprus-like sedge.
C. vesicaria. Large-fruited bladder sedge.
*C. ampullacea. Small-fruited bladder sedge.
Kobresia scirp. Cotton grass.
Schœnus rufus. Bog rush.
Scirpus palus. Common club grass.
S. cæspit. Scaly-stalked club rush.
S. setac. Brittle-stalked club rush.
*S. lacus. Bullrush.
Eriophorum capitat. Round-headed cotton grass.
E..angustifol. Narrow-leaved cotton grass.
E. latifol. Broad-headed cotton grass.

GRAMINEÆ.

Nardus stricta. Common mat grass.
Phleum praten. Common cat's-tail grass.
*P. β. nodosa.
P. alpina. Alpine grass.
Alopecurus genicul. Floating fox-tail grass.
Milium effus. Spreading millet grass.
*Arundo epigeios. Wood reed.
*A. varia.
*A. arenaria. Sea reed.
*A. phragmites. Common reed.
Agrostis canina. Brown bent grass.
A. alp. Alpine brown bristle-headed bent grass.
A. vulg. Fine bent grass.
A. stolonif. Marsh bent grass.
Aira aquat. Water whod grass.
A. subspic. Silky bent grass.
A. cæspit. Turfy hair grass.

Aira flexuo. Waved hair grass.
A. flexuo. β. Montana waved hair grass.
*A. atropur.
*A. alp. Smooth Alpine hair grass.
*A. præcox. Early hair grass.
*Melica cærul. Melic grass.
Holcus odorat. Soft grass.
*Sesleria cærul. Blue moor grass.
Poa flex. Meadow grass.
P. marit. Creeping sea hard grass.
*P. distans. Reflexed hard grass.
P. laxa. Wavy meadow grass.
P. alp. Alpine meadow grass.
P. alp. β. vivip.
P. praten. Smooth meadow grass.
P. trivial. Rough meadow grass.
P. nem. Grey meadow grass.
P. nem. j. firmula. Grey meadow grass.
*P. d. cæsia. Grey meadow grass.
*P. annua. Annual meadow grass.
*P. compressa. Flat-stalked meadow gras.
Festuca rub. Fescue.
F. rub β. arenar.
F. ovina. Sheep's fescue.
F. ovina β. vivip. Viviparous fescue grass.
F. duriusc. Hard fescue grass.
*F. elatior. Tall fescue grass.
*F. fluit. Floating fescue grass.
Elymus arenar. Upright sea lyme grass.
*Triticum rep. Couch grass.
*T. can. Dog's wheat.
Anthoxanthum ardor. Spring grass.

EQUISETACEÆ.

Equisetum arv. Corn horse-tail.
E. β. alp.
*E. sylv. Wood horse-tail.
E. palus. Marsh horse-tail.
*E. fluviat. Great water horse-tail.
E. limos. Smooth naked horse-tail.
*E. hyemale. Great rough horse-tail.

MARSILLEACEÆ.

Isoëtes lacustris.

LYCOPODIACEÆ.

*Lycopodium clavat. Common club moss.
*L. selago. Fir club moss.
L. complan.
L. alp. Savin-leaved club moss.

FILICES.

Polypodium vulg. Common polypody.
P. Phegop. Pale mountain polypody.
P. ilven. Woodsia ilvensis.
*P. dryop. Tender three-branched ilvensis.

Aspidium lonchitis. Rough Alpine shield fern.
A. filis mas. Male Alpine shield fern.
*A. filis fæm. Female fern.
A. frag. Brittle fern.
*A. thelyp. Marsh fern.
Pteris crispa. Marsh brake.
Botrych. lun. Common moonwort.
*Ophio glossum vulg. Common adder's tongue.
Asplen. trich. Common maiden hair spleenwort.
*A. septent. Forked maiden hair spleenwort.

ACOTYLEDONES.

Musci frondosi.

Sphagnum obtusifol. Blunt-leaved bog moss.
*S. squarros. Spreading-leaved bog moss.
*S. acutifol. Slender bog moss.
*Phaseum cuspidat. Cuspidate earth moss.
*P muticum. Common dwarf earth moss.
Gymnostomum lapp. Lapland beardless moss.
G. curviros. Curved-beaked beardless moss.
G. affine.
*Tetraphis pelluc. Pellucid tetraphis.
Diphysium folosium. Leafy diphyscium.
Splachnum sphær. Globe-fruited splachnum.
S. tenue. Slender splachnum.
S. mnioides. Brown tapering splachnum.
S. urceolat.
*S ampullac. Purple bottle moss.
*S. vasculos. Globe-fruited splachnum.
*Polytrichum hercynicum. Incurved hair moss.
P. lævigat.
P. pilifer. Bristle-pointed hair moss.
P. juniperifol. Juniper-leaved hair moss.
P. juniperifol β. strict. Variety of the former.
P. commune. Common hair moss.
P. commune β. formosum. A variety.
P. septent. Northern hair moss.
P. alp. Alpine hair moss.
P. alp β. arctic. Alpine hair moss.
*P. urnigerum. Urn-bearing hairmoss.
*P. nanum. Dwarf round-headed hair moss.

Conostomum bor. Northern conostomum.
Tortula ruralis. Great hairy screw moss.
T. subul. Awl-shaped screw moss.
T. tortuosa. Frizzled mountain screw moss.
Eucalypta vulg. Common extinguisher moss.
E. rhaptocarpa. Spiral-fruited extinguisher moss.
E. ciliata. Fringed extinguisher moss.
Grimmia apocarpe. Sesile grimmia.
G. apocarpe β. stricta. Variety of the former.
G. marit. Sea-side grimmia.
G. ovata. Ovate grimmia.
G. Donniana. Donian beardless moss.
Weissia lanceol. Lance-leaved weissia.
*W. controversa. Green-cushioned weissia.
W. acuta. Sharp-pointed weissia.
W. curviros. Curved-leaved weissia.
W. crisp. Curled weissia.
W. volcan.
Dicronum glauc. White fork moss.
D. cervicul. Red-necked fork moss.
D. virens. Green spur-fruited fork moss.
D. strumiferum. Many-headed fork moss.
D. foliatum. Sickle-leaved fork-moss.
D. crispum. Curled-leaved fork moss.
D. scottianum. Upright fruited fork moss.
D. polycarp. Many-headed fork moss.
*D. rupes.
*D. subal.
D. morikianum.
D. flexuos. Zigzag fork moss.
D. adianthoides. Adiantum fork moss.
Trichostomum lanuginos. Woolly-fringe moss.
*T. caneciens. Hoary-fringe moss.
T. heterostium. Serrated fringe moss.
T. acicu. Dark mountain fringemoss.
T. ellipt. Elliptical fringe moss.
T. fascic. Beardless hoary fringe moss.
Didymodon purp. Purple didymodon.
D. glaucesc. Glaucous didymodon.
D. trifurc. Three-ranked didymodon.
D. capillac. Fine-leaved didymodon.
*D. hetromall. Curved-leaved didymodon.
Funaria hygrometrica. Common cord moss.
F. β. minor. Variety.

APPENDIX. 363

Ærthotrichum anomal. Anomalous bristle moss.
Æ. cupulat. Single-fringed sessile-fruited bristle moss.
Æ. affine. Purple straight-leaved bristle moss.
Fontinalis antepyret. Greater water moss.
*F. squam. Alpine water moss.
*F. falcata.
Bartramia pomiform. Common apple moss.
B. ithyphylla. Straight-leaved apple moss.
B. fontana. Fountain apple moss.
Leskea dendroides.
*Hypnum denticulat. Fern-like feather moss.
H. serpens. Creeping feather moss.
H. molle. Soft-water feather moss.
H. schreberi. Hair-pointed feather moss.
H. moniliforme. Bearded feather moss.
H. stramineum β. sarmentos. Straw-like feather moss.
H. fluit. Floating feather moss.
H. pulchell. Elegant feather moss.
H. nitens. Shining feather moss.
H. lutesc. Roughed-stalked feather moss.
*H. curvat. Curved feather moss.
H. splen. Glittering feather moss.
*H. prolif. Proliferous feather moss.
*H. prælong. Very long feather moss.
H. abiet. Spruce-tree feather moss.
H. velutin. Velvet feather moss.
H. cusp. Pointed bog feather moss.
H. condifol. Heart-leaved feather moss.
*H. polymorph. Many-fruited feather moss.
H. stellat. Yellow starry feather moss.
H. loreum. Rambling mountain feather moss.
H. squarr. Drooping-leaved feather moss.
*H. filian. Lesser golden fern feather moss.
H. palus. Marsh feather moss.
H. adunc. Claw-leaved feather moss.
H. adunc. β. tenue. Claw-leaved feather moss.
H. rugos. Wrinkled-leaved feather moss.
H. silesian. Silesian feather moss.
H. uncin. Sickle-leaved feather moss.
H. scorpoides. Scorpion feather moss.
H. cupressifor. Cypress-leaved feather moss.
H. mollusc. Plumy-crested feather moss.

Bryum palus. Marsh thread moss.
B. pyrifor. Golden-thread moss.
B. julaceum. Slender-branched thread moss.
B. wahlenbergii. Pale-leaved thread moss.
B. cæspit. Lesser matted thread moss.
B. turbinat. Turbinate thread moss.
B. Duvalii.
B. nutans. Silky pendulous thread moss.
B. ventricos. Swelling bog thread moss.
B. punctat. Dotted thyme thread moss.
B. cuspidat. β. maj. (Buff.) Pointed-leaved thread moss.
Meesia ulig. Long-stalked thread moss.
*M. dealbata. Pale-leaved thread moss.
Andræ alp. Alpine split moss.

HEPATICÆ.

Jungermannia platyphylla. Flat-leaved jungermannia.
J. delatata. Dilated-leaved jungermannia.
J. tamariscifol. Tamarisk scale moss.
J. serpyll. Thyme-leaved jungermannia.
J. trichom. Maiden-hair scale moss.
J. compress. Cypress scale moss.
J. scalaris. Ladder scale moss.
J. Francisci. Francis' scale moss.
J. bidentata. Two-rooted scale moss.
J. albesc. Pallid scale moss.
J. barbata. Toothed scale moss.
J. tricophyll. Three-lobed scale moss.
J. ciliaris. Fringed scale moss.
J. setiform. Brittle-leaved scale moss.
J. julac. Ragged scale moss.
J. viticulos. Pouched scale moss.
J. pumila. Dwarf scale moss, or jungermannia.
J. cremulata. Crenulated jungermannia.
J. sphagni. Bog scale moss.
J. cordifol. Heart-leaved jungermannia.
J. sphærocarp. Round-fruited jungermannia.
J. asplenoides. Spleenwort scale moss.
J. laxifol. Lax-leaved scale moss.
J. concinnata.
J. emargin. Notched jungermannia.
J. inflata. Inflated scale moss.
J. excisa. Jagged-leaved scale moss.
J. connivens. Connivent scale moss.
J. byssacea.
J. bicuspid. Forked jungermannia.
J. muriata. Wall scale moss.
J. saxicola.
J. undulata. Wavy-leaved scale moss.
J. albicans. Whitish jungermannia.
J. nemorosa. Wood scale moss.
J. multifida. Many-lobed jungermannia.

Jungermannia blasia.
Marchantia polymorpha. Polymorphous marchantia.
*M. hæmispher. Hemispherical marchantia.
*M. tenella.
*M. conica.
*Riccia crystal. Clear crystal wort.
*R. glauca. Clear crystal wort.
*Anthoceros punctat.

LICHENES.

*Usnea barbata b. hirta. Common rough lichen.
Evernia jubata b. chalybæform. Thread-like.
*E. jubata c. implexa.
E. ochroleuca a. rig. Shrubby sulphureous lichen.
*E. ochroleuca c. sarment.
*E. prunast.
*E. furfurac. Branny lichen.
*Ramalinia calicaris a. fraxinea. Ragged-beaked lichen.
Ramalinia c. canalicul.

R. scopulorum.
Cetraria tristis.
C. aculea.
C. island. Rare.
C. island b. platyna.
C. island c. crispa.
C. cucullata.
C. nivalis. Snow lichen.
*Peltigera resupinatus.
P. aphtho. Thrush lichen.
P. canina. Ash-coloured ground liver wort.
P. rufesc. Dark-coloured ground lichen.
P. venosa. Green veiny lichen.
P. croc.
P. sacc.
*Stricta pulmonacea. Lung wort.
Parmelia saxat.
P. saxat β. omphal. Cork, corker, or Arcell.
P. physodes.
P. oliracea. Olive-coloured leafy lichen.
P. fahluncnsis.
P. stygia. Stygian lichen.

THE END.

VIRTUE AND CO., PRINTERS, CITY ROAD, LONDON.

www.ingramcontent.com/pod-product-compliance
Lightning Source LLC
Chambersburg PA
CBHW030343230426
43664CB00007BA/515